'The financial, digital, mobile revolution promises a borderless and frictionless world. A swift planet; an intelligent social order, free from poverty and inequality; a prosperous global family in which those marked out by gender, race or class are no longer excluded. In *The Exclusionary Politics of Digital Financial Inclusion: Mobile Money, Gendered Walls*, Serena Natile takes these new developmental promises and turns them upside down. Her unflinching exploration of the dark side of our fixation on quick, individualised and privatised solutions is socio-legal critique at its best. The result is a deeply grounded, theoretically savvy and globally relevant analysis, offered up at a moment when the most urgent demands for effective redistribution are being answered with clicks and taps on keyboards and touchscreens.'

Luis Eslava, Reader in International Law and
Co-Director of the Centre for Critical International Law
(CeCIL) at Kent Law School, University of Kent

'This book represents a breakthrough. Many analyses of Kenya's mobile money facility are celebratory and uncritical. This book draws on an impressive range of historical and contemporary literature to consider the implications of digital financial inclusion initiatives for gender equality. It argues that in its conception and regulation, M-Pesa purports to extend opportunities while having little redistributive effect. In this important book, Serena Natile confronts the limits of mobile money and the entrepreneurial economic model underpinning it.'

Ambreena Manji, Professor of Land Law and Development at Cardiff
Law School, Co-Director of the Law and Global Justice Centre,
President of the African Studies Association UK and former
Director of the British Institute in Eastern Africa (2010–2014)

'Natile's original and important social legal study draws upon feminist political economy and African feminism to explore the gendered dynamics of digital financial inclusion. *The Exclusionary Politics of Digital Financial Inclusion* deftly reveals how phone-enabled money transfer systems such as M-Pesa cannot, unless they are accompanied by measures that redistribute land and care responsibilities, tackle the structural problems that perpetuate Kenyan women's inequality.'

Judy Fudge, LIUNA Enrico Henry Mancinelli Professor
of Global Labour Issues at McMaster University, Canada

'A carefully argued in-depth study of the limits of what was achieved by Vodafone's M-Pesa mobile phone banking initiative in Kenya. Focusing on how and how far it led to more women being included in the economy, *The Exclusionary Politics of Digital Financial Inclusion* shows how this form of private-public partnership privileges neoliberal values and reinforces existing inequalities and social practices. A must read for those working in fields as varied as law and development, gender studies, financial regulation, sociology of law and transnational law.'

David Nelken, Professor of Comparative and Transnational
Law at the Dickson Poon School of Law, King's College London

'This volume examines one of the most iconic cases of digital financial inclusion in development – Kenya's M-Pesa programme. Natile's book brings together feminist political economy with socio-legal studies to provide a comprehensive view of the institutional landscape in Kenya and place this case study in global context. Her exploration is grounded in empirical research that centres the views of women who use M-Pesa as part of their livelihood strategies while juggling the multiple pressures of income generation, care and reproductive and community labour. The acute analysis unravels the nexus of financial inclusion and gender equality, and how the 'logic of opportunity' can disguise gendered burdens of labour which allow banks to profit from women's solidarity and survival practices on an often overstated promise of autonomy and success.'

Kate Maclean, Professor of Social Geography at the
Centre for International Development, University of Northumbria

The Exclusionary Politics of Digital Financial Inclusion

Focusing on Kenya's path-breaking mobile money project M-Pesa, this book examines and critiques the narratives and institutions of digital financial inclusion as a development strategy for gender equality, arguing for a politics of redistribution to guide future digital financial inclusion projects.

One of the most-discussed digital financial inclusion projects, M-Pesa facilitates the transfer of money and access to formal financial services via the mobile phone infrastructure and has grown at a phenomenal rate since its launch in 2007 to reach about 80 per cent of the Kenyan population. Through a socio-legal enquiry drawing on feminist political economy, law and development scholarship and postcolonial feminist debate, this book unravels the narratives and institutional arrangements that frame M-Pesa's success while interrogating the relationship between digital financial inclusion and gender equality in development discourse. Natile argues that M-Pesa is premised on and regulated according to a logic of opportunity rather than a politics of redistribution, favouring the expansion of the mobile money market in preference to contributing to substantive gender equality via a redistribution of the revenue and funding deriving from its development.

This book will be of particular interest to scholars and students in Global Political Economy, Socio-Legal Studies, Gender Studies, Law & Development, Finance and International Relations.

Serena Natile is a Lecturer in Socio-Legal Studies at Brunel Law School, Brunel University London, UK.

RIPE Series in Global Political Economy

Series Editors: James Brassett, *University of Warwick, UK*, Susanne Soederberg, *Queen's University, Canada* and Eleni Tsingou, *Copenhagen Business School, Denmark.*

The RIPE Series published by Routledge is an essential forum for cutting-edge scholarship in International Political Economy. The series brings together new and established scholars working in critical, cultural and constructivist political economy. Books in the RIPE Series typically combine an innovative contribution to theoretical debates with rigorous empirical analysis.

The RIPE Series seeks to cultivate:

- Field-defining theoretical advances in International Political Economy
- Novel treatments of key issue areas, both historical and contemporary, such as global finance, trade, and production
- Analyses that explore the political economic dimensions of relatively neglected topics, such as the environment, gender relations and migration
- Accessible work that will inspire advanced undergraduates and graduate students in International Political Economy.

The *RIPE Series in Global Political Economy* aims to address the needs of students and teachers.

Japanese Resistance to American Financial Hegemony
Global versus Domestic Norms
Fumihito Gotoh

Money-Power and Financial Capital in Emerging Markets
Facing the Liquidity Tsunami
Ilias Alami

The Exclusionary Politics of Digital Financial Inclusion
Mobile Money, Gendered Walls
Serena Natile

For more information about this series, please visit: www.routledge.com/RIPE-Series-in-Global-Political-Economy/book-series/RIPE

The Exclusionary Politics of Digital Financial Inclusion

Mobile Money, Gendered Walls

Serena Natile

Routledge
Taylor & Francis Group
LONDON AND NEW YORK

First published 2020 by Routledge

2 Park Square, Milton Park, Abingdon, Oxon OX14 4RN
605 Third Avenue, New York, NY 10017

Routledge is an imprint of the Taylor & Francis Group, an informa business

First issued in paperback 2021

Publisher's Note

The publisher has gone to great lengths to ensure the quality of this reprint but points out that some imperfections in the original copies may be apparent.

British Library Cataloguing-in-Publication Data
A catalogue record for this book is available from the British Library

Library of Congress Cataloging-in-Publication Data
Names: Natile, Serena, author.
Title: The exclusionary politics of digital financial inclusion : mobile money, gendered walls/Serena Natile.
Other titles: RIPE series in global political economy.
Description: Abingdon, Oxon; New York, NY: Routledge, 2020. | Series: RIPE series in global political economy | Based on the author's thesis (doctoral)–Kent Law School, 2016. | Includes bibliographical references and index.
Identifiers: LCCN 2019049128 (print) | LCCN 2019049129 (ebook) | ISBN 9780367179588 (hardback) | ISBN 9780367179618 (ebook)
Subjects: LCSH: Banks and banking, Mobile–Kenya. | Mobile commerce–Kenya. | Microfinance–Kenya. | Financial exclusion–Prevention–Technological innovations. | Women–Africa–Economic conditions.
Classification: LCC HG1616.M54 N495 2020 (print) | LCC HG1616.M54 (ebook) | DDC 332.1702854678096–dc23
LC record available at https://lccn.loc.gov/2019049128
LC ebook record available at https://lccn.loc.gov/2019049129

ISBN: 978-0-367-17958-8 (hbk)
ISBN: 978-1-03-217535-5 (pbk)
DOI: 10.4324/9780367179618

Typeset in Times New Roman
by Wearset Ltd, Boldon, Tyne and Wear

Contents

Preface

Mobile money, gendered walls

This drawing by artist Pawel Kuczyński illustrates the argument presented in this book. While mobile money platforms such as M-Pesa contribute to the inclusion of women in the financial system, they do not challenge the visible and invisible 'walls' that create and reproduce gendered exclusion, oppression and inequality. Digital financial inclusion imposes on women at the lower end of the income distribution, who are already overburdened by gendered responsibilities, the additional responsibility for transforming the opportunities offered by digital finance into success, in line with the international development framework of 'gender equality as smart economics'.

Acknowledgements

This book would have not been possible without the numerous people who have inspired, encouraged and supported me in this journey.

I began the research on which this book is based while doing my PhD at Kent Law School (KLS), and I am immensely grateful to KLS for the generous studentship that allowed me to undertake this journey and to all the friends and colleagues who shared the joy and pain, laughs and tears, challenges and discoveries and lots of fun. First, I would like to thank my PhD supervisors and pillars of support, Toni Williams and Donatella Alessandrini, for their invaluable guidance and friendship throughout and after my PhD, and for teaching me to be critical in my academic work and optimistic in my social justice activism.

I am equally grateful to my PhD examiners, Judy Fudge and Ambreena Manji, for making my viva an inspirational exchange of ideas and for their continuous advice and support for my research and career. I also thank all my colleagues at the Centre for Law, Gender and Sexuality (now Centre for Sexuality, Race and Gender Justice) who shaped my intellectual development significantly over the three years I served on the steering committee, particularly Davina Cooper, Didi Herman, Suhraiya Jivraj, Rosemary Hunter, Sally Sheldon, Kate Bedford, Emily Grabham, Joanne Conaghan, Doris Buss, Sinéad Ring, Anisa de Jong, Nicola Barker, Emily Haslam, Ruth Cain, Maria Drakopoulou, Máiréad Enright, Simone Wong and Flora Renz. I am also very grateful to Luis Eslava, Rose Parfitt, Anneli Albi, Amanda Perry-Kessaris, Iain Ramsay, Nick Grief and Martin Hedemann-Robinson at KLS. During and after my PhD I have really valued the friendship of Silvana Tapia Tapia, Asta Zokaityte, Josipa Saric, Will Mbioh and Mo Afshary. I also thank my MA supervisor at the University of Trento, Luisa Antoniolli, for motivating me to take on the PhD in the first place.

I am immeasurably grateful to Susanne Soederberg, who encouraged me to publish this book for the RIPE Series in Global Political Economy of Routledge, which I have always considered a fantastic forum for interdisciplinary critical research. Susanne's work and intellectual generosity are an inspiration for me. I am also thankful to the other RIPE Series editors, James Brassett and Eleni Tsingou, and to Routledge's editorial assistant, Claire Maloney. A particular thank you to the very talented Pawel Kuczyński, who created the image for the preface of this book. I am also very grateful to Sally Sutton for her patient proofreading and helpful comments.

Very special thanks go to all the people who made my research time in Kenya a joyful and enriching experience, in particular John Kariuki Ngethe, Jackline Onyancha, Beatrice Karore, Vincent Robi, Faith Odhiambo, Radha Upadhyaya, Rosemary Atieno, Winnie Mitullah, Wanjiku Mukabi Kabira, Peter Kimuyu, Mary Njeri Kinyanjui, Lucy Njoki, Winnie Kamau, Kaltum Guyo, Jemimah Muriithi, Allan Mugeni, Timothy Simiyu, Cecilia Noolamal, the Kawangware Jitahidi Women Group and the Wanawake Mashinani Initiative, Shiro Mogeni-Shilako, Alice Maranga, the Federation of Women Lawyers (FIDA) Kenya, the Institute for Development Studies at the University of Nairobi, everyone who participated in my fieldwork and all the feminist groups who involved me in their protests for gender justice.

This book has benefited from my involvement in two research projects: Inclusionary Practices, led by Toni Williams at KLS and Fabricio Bertini Pasquot Polido at the Federal University of Minas Gerais, and Mapping Digital Humanitarianism, with David Nelken. The Inclusionary Practices project was a wonderful opportunity to work with talented research partners and dear friends Toni Williams, Fabricio Polido, Luis Eslava, Pedro Nicoli, Marcelo Ramos, Lina Buchely, Emilio Peluso, Maria Fernanda Salcedo Rapolês and Thomas Bustamante. I am also grateful to research partner and beloved friend Ana Paula Camelo at FGV São Paulo. I greatly appreciate David Nelken's mentorship during my postdoc at King's College and our collaboration on the editorial team of the *International Journal of Law in Context*. Thanks also to my postdoc buddy at King's College, Katrien Steenmans, and to the organisers of the King's Transnational Law Summit where I had the opportunity to engage in conversation and build collaborations with brilliant colleagues such as Kate Maclean, Celine Tan and Vitor Ido.

Over the last year I have relied on the support of colleagues at Brunel University London and I am particularly grateful to my inspiring and encouraging mentors William Spurlin and Felicity Kaganas, the Head of Brunel Law School Arad Reisberg, my multi-talented and supportive line manager Abimbola Olowofoyeku, and my partners in critical thinking and social justice activism Royona Mitra, Josh Bowsher, Mike Thomas, Henrietta Spalding, Adrienne Barnett, Kathrin Hamenstaedt, Jurgita Malinauskaite, Paula Westenberger and Jessica Corsi. Special thanks go to all my students at Brunel, Kent and King's College who constantly motivate my research.

I thank all my friends and fellow feminists across the world who provide me with pleasant memories, the excuse to travel and a place where I can always feel at home. Particular thanks to Martina Tortis for her friendship and tireless sense of humour. Finally, I am very thankful to my family for their unbounded love and support despite the difficult times, in particular to my beloved nephew Peppe and to my parents, Isabella Ragusa and Giuseppe Natile, who taught me to be bold, audacious, honest and never afraid to stand up for what I care about. This book is dedicated to them.

Abbreviations

ACP	African, Caribbean and Pacific Observatory on Migration
AFI	Alliance for Financial Inclusion
AML	anti-money laundering
ASCA	accumulating savings and credit association
BoP	bottom of the pyramid
CBA	Commercial Bank of Africa
CBK	Central Bank of Kenya
CDD	customer due diligence
CEDAW	Convention on the Elimination of all Forms of Discrimination Against Women
CGAP	Consultative Group to Assist the Poor
CTF	counter-terrorist financing
DFID	Department for International Development
FDCF	Financial Deepening Challenge Fund
FIDA	Federation of Women Lawyers
FIEG	Financial Inclusion Experts Group
FSD	Financial Sector Deepening Kenya
GAD	Gender and Development
GBP	British Pound Sterling
GPFI	Global Partnership for Financial Inclusion
GSMA	Groupe Spéciale Mobile Association
ICESCR	International Covenant on Economic, Social and Cultural Rights
ICT	information and communication technology
IMF	International Monetary Fund
IMTFI	Institute for Money, Technology and Financial Inclusion
KES	Kenyan shilling – currency of Kenya
KWFT	Kenya Women Finance Trust
KYC	know your customer
MDGs	Millennium Development Goals
MNO	mobile network operator
MYWO	Maendeleo Ya Wanawake Organisation
NIEO	New International Economic Order
NGO	non-governmental organisation

NPS	National Payment System
OECD	Organisation for Economic Co-operation and Development
OPM	Oxford Policy Management
ROSCA	rotating savings and credit association
SACCO	Savings and Credit Co-operative
SAPs	structural adjustment programmes
SDGs	Sustainable Development Goals
SIMBA	Skills and Innovation for Micro-Banking in Africa
UN	United Nations
UNCDF	United Nations Capital Development Fund
USAID	United States Agency for International Development
USD	United States Dollar
WID	Women in Development
WEF	World Economic Forum
WSF	World Social Forum
WTO	World Trade Organization

Introduction

Financial inclusion and its digital turn: a gendered story?

In the summer of 2011, I was conducting research on the gender aspects of South–South migration for the European Commission–United Nations Joint Migration and Development Initiative. In the course of an interview with a representative from the African, Caribbean and Pacific Observatory on Migration (ACP) I learnt of the common practice in Kenya of sending remittances between the urban and rural areas via a mobile phone-enabled money transfer system called M-Pesa (ACP Observatory 2011: 20). M-Pesa (M for mobile and *pesa*, Swahili for money) was explained to me as an initiative for local development aimed at facilitating financial management and small financial transactions for those who had no access to financial services. However, in piecing together its background and the various institutions involved in its implementation I realised that M-Pesa would be useful as a case study to unravel some key debates around international development and understand the aims and governance of the increasingly influential digital financial inclusion agenda.

M-Pesa was launched in March 2007 when the Western world was seeing the first signs of the financial crisis and Apple had just released the first iPhone. The idea for M-Pesa originated from the grassroots practice of sending prepaid airtime in small denominations following the rapid spread of mobile phones in African countries, and it was institutionalised via a public-private partnership between the UK Department for International Development (DFID), the UK-based telecommunications corporation Vodafone and its local partner Safaricom (of which Vodafone owns 40 per cent). As a development project M-Pesa was created to contribute to financial development in Kenya by facilitating access to formal financial services for those who were otherwise excluded from the mainstream banking infrastructure. While Vodafone and DFID initially saw it as a service to facilitate microfinance transactions, with the pilot it emerged that local users were more interested in using it to transfer money, and this subsequently became its main focus.

Since its launch in 2007, M-Pesa has grown at a phenomenal rate in Kenya and is now used by over 70 per cent of the population.[1] It has been rapidly adopted to facilitate transactions in finance and commerce but also healthcare, education, energy and transport sectors, among others, increasing access to formal finance across the urban/rural, socio-economic and gender divides. According to a series of surveys coordinated by Financial Sector Deepening (FSD) Kenya, following the introduction of M-Pesa the number of people in the country with access to formal finance increased from 20 per cent in 2006 to 80 per cent in 2019 (FSD 2007, 2019). The number of people using informal financial methods decreased from 32 per cent in 2006 to 6 per cent in 2019 and the number of those who are financially excluded from 41.3 to 11 per cent (FSD 2019: 8). As a consequence, M-Pesa captured global attention as the archetype of digital financial inclusion in the Global South,[2] able to contribute to economic growth, financial stability and the achievement of the UN Sustainable Development Goals (SDGs).[3] Since the launch of M-Pesa, mobile money services have been established in about 90 countries across the Global South with a total of 866 million registered accounts and daily transactions to the value of 1.3 billion USD (GSMA 2019).

'Financial inclusion' commonly refers to the process of providing those excluded from the mainstream banking infrastructure with access to affordable and convenient formal financial products and services. The term 'unbanked' is often used to describe people who do not conform to the standard conventions of bankability, lacking collateral, credit history and a fixed and regular income (Cull, Demirguc-Kunt and Murdoch 2013). These conditions denote the nexus between financial exclusion and the structural inequalities determined by intersecting relations of power, gender, race, class and poverty (see for example Young, Bakker and Elson 2011; Rankin 2013; Soederberg 2014).

Financial inclusion is premised on the idea that people, particularly those living in poverty or on a low income, are in need of financial services such as credit, savings, insurance and money transfer to manage their small amount of money effectively, cope with their everyday needs and potentially improve their livelihoods via savings and/or the opportunity to start an income-generating activity. Financial inclusion policies and interventions supported by governments, international organisations such as the International Monetary Fund (IMF), the World Bank and the UN and donors are based on the premise that affordable and available financial services are instrumental in or even necessary for the achievement of important social objectives such as access to water and healthcare, poverty reduction and gender equality. However, they do not explicitly address the socio-economic inequalities that cause financial exclusion.

Financial inclusion has been discussed as a development strategy in the Global South since the 1980s, particularly in relation to microcredit programmes, and gained increased public attention in the Global North following the 2007–2008 financial crisis. Research on microfinance in the Global South has long questioned the ability of financial inclusion to contribute to poverty reduction, gender equality and development more generally, pointing out that it has become an increasingly lucrative industry (Goetz 1996; Rahman 1999; Kabeer 2001; Williams 2001; Mayoux 2002; Rankin 2002; Maclean 2010, 2013; Karim 2011; Roy 2010). The 2007–2008 financial crisis also exposed the limits of the use of financial inclusion in the Global North for the realisation of social objectives such as housing, and how it can disproportionately affect more vulnerable subjects across the income, gender and racial spectrums (Young, Bakker and Elson 2011; Soederberg 2007; Montgomerie and Young 2011; Roberts 2012). Scholars have argued that both microfinance programmes in the Global South and subprime lending in the US are forms of 'poverty finance' (Rankin 2013) and 'debtfarism' (Soederberg 2013, 2014), highlighting the limits of financial inclusion in the Global North as in the Global South. However, the view of financial inclusion as a development strategy in the Global South also requires an analysis of how colonialism and development interventions have shaped financial exclusion and defined the conditions of inclusion, and of the historical, political, legal and socio-economic relations framing the developing/developed and South/North divide.

These reflections are particularly relevant because in 2009 the G20 leaders adopted a global agenda promoting universal financial inclusion as a policy instrument for financial stability, economic growth and the realisation of social goals, in response to the financial crisis. This commitment to financial inclusion, affirmed at the 2009 Pittsburgh G20 Summit, resulted in the creation of the Financial Inclusion Experts Group (FIEG) and is now supported by governments and well-known international institutions such as the IMF, the World Bank and the UN, as well as by emerging actors in the field of financial inclusion such as the Alliance for Financial Inclusion (AFI), the Groupe Spéciale Mobile Association (GSMA) and the Better Than Cash Alliance as well as governmental and non-governmental organisations, corporations and philanthropic foundations such as the Bill and Melinda Gates Foundation.

In 2010 the FIEG subgroup Access through Innovation developed its Principles for Innovative Financial Inclusion, a non-binding regulatory framework built on the World Bank's (2008) *Finance for All?* report focusing on improving access to finance via new types of financial services.[4] The Principles, endorsed by the G20 at their Toronto Summit, support the use of digital technology to reach the financially excluded via mobile phones, banking agents and payment services provided by retail outlets in grocery stores, pharmacies, kiosks and petrol stations, among others (Principle 3, Innovation). M-Pesa has become an example of digital financial innovation that extends financial services to those unserved and under-served by mainstream finance. Its rapid expansion and the fact that it originated in a country of the Global South has been used to promote the idea that successful digital financial inclusion projects can be realised even in contexts with a dominant informal sector, limited infrastructure and financial resources. The agenda for universal financial inclusion sees mobile money as more transparent and secure than informal finance and more convenient, available and inclusive than mainstream banking. The development of M-Pesa following the general loss of trust in finance engendered by the financial crisis has been used to support the idea that digital financial platforms such as mobile money can contribute to development goals such as poverty reduction and gender equality (UNCDF 2018).

The research presented in this book was motivated by a strong interest in unravelling the 'success' of M-Pesa and interrogating the nexus between digital financial inclusion and gender equality. Gender equality has become a key policy objective of the digital financial inclusion agenda,[5] and M-Pesa is often used as a successful example in this regard (Suri and Jack 2016). While M-Pesa, unlike microcredit programmes, does not specifically target women, it has become the only financial service that women living on a low and irregular income can afford. The FSD surveys (2007: 13, 2009: 19, 2013: 13–14, 2016: 6, 2019: 9) and the World Bank's Global Findex (World Bank 2018: 25) show that since the launch of M-Pesa the percentage of women and men with access to formal finance, including both banking and mobile money services, has increased evenly, although men are more likely to have a bank account or both a bank and a mobile account, while women are more likely to have only a mobile money account. Studies conducted by the FSD (Mintz-Roth 2018) and the Institute for Money, Technology and Financial Inclusion (Kusimba *et al.* 2013) show that women have integrated M-Pesa in their informal financial practices, micro-businesses and social networks.

This process of inclusion, which has extended the purview of financial markets to informal finance, has been promoted as an achievement in terms of gender equality which is celebrated and supported by governments, development institutions, donors, corporations and all the institutions supporting the digital financial inclusion agenda. Institutions such as the World Bank, the IMF, the UN, the GSMA, the AFI and the Bill and Melinda Gates Foundation draw on these data (FSD 2007, 2009, 2013, 2016, 2019; World Bank 2018) to promote mobile money as an opportunity for women and an instrument for universal financial inclusion and development. They target the reduction of the male-female gap in access to finance as a main policy objective of digital financial inclusion, but fail to consider the unequal social structures and relations and gendered socio-economic disadvantages that created that gap in the first place, and still limit access to mainstream banking.

This book engages with these questions and considers gender a relevant and revealing aspect of financial inclusion, not only because statistics present women as numerically predominant among the financially excluded and gender equality is a key policy component of digital finance but also, and particularly, because an investigation of gender relations can help with recognising and examining the social, economic and legal conditions that define financial exclusion and the logic and politics of inclusion. As Conaghan argues, 'gender functions [...] as a category of social ordering and can therefore be deployed as an analytical tool to interrogate particular social relational configurations and their effects' (2013: 24). Gender relations are not isolated from other social relations such as those of race, ethnicity, class and poverty, or from the macro-power relations created, for instance, by colonialism and globalisation. Looking at gender can help with investigation of the norms and patterns that are produced, reproduced and changed as a result of the intersection of these different power relations. In this context gender is an important analytical concept and a relevant methodological research tool (Mauthner 2000; Mohanty 2003), and the gender analysis presented in this book reflexively engages with, makes visible and addresses the complex economic, social and legal dynamics of digital financial inclusion.

A gender analysis of financial inclusion not only illustrates the socio-economic and legal disadvantages that determine financial exclusion, but can also help to interrogate the rationale of digital financial inclusion projects and measures and to reflect on whether and how the sphere of finance can be repoliticised as a site of struggle for social justice. Financial inclusion policies promote access to finance for women as a necessary condition of their own, their families' and their communities' autonomy and future wellbeing, in line with the development framework of 'gender equality as smart economics' (World Bank 2006, 2012), which advocates gender equality as a valuable instrument for economic efficiency and development, rather than recognising its intrinsic importance (Chant and Sweetman 2012; Roberts and Soederberg 2012; Prügl 2016). According to this logic, financial exclusion undermines women's ability to cope with uneven income flows, lack of resources and unexpected events; to engage in productive activities; and to juggle both paid and unpaid work. In the specific case of digital platforms such as M-Pesa, financial inclusion is seen as mitigating the precarity and vulnerability of women living in poverty and on a low and irregular income, increasing their mobility and security and placing them in a better position to access resources and services and a variety of entrepreneurial opportunities.

The Exclusionary Politics of Digital Financial Inclusion: Mobile Money, Gendered Walls problematises these claims, the assumptions on which they are based and the narratives and institutions that underpin them, and investigates the limits as well as the potential of digital financial inclusion as a development strategy for gender equality. Using Kenya's M-Pesa as a central case study, it examines whether digital financial inclusion can contribute to challenging and transforming unequal gender relations and interrogates the logics and politics of financial inclusion and gender equality in international development.

Situating the study

The analysis in this book is built around the example of M-Pesa in Kenya. M-Pesa offers a relevant case study not simply because of its rapid growth and perceived success, but also because of its influence on the international development agenda. M-Pesa allows the exploration of broader questions about the colonial legacy of financial exclusion, the gendered political economy of development, the regulation of digital financial platforms, the changing architecture of global financial governance and the multi-polar reconfiguration of South-North relations according to intersections of gender, race, socio-economic status and poverty. These questions follow the trajectory of the book, which begins by illustrating how global processes such as colonialism, globalisation and financialisation created the conditions for M-Pesa in Kenya; how the local development of M-Pesa shaped the role of digital financial inclusion at the global level; and how these global changes influenced the further development of M-Pesa and digital finance in Kenya.

Most studies of digital financial inclusion and M-Pesa have been produced by an interlinked network of mobile money professionals or, in Maurer's (2012: 301) words, 'mobile money intellectuals'. These mobile money experts are mostly based in and funded by the institutions involved in the mobile money market and its regulation including FSD Kenya, the World Bank's Consultative Group to Assist the Poor (CGAP), the United Nations Capital Development Fund (UNCDF), GSMA, AFI, the Better Than Cash Alliance and the Bill and Melinda Gates Foundation, which has been called the 'philanthropic arm' of the mobile money industry (Donovan 2015). They also include consultants and researchers funded by sectors such as the telecommunications and payment industries and financial institutions or associated with specialised research institutes such as the University of California, Irvine's Institute for Money, Technology and Financial Inclusion (IMTFI), which was also founded with a grant from the Bill and Melinda Gates Foundation. Some of these institutions, such as the donors' forum CGAP, were already involved in the global dissemination of microfinance, while others such as GSMA and AFI have become key actors in the digital financial inclusion agenda since 2008.

These studies initially focused on the rapid growth of M-Pesa in Kenya to identify lessons learned for the benefit of other countries (Heyer and Mas 2009; Mas and Morawczynski 2009; Mas and Radcliffe 2010; Jack and Suri 2011, 2014), and later more broadly on digital financial inclusion as a key instrument for realising the SDGs (Suri and Jack 2016). The above literature includes a variety of quantitative and qualitative analyses that assume that financial inclusion is a desirable outcome contributing to economic growth, poverty reduction and gender equality. Gender equality is overall considered a quantifiable goal whose measurement is mainly determined by the number of women able to access financial services.

There is, however, an emerging body of literature (Gabor and Brooks 2017; Bateman, Duvendack and Loubere 2019) that is more critical of the digital financial inclusion agenda, questioning the claim that financial technologies contribute to poverty reduction and local development. It points out the emerging practice of 'digital mining' for the benefit of telecommunication and financial corporations and the risk of repeating some of the negative patterns of microcredit, such as difficulties with creating a secure source of income and the trap of over-indebtedness, both in connection with micro-entrepreneurship. This literature adds to the extensive critique of microfinance and financialisation on which this research draws.

This book contributes to this literature by providing a feminist critique of digital financial inclusion which considers the history of colonialism, the implications of development discourses and interventions, and structural inequalities and power relations. It places gender at the centre of the analysis as an analytical and methodological tool to illustrate the limits of digital financial inclusion, but also to reflect on the potential for change. It looks at the gendered dynamics underpinning the governance of digital financial inclusion and at how gender equality policies are deployed in development discourse on financial inclusion. The investigation brings together socio-legal enquiry and feminist political economy analysis, using insights from law and development, post-colonial literature, feminist debates and fieldwork conducted in Nairobi, Kenya.

This methodological approach aims to capture the 'interconnectedness' (Perry-Kessaris 2014, 2015) of the global and local social, economic and legal dynamics that frame the development of M-Pesa and its role in the digital financial inclusion agenda. The socio-legal enquiry examines the structure, purpose and implications of the institutional and regulatory arrangements of M-Pesa, distinguishing between its inclusionary techniques and its potential to challenge gender and other social inequalities. This analysis cannot be detached from consideration of the gendered political economic context of M-Pesa, as shaped by colonialism and development interventions.

The fieldwork that prompted this study was conducted in 2012 and 2013 at the initial stage of this research project, with some follow-up interviews to monitor the development of M-Pesa's regulatory framework. The fieldwork served as a foundation from which to understand the context, institutions and functioning of M-Pesa and identify the key debates emerging as it has developed, rather than an interview-based or ethnographic study. This approach was motivated by a reflexive evaluation of the difficulty of giving a voice to M-Pesa users living in poverty or on a low income, in particular women, without reproducing the patterns and to some extent the politics created by the numerous institutions involved with M-Pesa and the mobile money market.

Unlike many development projects, M-Pesa is characterised by not the lack but the overproduction of data, most of which is collected and disseminated by the institutions mentioned above and provide detailed accounts of M-Pesa's users and uses which have been instrumental in the development of new mobile money products and services and in the expansion of the mobile money market. These data are presented around a main narrative of success demonstrating how M-Pesa has contributed to financial inclusion (FSD 2019). However, analysis of these data did not contextualise M-Pesa within the broader structures and power relations that define the development project, which is a main aim of this book.

The fieldwork in Nairobi involved observations, interviews and focus groups. Observation of day-to-day use of M-Pesa and how it is employed in markets, shops and informal finance meetings such as ROSCAs was necessary to understand how the service functions and its uses. To gather information on the institutional and regulatory framework of M-Pesa I conducted semi-structured interviews with representatives of the Central Bank of Kenya (CBK); FSD Kenya; Safaricom and other mobile network operators (MNOs); microfinance and financial institutions such as the Small and Micro Enterprise Programme, Jami Bora Bank, the Kenya Women Finance Trust (now the Kenya Women Microfinance Bank), Equity Bank, the Kenya Bankers' Association and the Association of Microfinance Institutions; governmental organisations such as the Kenya National Commission for Gender Equality, the Commission for Human

Rights and the Women Enterprise Fund; and non-governmental organisations such as the Kenya Human Rights Commission, the Kenya Law Reform Commission, the Law Society of Kenya and the Institute for Economic Affairs. I also interviewed mobile money agents in two districts in Nairobi, Kawagware and Ngando, to obtain insights from the people that run the M-Pesa network on the ground.

The core of the fieldwork was the focus groups of M-Pesa users in three low-income districts of Nairobi: Kawangware, Ngando and Mathare.[6] The use of focus groups was motivated by the need for dynamic and unstructured discussions that would help to define the key themes of the investigation. The groups were organised with the help of two social workers introduced to me by the Federation of Women Lawyers (FIDA), John Kariuki Ngethe and Jackline Onyancha. They helped me to establish a relationship of trust with the participants, and my collaboration with FIDA allowed me to position myself as a researcher working on gender rights rather than, for instance, working for one of the mobile money-related institutions. The relationship I built with the participants allowed me to take part in various local demonstrations demanding gender equality and social rights.

The focus group participants, most of whom earned income irregularly and were on or slightly above the poverty line of 1.90 USD per day (about 195 KES), included members of informal rotating credit and savings associations (ROSCAs, known as *chamas* in Kenya), members of other local support groups, casual workers and micro-entrepreneurs. They described the precarity of their informal jobs and how casual work and micro-entrepreneurship are often their only option. They considered their irregular and limited earnings a major reason for their inability to access formal financial services. Informal financial practices such as those provided by *chamas* were mentioned as a main source of support, particularly for women, helping them to cope with everyday necessities such as food, healthcare and children's school fees.

All the women in the focus groups were juggling paid and unpaid work, including care and community work, while searching for new ways to improve their livelihoods. M-Pesa was introduced to them by Safaricom as a more affordable – although still not cheap – payment service than those offered by banks, and for this reason useful for daily transactions, sending money to family in rural areas and creating entrepreneurial opportunities such as working as a mobile money agent. Our conversations on financial inclusion and the use of M-Pesa were directly or indirectly related to structural inequality, women's socio-economic disadvantage and the increasing influence and economic power of mobile network operators such as Safaricom.

These discussions revealed the need to link socio-legal enquiry with feminist political economy analysis in the methodology. The socio-legal enquiry shows how social and legal norms shape the gendered dynamics of financial exclusion and inclusion on the one hand, and illustrates the social implications of the institutional arrangements and regulatory frameworks of digital financial inclusion on the other. Feminist political economy analysis is necessary to examine the gender implications of apparently gender-neutral projects by illuminating women's visible and hidden socio-economic disadvantages and disproportionate responsibility for unpaid 'social reproduction' work. Feminist political economy scholars have coined the term social reproduction to denote the social relations, processes and labour that go into the daily and generational maintenance of the population across space and time (Katz 2001; Picchio 2003; Bakker and Silvey 2008). The concept of social reproduction has been deployed to analyse the disadvantaged status of women in Western capitalist societies (Elson 1979; Fortunati 2007; Federici 2012), but can also be used to understand the exclusionary and discriminatory impact of colonial norms and development interventions on gender relations (Rogers 1980; Elson 1989, 1991; Kabeer 1994). This point links back to the socio-legal investigation, as gendered disadvantages and disproportionate responsibilities can be created, exacerbated, ignored or mended by legal, policy and regulatory measures.

This methodological approach is integrated within the wide body of feminist knowledge that has shaped my orientation to research, questions and arguments, in particular African and Kenya feminism(s) and postcolonial and decolonial feminist thinking, gender and development literature and feminist legal theory. My fieldwork in Kenya was also important in that it provided the opportunity to access local libraries and engage with sources and literature not easily available in Western libraries that I would otherwise not have been able to explore.

Aims, trajectory and outline

This book was motivated by interest in investigating the development of M-Pesa, interrogating the relationship between digital financial inclusion and gender equality in the process. Throughout the analysis I engage with debates on the colonial legacy of financial exclusion; the rationale of 'inclusion' in the international development project; the embracement of the 'gender equality as smart economics' framework in the governance of mobile money; the links between philanthropy, business and digital financial inclusion; the regulation of digital financial platforms; and feminist discussions on socio-economic rights, social justice and redistribution, with the ultimate aim of understanding whether and how digital financial inclusion can contribute to challenging gender inequality at the lower end of the income distribution.

In addressing these questions I argue that while digital financial platforms such as M-Pesa facilitate access to formal financial services for women living on a low and irregular income, if they are to contribute to gender equality these platforms need to be accompanied by redistributive measures addressing the gendered socio-economic inequalities that have caused and reproduce financial exclusion. In a postcolonial context such as that of Kenya, the socio-economic inequalities that cause financial exclusion have been shaped by colonial rule and reproduced by development interventions that often use the rhetoric of inclusion to reframe rather than challenge exclusions (Cornwall and Rivas 2015). Possible redistributive measures include public healthcare, education and other social services, infrastructure and welfare schemes.

Throughout the analysis I show how M-Pesa and the narratives, partnerships and policies governing the digital financial inclusion agenda are premised on a logic of opportunity rather than a politics of redistribution. The politics of redistribution takes the view that people are entitled to the fair distribution of resources, the power that influences discourses and decisions, and gendered responsibility for social reproduction work. Drawing on postcolonial and critical development scholarship (Fanon 1963: 64; Nkrumah 1965; Manley 1991; Nyerere 2011; Anghie 2013, 2015; Ferguson 2015; Getachew 2019), I regard a politics of redistribution attentive to colonial history, unfair economic rules and structural and social inequalities, as essential to achieve decent standards of living for all people in the Global South, as in the Global North.

The logic of opportunity tends not only to ignore past and present political, economic and legal dynamics that have shaped gendered forms of exclusion but also risks furthering unequal gender relations by charging women with the responsibility for using the opportunities offered by mobile money to create improved livelihoods for themselves, their families and their communities in line with the mentioned development framework of 'gender equality as smart economics'. In other words, the logic of opportunity adds a further layer to what Chant (2008) calls the 'feminisation of responsibility and obligation' imposed on women by development. This exposes a general problem of financial inclusion as a development strategy for gender equality: the potential benefits can very easily become burdens when strategies to enhance women's autonomy and inclusion simply increase the load they bear and the number of demands to which they must respond (Kabeer 2015). The increased revenue, funding and investment deriving from M-Pesa and other digital financial platforms is not redistributed to provide women with the resources and social support necessary for them to take advantage of financial inclusion, but used to create further opportunities via new mobile money-enabled products and services that constitute a secure source of profit for the mobile network operator and the institutions involved in the mobile money business.

This book presents the above arguments in five chapters. To situate the book's contribution, Chapter 1, 'A brief herstory of gender, development and financial inclusion', introduces the debates around financial inclusion and gender equality as two interrelated aspects of the international development project. It begins with an examination of the economic, social and legal norms introduced during colonialism that excluded women from formal finance and presents the ensuing progressive development interventions seeking to provide them with access to financial services. The chapter analyses the relationship between financial inclusion and gender equality at different stages of the development project, looking in particular at the shifts from microcredit to microfinance and from microfinance to financial inclusion, and at the recent turn to digital finance. It argues that the rhetoric of financial inclusion exploits existing unequal gender relations to extend financial logic to areas that typically fall outside the purview of capitalist markets, without challenging the gendered socio-economic disadvantages that cause financial exclusion.

Chapter 2, 'Theorising gender and financial inclusion: opportunity v. redistribution', sets out the conceptual framework of the analysis. Drawing on feminist political economists' claim that a gender-equitable system requires the spheres of finance and production to serve the needs of social reproduction (Elson 2010, 2014), it examines digital financial inclusion within the nexus of finance, production and social reproduction in a postcolonial context such as that of Kenya. It investigates the possibility for financial inclusion to contribute to gender equality by looking at the interrelated concepts of autonomy and solidarity and of opportunity and redistribution and shows how digital financial inclusion is based on a logic of opportunity that encourages women's autonomy, relying on and even profiting from their solidarity and survival practices. These practices are often promoted as ones of resilience and even empowerment, rather than prompting the adoption of measures to ensure decent living standards that take into consideration women's disproportionate responsibility for social reproduction work and support them in managing it. Such thinking risks exacerbating gender inequality by imposing a further burden on women: the obligation to transform opportunity into success. The chapter argues that rethinking digital financial inclusion according to a politics of redistribution would contribute to more equal distribution of power, resources and responsibilities, and thus to more equal gender relations.

The centre of the book, Chapter 3, 'The story of M-Pesa in Kenya: a gender reading', explores the key case study, M-Pesa, highlighting its gendered characteristics. It starts by providing an overview of Kenya's postcolonial political economy and its gender implications, its formal and informal financial sectors and the increasing centrality of financial inclusion policies. It then shows how M-Pesa is the result of interaction between global and local dynamics and examines the institutional arrangements and regulatory framework that have contributed to defining it as an archetype of digital financial inclusion. While M-Pesa, unlike microcredit, does not target women specifically, the analysis shows how its development is embedded in gendered political, economic and social relations and institutions. The chapter argues that the rapid expansion of the M-Pesa service has relied on existing socio-economic inequality and exclusion and has created new gendered responsibilities by promoting the idea that poor people can live well on a small and irregular income if they have access to a financial instrument such as M-Pesa to help them manage their money efficiently.

Chapter 4, 'The gendered narratives of mobile money: from social entrepreneurship to philanthrocapitalism', locates the evolution of M-Pesa within the social entrepreneurship narrative, which has become increasingly dominant in mainstream development discourse. It maintains that M-Pesa is premised on a narrative of social entrepreneurship, promoting the idea that digital financial inclusion can both address social problems and produce profit. It analyses the articulations of this narrative in relation to digital financial inclusion, tracing the shift from social entrepreneurship to philanthrocapitalism, a type of philanthropy that emulates for-profit business in the capitalist world. It examines the gender implications of these narratives within the M-Pesa system by looking at the mobile money-enabled products and services built on its infrastructure and the opportunity to work as mobile money agents. It argues that M-Pesa has contributed to the reconceptualisation of access to basic resources and services as an entrepreneurial opportunity, resulting in public and private funding and investment being channelled into the mobile money market rather than into public social services and assistance. While the resources generated by the rapid development of mobile money are not redistributed, possible rewards are offered through opportunities which, however, leave the responsibility and risks inherent in taking advantage of them to the target beneficiaries – the financially excluded – often increasing gendered responsibility for social reproduction rather than challenging unequal gender relations.

Chapter 5, 'The gendered governance of mobile money: from local to global and back', illustrates the trajectory of the regulation and governance of mobile money and its gender implications. It explains how Kenya's main legal and policy frameworks for financial inclusion and gender equality, Kenya Vision 2030 and the 2010 Kenyan Constitution, are the results of interaction between global influences and local norms. While Kenya Vision 2030 focuses on economic growth and financial development, with an emphasis on gender equality as instrumental to these aims, the Constitution is seen as the result of a long grassroots struggle for national recognition of the importance of gender justice and socio-economic rights, among other principles. The chapter shows how M-Pesa's regulatory framework aims to create an enabling environment for financial inclusion and the expansion of the mobile money market, as proposed by the Kenya Vision, in preference to the more redistributive measures necessary for the realisation of the rights and purposes enshrined in the Constitution. This regulatory approach is endorsed by the institutions that constitute mobile money's global governance, in particular the FSD, GSMA, CGAP, the AFI, the Better Than Cash Alliance and the Bill and Melinda Gates Foundation, which promote gender equality as a measurable and profitable goal in order to ensure the social legitimacy of the business of the digital financial inclusion agenda.

In the concluding chapter I draw together the book's themes and arguments and argue for a politics of redistribution to guide financial inclusion projects, platforms and policies, considering the redistribution of power, resources and gendered responsibilities as necessary for social justice.

Notes

1 See S. Di Castri and L. Gidvani (2013) *The Kenyan Journey to Digital Financial Inclusion*, GSMA, www.gsma.com/mobilefordevelopment/wp-content/uploads/2013/07/MMU-Infographic-The-Kenyan-journey-to-digital-financial-inclusion.pdf (accessed 15 June 2019). According to the Safaricom Annual Report 2018, M-Pesa currently has 20.5 million active customers, www.safaricom.co.ke/images/Downloads/Safaricom_annual_report_070818.pdf (accessed 30 April 2019).

2 This research recognises the limits and problematic aspects of the terms Third World/First World, developing/developed and Global South/Global North, particularly concerning their simplistic and monolithic representation of highly heterogeneous countries. The idea of the Third World developed in relation to the First (capitalist) and Second (communist) Worlds and evokes ideas of poverty, tradition and non-industrialisation. 'Developing' and 'developed' refer mainly to the power relations whereby some countries are considered 'donors' of development (developed countries) and others as 'recipients' (developing countries). Similarly, the terms Global South and Global North and East and West are not used in reference to geographical location but rather to the political, economic, social and legal processes that have defined this division. In the same way, according to the Congolese philosopher Mudimbe (1988), the idea of 'Africa' as a 'paradigm of difference' means that it has served as a prism through which Westerners reflect images of the Other and of themselves.

3 The UN Sustainable Development Goals (SDGs) replaced the Millennium Development Goals (MDGs) as a set of human development goals supported by specific targets and indicators, to be achieved through global cooperation. The MDGs were adopted in 2000 with the aim of attaining them by 2015. Although the MDG Report of 2015 describes them as 'the most successful anti-poverty movement in history', the goals have not been met. The post-2015 development agenda built on the MDGs and led to the adoption of the SDGs in 2015, with the aim of achieving these by 2030. See General Assembly, *Transforming Our World: The 2030 Agenda for Sustainable Development*, A/RES/70/1, 21 October 2015.

4 G20 Financial Inclusion Experts Group, Innovative Financial Inclusion: Principles and Report on Innovative Financial Inclusion from the Access through Innovation Sub-Group of the G20 Financial Inclusion Experts Group, www.gpfi.org/sites/gpfi/files/documents/Principles%20and%20Report%20on%20Innovative%20Financial%20Inclusion_0.pdf (accessed 20 August 2019).

5 Gender Equality is a key development objective (Goal 5, UN SDGs) and for this reason has been embraced by the institutions supporting the digital financial inclusion agenda. In its Gender Equality Strategy, the Bill and Melinda Gates Foundation regards the opportunities offered by mobile money services such as M-Pesa as contributing to gender equality, see www.gatesfoundation.org/What-We-Do/Global-Growth-and-Opportunity/Gender-Equality (accessed 10 August 2019). Similarly, GSMA has a Connected Women Programme, www.gsma.com/mobilefordevelopment/programmes/connected-women/ (accessed 29 August 2019) and the Alliance for Financial Inclusion adopted the Denarau Programme aimed at bridging the gender gap in access to financial services, www.afi-global.org/gender-women-financial-inclusion (accessed 29 August 2019). Gender equality as a policy objective of digital financial inclusion is discussed in Chapter 5, fourth section: 'Gender in mobile money governance'.

6 The fieldwork involved six focus groups of five to seven informants each in Kawangware, Ngando and Mathare, and a final discussion with one or two informants from each group on the most relevant issues emerged from the fieldwork; observation and semi-structured interviews with 28 M-Pesa agents, 14 in Kawangware and 14 in Ngando; and 27 semi-structured interviews with representatives of financial institutions, MNOs and mobile money-related institutions, governmental and non-governmental organisations, regulatory institutions and research centres. Mathare, one of the places chosen for M-Pesa's pilot project, is one of the poorest slums in terms of infrastructure, services and security. It is characterised by precarious land rights as the land, officially owned by the government, has been appropriated by so-called 'structure owners' who

rent it to people who often struggle to pay the rent. Ngando is part of Nairobi's Dagoretti slum and is also characterised by poor infrastructure and services. In Ngando landowners build shelters and rent them out, but according to locals, richer people are buying land from poorer families in need of money and building bigger, expensive houses. In Kawangware most of the residents I interviewed were tenants; the district is considered a more entrepreneurial slum with numerous shops, markets and micro-businesses and many community initiatives such as schools and a support centre for people with disabilities. I selected these areas on the suggestion of John Kariuki Ngethe and Jackline Onyancha, the two social workers who helped me to organise the focus groups.

References

ACP Observatory on Migration (2011) *Remittances in the African, Caribbean and Pacific Countries, ACP Background Note*. Brussels: ACP Observatory on Migration.

Anghie, A. (2013) Whose Utopia? Human Rights, Development, and the Third World. *Qui Parle Special Issue: Human Rights between Past and Future*, 63–80.

Anghie, A. (2015) Legal Aspects of the New International Economic Order 6(1). *Humanity: An International Journal of Human Rights, Humanitarianism and Development*, 145–158.

Bakker, I. and Silvey, R. (eds) (2008) *Beyond States and Markets: The Challenges of Social Reproduction*. New York: Routledge.

Bateman, M., Duvendack, M. and Loubere, N. (2019) Is Fin-tech the New Panacea for Poverty Alleviation and Local Development? Contesting Suri and Jack's M-Pesa Findings Published in Science. *Review of African Political Economy*. DOI: 10.1080/03056244.2019.1614552

Chant, S. (2008) The 'Feminisation of Poverty' and the 'Feminisation' of Anti-Poverty Programmes: Room for Revision? *Journal of Development Studies* 44(2), 165–197.

Chant, S. and Sweetman, C. (2012) Fixing Women or Fixing the World? 'Smart Economics', Efficiency Approaches, and Gender Equality in Development. *Gender and Development* 20(3), 517–529.

Conaghan, J. (2013) *Law and Gender*. Oxford: Oxford University Press.

Cornwall, A. and Rivas, A. M. (2015) From Gender Equality to Global Justice: Reclaiming a Transformative Agenda for Gender and Development. *Third World Quarterly* 36(2), 396–415.

Cull, R., Demirguc-Kunt, A. and Murdoch, J. (2013) *Banking the World: Empirical Foundations of Financial Inclusion*. Cambridge: MIT Press.

Di Castri, S. and Gidvani, L. (2013) *The Kenyan Journey to Digital Financial Inclusion*, GSMA, www.gsma.com/mobilefordevelopment/wp-content/uploads/2013/07/MMU-Infographic-The-Kenyan-journey-to-digital-financial-inclusion.pdf (accessed 15 June 2019).

Donovan, K. P. (2012) Mobile Money, More Freedom? The Impact of M-Pesa's Network Power on Development as Freedom. *International Journal of Communication* 6, 2647–2669.

Donovan, K. P. (2015) Mobile Money, in R. Mansell and P. Hwa Ang (eds), *The International Encyclopedia of Digital Communication and Society*, Hoboken, NJ: Wiley-Blackwell.

Elson, D. (1979) The Value Theory of Labour, in Diane Elson (ed.) *Value: The Representation of Labour in Capitalism*. London: CSE Books.

Elson, D. (1989) The Impact of Structural Adjustments on Women: Concepts and Issues, in B. Onimode (ed.) *The IMF, The World Bank and the African Debt, Volume 2: The Social and Political Impact*. London: Zed Press.

Elson, D. (1991) Structural Adjustment: Its Effect on Women, in T. Wallace and C. March (eds) *Changing Perceptions: Writings on Gender and Development*. Oxford: Oxfam.

Elson, D. (2010) Gender and the Global Economic Crisis in Developing Countries: A Framework for Analysis. *Gender and Development* 18(2), 201–212.

Elson, D. (2014) Economic Crises from the 1980s to the 2010s: A Gender Analysis, in S. M. Rai and G. Waylen (eds) *New Frontiers in Feminist Political Economy*. Oxford: Routledge.

Fanon, F. (1963) *The Wretched of the Earth*. London: Penguin.

Federici, S. (2012) *Revolution at Point Zero: Housework, Reproduction and Feminist Struggle*. Brooklyn: PM Press.

Ferguson, J. (2015) *Give a Man a Fish: Reflections on the New Politics of Redistribution*. Durham: Duke University Press.

Fortunati, L. (2007) Immaterial Labour and its Machinization. *Ephemera: Theory and Politics in Organisation* 7(1), 139–157.

FSD Kenya and The Steadman Group Research Division (2007) *Financial Access in Kenya: Results of the 2006 National Survey*. Nairobi: FSD Kenya.

FSD Kenya and Central Bank of Kenya (2009) *FinAccess National Survey 2009: Dynamics of Kenya's Changing Financial Landscape*. Nairobi: FSD Kenya.

FSD Kenya and Central Bank of Kenya (2013) *FinAccess National Survey 2013: Profiling Developments in Financial Access and Usage in Kenya*. Nairobi: FSD Kenya.

FSD Kenya, Central Bank of Kenya, Kenya National Bureau of Statistics (2016) *The 2016 FinAccess Household Survey on Financial Inclusion*. Nairobi: FSD Kenya.

FSD Kenya, Central Bank of Kenya, National Bureau of Statistics (2019) *2019 FinAccess Household Survey*. Nairobi: FSD Kenya.

Gabor, D. and Brooks, S. (2017) The Digital Revolution in Financial Inclusion: International Development in the fintech Era. *New Political Economy* 22(4), 423–436, www.tandfonline.com/doi/abs/10.1080/13563467.2017.1259298

Getachew, A. (2019) *Worldmaking After Empire*. Princeton, NJ: Princeton University Press.

Goetz, A. M. (1996) Who Takes Credit? Gender, Power and Control over Loan Use in Rural Credit Programs in Bangladesh. *World Development* 24(1), 45–63.

GSMA (Francesco Pasti) (2019) State of the Industry Report on Mobile Money 2018. London: GSMA.

Heyer, A. and Mas, I. (2009) *Seeking Fertile Grounds for Mobile Money*. London: GSMA, Seattle, WA: Bill and Melinda Gates Foundation.

Jack, W. and Suri, T. (2011) *Mobile Money: The Economics of M-Pesa*. Cambridge, MA: MIT Sloan.

Jack, W. and Suri, T. (2014) Risk Sharing and Transactions Costs: Evidence from Kenya's Mobile Money Revolution. *American Economic Review* 104 (1), 183–223.

Kabeer N (1994) *Reversed Realities: Gender Hierarchies in Development Thought*. London: Verso.

Kabeer, N. (2001) Conflicts over Credit: Re-evaluating the Empowerment Potential of Loans to Women in Rural Bangladesh. *World Development* 29(1), 63–84.

Kabeer, N. (2015) Evolving Meanings of 'the Social' in the International Development Agenda. *Journal of International and Comparative Social Policy* 31(2), 114–131.

Karim, L. (2011) *Microfinance and its Discontent: Women in Debt in Bangladesh.* Minneapolis: University of Minnesota Press.

Katz, C. (2001) Vagabond Capitalism and the Necessity of Social Reproduction. *Antipode* 33(4), 709–728.

Kusimba, S., Chaggar H., Gross, E. and Kunyu, G. (2013) *Social Networks of Mobile Money in Kenya.* Irvine, CA: IMTFI, www.imtfi.uci.edu/files/2013-1_kusimba_1.pdf

Maclean, K. (2010) Capitalizing on Women's Social Capital? Women-Targeted Microfinance in Bolivia. *Development and Change* 42(3), 495–515.

Maclean, K. (2013) Gender, Risk and Micro-financial Subjectivities. *Antipode* 45(2), 455–473.

Manley, M. (1991) *The Poverty of Nations: Reflections on Underdevelopment and the World Economy.* London: Pluto.

Mas, I. and Morawczynski, O. (2009) Designing Mobile Money Services: Lessons From M-Pesa. *Innovations* 4(2), 77–92.

Mas, I. and Radcliffe, D. (2010) *Mobile Payments go Viral: M-Pesa in Kenya*, Seattle: Bill and Melinda Gates Foundation.

Maurer, B. (2012) Regulation as Retrospective Ethnography: Mobile Money and the Arts of Cash, *Banking and Finance Law Review* 27, 299–313.

Mauthner, M. (2000) Snippets and Silences: Ethics and Reflexivity in Narratives of Sistering. *International Journal of Social Research Methodology* 3(4), 287–306.

Mayoux, L. (2002) *Women's Empowerment or Feminisation of Debt? Towards a New Agenda in African Microfinance.* Report based on One World Action Conference London March 2002, One World Action.

Mintz-Roth, M. (2018) *The Gender and Age Dimensions of Mobile Money Adoption in Kenya*, FSD Research Brief 3, March. Nairobi: FSD Kenya.

Mohanty, C. M. (2003) *Feminism Without Borders: Decolonizing Theory, Practicing Solidarity.* Durham, NC: Duke University Press.

Montgomerie, J. and Young, B. (2011) *Home is Where the Hardship is: Gender and Wealth (Dis)Accumulation in the Subprime Boom.* Centre for Research on Socio-Cultural Change (CRESC) Working Paper Series 79, Milton Keynes: CRESC.

Mudimbe, V. Y. (1988) *The Invention of Africa.* Bloomington: Indiana University Press.

Nkrumah, K. (1965) *Neocolonialism: The Last Stage of Imperialism.* New York: International.

Nyerere, J. K. (2011) *Freedom and a New Economic Order: A Selection from Speeches, 1974–1999.* Dar es Salaam: Oxford University Press.

Perry-Kessaris, A. (2015) Approaching the Econo-socio-legal. *Annual Review of Law and Social Science* 11, 57.

Picchio, A. (2003) *Unpaid Work and the Economy: A Gender Analysis of the Standards of Living.* London-New York: Routledge.

Prügl, E. (2016) Neoliberalism with a Feminist Face. *Feminist Economics* 23(1), 30–53.

Rahman, A. (1999) *Women and Microcredit in Rural Bangladesh.* Boulder, CO: Westview Press.

Rankin, K. N. (2002) Social Capital, Microfinance, and the Politics of Development. *Feminist Economics* 8(1), 1–24.

Rankin, K. N. (2013) A Critical Geography of Poverty Finance. *Third World Quarterly* 34(4), 547–568.

Roberts, A. (2012) Financial Social Reproduction: The Gendered Relations of Debt and Mortgage Finance in Twenty-first-century America. *New Political Economy* 18(1), 21–42.

Roberts, A. and Soederberg, S. (2012) Gender Equality as Smart Economics? A Critique of the 2012 World Development Report. *Third World Quarterly* 33(5), 949–968.

Rogers, B (1980) *The Domestication of Women: Discrimination in Developing Societies*. London: Kogan Page.

Roy, A. (2010) *Poverty Capital: Microfinance and the Making of Development*. New York: Routledge.

Soederberg, S. (2007) Freedom, Ownership and Social (In-)Security in the United States. *Cultural Critique* 65, 94–114.

Soederberg, S. (2013) Universalising Financial Inclusion and the Securitisation of Development. *Third World Quarterly* 34(4), 593–612.

Soederberg, S. (2014) *Debtfare States and the Poverty Industry*. Oxford and New York: Routledge.

Suri, T. and Jack, W. (2016) The Long-run Poverty and Gender Impacts of Mobile Money. *Science* 354 (6317), 1288–1292.

UNCDF (United Nations Capital Development Fund) (2018) UNCDF and the SDGs: Financial Inclusion and the SDGs, www.uncdf.org/financial-inclusion-and-the-sdgs

Williams, T. (2001) Requiem for Microcredit? The Decline of a Romantic Ideal. *Banking and Finance Law Review* 19(2), 145.

World Bank (2006) *Gender Equality as Smart Economics: A World Bank Group Gender Action Plan*. Washington, DC: World Bank.

World Bank (2008) *Finance for All? Policies and Pitfalls in Expanding Access*. World Bank Policy Research Report. Washington, DC: World Bank.

World Bank (2012) *World Development Report 2012: Gender Equality and Development*. Washington, DC: World Bank.

World Bank (2018) *The Global Findex Database 2017: Measuring Financial Inclusion and the Fintech Revolution*. Washington, DC: World Bank Group.

Young, B., Bakker, I. and Elson, D. (eds) (2011) *Questioning Financial Governance from a Feminist Perspective*. London: Routledge.

1 A brief herstory of gender, development and financial inclusion

The international development project: an overview

People in various territories of the Global South have found themselves and their indigenous norms and institutions subjected to increasing Western intervention, starting with colonialism in the sixteenth and seventeenth centuries onwards and continuing as targets of the development project. Colonised nations became part of the capitalist world market by supplying labour, raw materials and other commodities to the West, and were forced to 'modernise' their institutions to follow the 'developed' Western path (Mugo 2012: 198). Even after independence, the autonomy of the newly created nation states remained conditional on rules of international law and development shaped by the liberal vision of the world order and designed to protect Western economic interests (Pahuja 2011). Following the end of the Cold War in 1991 and what has been called the global victory of Western liberal democracy and capitalism over communism (Fukuyama 1992), Western countries have increasingly exercised a powerful influence over the policies of newly independent governments, both directly and through institutions such as the United Nations (UN), the World Bank, the International Monetary Fund (IMF), the Organisation for Economic Co-operation and Development (OECD), aid agencies such as the UK Department for International Development (DFID) and the US Agency for International Development (USAID), non-governmental organisations (NGOs), corporations and the all-pervasive ramifications of international finance including loans and aid.[1]

Particularly relevant measures that have framed the development project are the Washington Consensus and the adoption of structural adjustment programmes (SAPs) in the 1980s and 1990s; the UN Millennium Development Goals (MDGs) and the post-Washington Consensus in 2000 and the Sustainable Development Goals (SDGs) that replaced the MDGs in 2015. SAPs represented a package of loans conditional on the adoption of neoliberal policies imposed on developing countries by the Washington-based World Bank and IMF. Such policies included measures to stabilise, liberalise and globalise economies by lowering barriers to foreign capital, controlling inflation by reducing government spending, and privatising public services and state-owned industries. However, much research has shown that SAPs contributed to increasing economic and social inequality and poverty with devastating consequences for a large proportion of the population living on a low income, in particular women, who became disproportionately responsible for social provisioning in the household (Elson 1989, 1991, 1992; Benería 2003: 3; Bergeron 2004: 130; Jaquette and Summerfield 2006: 27). The MDGs, drawing on criticism of SAPs, proclaimed the need for greater attention to the social dimension of development and to expanding development institutions' competency, cooperation and intervention to include social objectives such as poverty reduction and gender equality (Rittich 2006). This expansion was driven by principles of good governance and the rule of law and supported by a parallel apparatus of international institutions, governments and donors with the task of coordinating the funds and financing for the evaluation and realisation of these goals (White and Black 2004). In replacing the MDGs, the SDGs reframed the social aims of development around the ideas of inclusion, economic, social and environmental sustainability and 'leaving no one behind' (Weber 2017). They continue to promote free market policy but added an additional layer of interventions focusing on good governance, people's empowerment and new collaborations with non-state actors, philanthropic foundations and the private sector.

The development project can be seen as the process of offering to formerly colonised countries a variety of conditional opportunities to align themselves with Western societies and become active participants in the global economic order. These conditions, defined by more powerful Western states and international institutions, are based on trade, financial rules and principles related to liberal democracy, resonating with US President Truman's view of the way to development, as he stated in his 1949 inaugural speech: through productive activities, technological resources, business and private capital and liberal values.[2] In the development project the realisation of decent standards of living for all people and socio-economic rights such as food, water, shelter and healthcare is not considered a priority per se, but it is linked to the aim of economic growth and, increasingly, financial development. In the immediate postcolonial period this resulted in the failure to implement the Declaration on the Right to Development, proposed by former colonial countries in 1986 following the adoption of the International Covenant on Economic, Social and Cultural Rights (ICESCR) in 1966.[3] The Declaration on the Right to Development was part of the Third World campaign for a New International Economic Order (NIEO), which started in the 1970s and argued for the economic reconstruction and redistribution necessary to ensure a decent standard of living for all people in former colonies (Bedjaoui 1979; Cheru 2016; Slaughter 2018; Getachew 2019). The NIEO pointed to the unequal economic relations between Southern and Western countries and emphasised the collective duty of all states to eliminate unfair trade rules and commodity prices, ensure permanent sovereignty over resources and build world food security (Anghie 2013). These proposals were rejected by Western countries, which saw them as one-sided obligations and socialist projects incompatible with Western liberal values and therefore problematic during the Cold War (Cornwall and Nyamu-Musembi 2004: 1422). Even since the Cold

War, development concerns regarding socio-economic rights have been deliberately framed as social objectives rather than rights and have mainly been promoted through market initiatives rather than public action for universal social provisioning.

This overview is an important starting point for the analysis of digital financial inclusion as a development strategy for gender equality. Gender equality has become a main social objective of the international development project, which promotes financial inclusion as a key instrument for achieving it. Analysis of the colonial legacy, the narratives and institutions that have framed the mainstream development project and the alternative ideas of economic and social development presented in the NIEO can help us understand the assumptions, rationale and limits of digital financial inclusion and its gender implications. To better situate the arguments developed in this book within the academic and policy debates to which it aims to contribute, this chapter provides an overview of the relationship between gender equality and financial inclusion as interrelated aspects of the development project. Drawing on the literature on law and development and international political economy, and engaging with feminist critiques of microfinance and financial inclusion, it discusses three key aspects of financial inclusion as a gendered issue: the second section looks at the legacy of colonialism in defining the socio-economic disadvantage of women that determines financial exclusion; the third section examines the rise in access to finance as a development strategy in the form of microcredit and the shift to a broader financial inclusion policy framework; and the fourth section presents the more recent turn to digital financial inclusion.

This chapter shows how the financial exclusion of women, presented as a general assumption in financial inclusion policy, is in reality strictly linked to socio-economic and legal structures and norms developed since colonialism and aimed at creating a capitalist world market. Rules on such issues as the commodification of land, the wage economy and customary norms introduced during colonialism created a gendered disadvantage that has excluded women from economic development and undermined their entitlements. Addressing this exclusion, the development project has increasingly promoted access to financial services as a useful or even necessary opportunity to include women in the economic system, increase their autonomy and improve their own, their families' and their communities' wellbeing. However, the rhetoric of inclusion has taken the form of inclusionary techniques that fail to address the socio-economic inequalities that caused financial exclusion in the first place. At the same time, financial inclusion and its digital development has become a profitable instrument for corporations, financial institutions, philanthropic foundations and other new influential development actors.

The legacy of colonialism

No investigation of the relationship between gender, development and financial inclusion can be isolated from an analysis of the gendered implications of colonial rule. As this book is concerned with digital financial inclusion in Kenya, the main focus of the analysis is on Africa and in particular on Sub-Saharan Africa. As Okeyo (2005: 299) argues

> the position of women in contemporary Africa needs to be considered at every level of analysis as an outcome of structural and conceptual mechanisms by which African societies have continued to respond to and resist the global processes of economic exploitation and cultural domination.

Gender inequality in Africa is bound up in the African people's struggle to free themselves from the poverty caused by colonialism. Okeyo (2005: 299–300) points out that while men and women under colonialism shared a similar subordinate structural position in relation to the dominant culture, colonial rules had a differential impact on them and affected gender relations. This section considers three interrelated aspects of how colonialism has shaped women's socio-economic disadvantage and excluded them from formal finance: the commodification of land and the introduction of property rights, the rules governing the wage economy and the creation of customary law.

Colonialism in Africa involved the expropriation of land from indigenous people, restructuring access to it on a monetary basis (Manji 2006). The introduction of property rights undermined the previous 'egalitarian pattern of social organisation' (Laesthaeghe 1989: 51) in favour of patriarchal relations that saw men as the household heads and holders of land titles (Maathai 2008; Federici 2011). The introduction of the wage economy targeted men as paid workers and the family breadwinners (Hodgson 1999; Obeng 2003), relegating women to the position of secondary unpaid workers (Boserup 1970; Manji 1999; Okeyo 2005). Most men earned wages in a discriminatory and often exploitative labour market in mines, farms and infrastructure construction, and often had to migrate to newly created urban areas or fight in colonial wars (Okeyo 2005: 301). Most women, on the other hand, were excluded from paid labour and engaged in unpaid subsistence agriculture, selling surplus produce to acquire goods, and housework including fetching water and firewood from several kilometres away (Maathai 2008: 281; Nixon 2013: 16). This contributed to the framing of women as responsible for unpaid household work, depending on men for money and excluded from financial services (Guyer 1991).

The wage economy also favoured reshaping the family structure and values with a shift to the nuclear family that was seen as the emblem of Western modernity (Zeitlin *et al.* 1995). Imported Christian values and missionary education contributed to limiting households to the heterosexual conjugal relationship rather than, as previously, extended households including other kin (Afonja 1981; Guyer and Peters 1987; Whitehead 1990; Oyèwùmí 2005: preface; Tamale 2011: 18). Christian missionaries instilled the ideals of obedience, domesticity and 'appropriate' female behaviour such as monogamy, marital fidelity and conjugal intimacy, and reinforced the roles of the male breadwinner and the dependent wife who manages the household (Cornwall 2005: 6;

Ngaruiya and O'Brien 2005: 145). The dismantling of the extended household deprived women of the support that had acted as a protective buffer for social provisioning, and was not replaced by state welfare services (Maathai 2010: 274).[4] Instead women, responsible for the daily needs of the household, found support in churches and other religious institutions, women's self-help groups, and later, development programmes and NGOs (Gaitskell 1990).[5]

Customary law contributed to women's socio-economic disadvantage by normalising the gender biases caused by land ownership and the wage economy, resulting in the consideration of women as what Oyèwùmí defines as 'second-class colonial subjects' (1997: 127). Chanock (1982) describes customary law as a product of the relationship between the colonial state and male clan elders, while Oyèwùmí (1997) defines customary rules as reinvented traditions, as their ultimate source was the colonial government and administration. Customary laws were in fact filtered according to colonial values via the 'repugnancy' clause with the aim of controlling government matters, protecting the economic interests of the West and favouring its economic expansion (Juma 2002; Banda 2003; Ocran 2006).[6] In this way customary law facilitated and legitimised the subordination of women in areas such as property and domestic and family law including marriage, divorce, inheritance, land and burial rights (Hay and Wright 1982; Stamp 1991; Manji 1999).

These discriminatory laws and women's exclusion from land ownership and the wage economy prevented them from owing or even inheriting property and capital, undermining their ability to open a bank account or access formal financial services (Guyer 1991). While men living in poverty and on a low income did not have easy access to finance either, women were at a greater disadvantage in accessing formal finance. This clarification is important, because early development interventions tended to portray African women as victims of African culture and African men (Cutrufelli 1984) without considering the structural subordinate position shared by men and women under the colonisers. Their economic and financial exclusion meant that women had to find ways of coping with daily household social and economic needs which, particularly for low-income women, resulted in the creation of self-help groups (Oduol and Kabira 1995: 187). Some of these groups developed into informal credit and savings associations such as *chamas* in Kenya (Kinyanjui 2012).

The gender roles and relations shaped by colonial rule continued to resonate in the postcolonial period. In many parts of Africa, normative discourses reinforced by Christian religious influences emphasised the importance of women's obedience and subjection while institutionalising men in their role as the household head and breadwinner (Cornwall 2005: 6). Although women played an active role in the struggles for independence in Africa, they were mainly constructed as 'the bearers and upholders of traditions and customs' (Mama 1997: 54). These gender roles resulted in a male bias in the organisation of newly independent nation states as well as in early development interventions (Mikell 2007). The political and economic marginalisation of women has been denounced by local feminist movements (Basu 1995) and, in response to this, the development project has increasingly targeted women's exclusion from market opportunities with policies and programmes for economic and financial inclusion.

From microcredit to universal financial inclusion

The relationship between gender equality and financial inclusion can be linked first of all to the process of including women in the development project, originating in the 1970s and culminating in the adoption of gender quality as a development goal in its own right in the MDGs 2000, and restated in the SDGs in 2015.[7] This process has focused on women's economic inclusion as a way of overcoming all other barriers to equality, generally ignoring the role of colonialism and of development itself in engineering gendered forms of exclusion.

In 1962 the UN General Assembly asked the Commission on Women's Status, established in 1946, to compile a report on the role of women in development. Ester Boserup's study, *Women's Role in Economic Development*, published in 1970, demonstrated the negative impact of colonialism on women, showing how the wage economy that targeted male workers resulted in women's exclusion from economic development and education and in the erosion of their political authority and entitlements, undermining their social status. The report combined an argument for the inclusion of women with one for efficiency, as women's participation in the wage economy would have improved production and the expansion of the cash economy, improving their status at the same time. These two arguments came to characterise the theorisations and policy debates constituting the Women in Development (WID) approach, largely inspired by Western liberal feminism. From the 1980s this approach was gradually replaced by the Gender and Development (GAD) framework, which drew upon postcolonial and Third World feminist critiques of inclusion and encouraged development institutions to pay more attention to the contextual construction of gender roles. Although GAD has shed light on unequal gender structures and relations, development policies have continued to focus mainly on women, often without challenging structural inequalities. In this way, GAD provided a framework for adverse and/or converging interests in gender equality among grassroots feminists, Western feminist groups, NGOs, national governments, international organisations, transnational networks and, increasingly, corporations.

Since the publication of Boserup's report international development organisations, bilateral and multilateral donors and local governments began to fund and support programmes and projects to provide women with opportunities for economic and financial inclusion (Tripp 2000: 9–10; Lewis 2005: 389). Women's inability to access finance was soon seen as a constraint to their economic inclusion and to their ability to provide for their families, and financial inclusion seemed the 'common missing piece' in development policies (McKee 1989: 995).

In the immediate postcolonial period access to finance was a secondary concern by both Western and local governments, as also for development institutions such as the IMF and World Bank, which tended to view the challenge of economic development as a matter of building visible infrastructure such as roads, power plants and canals (Caufield 1996). However, people were already engaging in informal financial practices to manage their everyday needs. They included money-lending and rotating credit and savings associations (ROSCAs), also known as 'merry-go-round', where members meet regularly and contribute to a common pot, which is given to one member on a rotating basis so that every participant receives the money over time (Geertz 1962; Bouman and Houtman 1988; Austin and Sugihara 1993; Ardener and Burman 1995).

The initial donor-funded and state-led poverty lending programmes provided subsidised credit to small farmers, usually male household heads (Rankin 2013: 553). Subsidised credit, however, was seen by the World Bank and IMF as inefficient and expensive as governments charged farmers less than the cost of the credit and had to support the costs of these programmes (Roodman 2012). For this reason, the microcredit experiment that would charge borrowers prices much closer to the cost of delivery and hold them fully accountable for repayments was soon acclaimed. It became central to the neoliberal development agenda that had introduced the SAPs of the 1980s and 1990s. In gender terms, microcredit marked a shift in approach from state-subsidised access to credit for male-headed households to third-sector microfinance institutions targeting poor women as entrepreneurial agents (Rankin 2002: 11–12).

Microcredit, seen for years as the archetype of financial inclusion in the Global South, involves the extension of small collateral-free loans to jointly liable groups of poor women to be used for income-generating activities, mainly in the form of micro-entrepreneurship. The typical microcredit contract, referred to as the Grameen model, involves loans to a group of poor women considered not creditworthy due to their lack of assets and stable wages. The borrowers are held liable for each other's loans, and possible future loans to all group members are withheld if any borrower has not repaid a previous loan. The roots of microcredit can be found in informal financial methods such as ROSCAs, but the beginning of institutional microcredit is usually linked to Muhammad Yunus and the founding of Bangladesh's Grameen Bank (Yunus 1999). Yunus is a former economics professor who returned from the US to take up a position in Bangladesh in 1972, and in 1976 started a series of experiments in the form of an action research project. He began by lending small amounts of his own money to poor households in the village of Jobra to enable them to start small business activities in the informal sector. Convinced that this project could contribute to reducing poverty, in 1976 he persuaded the Central Bank of Bangladesh to help him set up a special branch, first for the poor people of Jobra and later for those in other villages in Bangladesh. In 1983 a government ordinance officialised the Grameen Project as the Grameen Bank, a specialist credit institution with a mandate to provide credit services to poor people in rural Bangladesh, and in 1989 the Grameen Trust, a non-profit organisation using microcredit to fight poverty, was established.[8]

The programmatic success of the Grameen Bank (Rahman 1999: 21)[9] resulted in microcredit being incorporated in various development programmes such as the SAPs by international organisations and embraced by NGOs, well-established financial institutions, non-bank financial corporations and philanthropic foundations. The internationalisation of microcredit and its promotion as a development panacea also resulted in the proclamation by the UN of the International Year of Microcredit in 2005, legitimising microcredit as an important instrument for meeting the MDGs, and in particular poverty reduction and gender equality. This was followed by the awarding of the Nobel Peace Prize to Yunus and the Grameen Bank in 2006. These events increased support and funding for microcredit initiatives, which resulted in microfinance becoming an extremely profitable industry (Roy 2010).

Since the 1990s the term ‘microcredit’ has been gradually replaced by ‘microfinance’, referring to a broad range of small-scale financial products for the poor beyond credit for starting a microenterprise including savings, insurance and payment services (Armendariz and Morduch 2010: 15). While the terms ‘microcredit’ and ‘microfinance’ are often used interchangeably, ‘microfinance’ denotes a shift in the approach to access to finance. The initial focus of microcredit was poverty reduction and the economic inclusion of poor women, and the key providers were NGOs. With the change in language came a change in orientation towards a variety of financial products and providers, including self-sustaining, commercially oriented and regulated microfinance institutions that function according to financial markets, adopting mainstream financial tools such as credit bureaus and credit scoring, and also targeting less-poor low-income people for inclusion in the mainstream financial system (Armendariz and Morduch 2010: 15). This expansion in access to finance, however, risks excluding the poorest and placing those with a low income on a particular grid of risk based on their social and economic status, pricing their inclusion accordingly (Allon 2014: 23).

Although microcredit and microfinance schemes have been promoted as more effective ways of achieving development, poverty reduction and gender equality than the earlier state-subsidised credit, they remain largely dependent on external funding, often provided by donors. This is essential to ensure that microfinance institutions can serve poorer consumers, and for this reason the development sector has increasingly engaged with the private sector and multinational corporations to offer microfinance schemes. The Bill and Melinda Gates Foundation, for instance, launched its Financial Services for the Poor initiative in 2006 and since then has invested a large amount of money in financial inclusion, often in partnership with the private sector. These initiatives have resulted in ongoing debate on the correlation between the financial sustainability and profitability of microfinance institutions and their development aims (Conning 1999; Morduch 2000; Hermes 2011). This relationship is particularly relevant to analyse the nexus between financial inclusion and gender equality in development discourse.

The fact that microcredit targets predominantly women and that most borrowers are female was initially seen as proof of a successful gender equality project (Rahman 1999: 14, 74). By giving women access to financial services and economic opportunities, microcredit has been acclaimed for strengthening their position in the household, reducing their vulnerability and economic dependence on men, improving their status in the community and providing them with financial knowledge, capital and organisational skills to manage the loans. However, feminist, critical development and international political economy scholars have long investigated and questioned these potential gains, pointing out the limits to these claims.

First of all, such claims do not consider the unequal gender roles and relations in both the household and microcredit institutions. For instance, research has shown how patriarchal structures defined by gender roles such as 'male household head' and 'breadwinner' resulted in males controlling the use of loans and an escalation of household violence (Goetz 1996; Rahman 1999: 126, 149; Kabeer 2001). The exclusive focus on women as the target of a development strategy for financial inclusion singled them out without corresponding attention to men, contributing to further distortions in the understanding of gender relations and reinforcing the gender stereotypes created during colonial rule (Cornwall and White 2000). Second, the practice of group lending with joint responsibility for repaying loans and the gendered notion of shame have been used as social control mechanisms to guarantee micro-loan repayments and ensure microfinance institutions' financial sustainability (Williams 2001; Rankin 2002; Maclean 2010; Roy 2010). Third, the pressure to repay loans has created a risk of ever-expanding cycles of debt, often forcing women to borrow money to repay loans and affecting their ability to provide for the household (Rahman 1999; Williams 2001; Mayoux 2002; Taylor 2012).

The risk of over-indebtedness also relates to the limits of micro-entrepreneurship for generating profit. Women can only access micro-loans to produce goods and services for sale in the market, a condition that is presented as providing them with access to remuneration from work. However, micro-entrepreneurship does not provide the same possibilities as paid wage labour, particularly in terms of guaranteeing an adequate income level to meet basic needs (Kabeer 2012). The micro-entrepreneurship promoted by microcredit manifests primarily in small-scale informal sectors of the economy, or 'micro-informality' (Elyachar 2002), involving activities such as hairdressing or selling fish, flowers or unprocessed food. These informal micro-businesses require only a small amount of money to get started and can often be combined with household work. However, they involve low productivity and low returns, have limited local demand (Breman 2003) and often compete with cheap imports (Lairap-Fonderson 2002). While providing women with some income, microcredit excludes them from large-scale enterprise and makes them dependent on microcredit institutions.

Research has consistently shown that poor women seek loans for reasons beyond micro-entrepreneurship such as to buy food and water, to pay school and health fees and to cope with everyday needs in general (Lairap-Fonderson 2002; Lingam 2008; Shakya and Rankin 2008). This point was widely demonstrated by the gendered impact of SAPs. Studies have incisively shown that the process of privatising common resources, utilities and services that began with SAPs had a negative impact on people at the lower end of the income distribution, and particularly women (Elson 1989, 1991, 1992; Benería 2003: 3; Bergeron 2004: 130; Jaquette and Summerfield 2006: 27). Charging fees for healthcare and education and ending food subsidies forced families to rely on their own resources or resort to moneylenders and microcredit schemes. This had important consequences for gender relations, as it placed particular burdens on women's shoulders, increasing their responsibilities for social provisioning (Benería 2003; Eisenstein 2005). Importantly in this regard, microcredit and microfinance programmes have been coordinated neither with the reform of land, property and family legislation nor with policy measures to facilitate women's access to resources, employment, housing, healthcare and education.

This demonstrates how rather than addressing women's socio-economic disadvantages microcredit has relied on and even reinforced unequal gender roles and relations. Targeting women as the main customers for microfinance not only aimed at their financial inclusion but was also a strategy for careful financial management to benefit the microfinance institution (Williams 2001). Women, who are seen as responsible and risk-averse, were expected to use microcredit to work as micro-entrepreneurs and repay their loans while simultaneously producing a household income to feed and educate their children and contributing to the wellbeing of their community. According to Rahman (1999: 148), women became the preferred microcredit customers because of their 'positional vulnerability': they were seen as submissive, immobile and easy to discipline. In this way they met the requirements of the micro-lending structure, which includes borrowers' attendance at weekly meetings and a rigid repayment schedule. According to this logic, lending to women ensures not only the sustainability but also the profitability of the microcredit industry (Rankin 2001; Roy 2010). The portrayal of women as hardworking and more caring, responsible and reliable than men framed the narrative of women and girls as instrumental in and even profitable for development (Cornwall and Rivas 2015: 399). This logic has been formalised in the World Bank's 'gender equality as smart economics' framework (World Bank 2006, 2012), which advocates gender equality as a valuable instrument for economic efficiency and development, rather than recognising its intrinsic importance for social justice.

In this way microcredit and microfinance programmes and services, promoted as development strategies for gender equality, have contributed 'to the broader goals of deepening financial markets to areas that typically fall outside the purview of capitalist markets' (Rankin 2001: 28), such as the household, the informal economy and grassroots financial practices (Young 2010; Manji 2010; Rankin 2013). The idea of extending financial services to poor households and possibly formalising their informal financial practices has characterised the shift from microcredit programmes and microfinance services to a broader financial inclusion strategy. This shift is the result of development institutions' increasing interest in grassroots financial practices other than microcredit (Collins *et al.* 2009) and was prompted by the 2007–2008 financial crisis, in the aftermath of which financial inclusion became a policy instrument for financial stability, growth and development (Soederberg 2013). Following the crisis, the G20 leaders at the 2009 Pittsburgh Summit committed to improving access to financial services for people at the lower end of the income distribution via new modes of financial services, and for this purpose they created the Financial Inclusion Experts Group (FIEG). The FIEG subgroup, Access through Innovation, adopted the Principles for Innovative Financial Inclusion endorsed at the Toronto G20 Summit in 2010, a non-binding regulatory framework that builds on earlier World Bank documents, in particular the World Bank policy research report *Finance for All?* adopted in 2008.[10] The Principles were followed by the launch of a Global Partnership for Financial Inclusion (GPFI) to implement the agenda. This partnership has been facilitated by the UN's SDG framework, which encourages collaboration between different development actors including governments, NGOs, private sector and philanthropic foundations, all committed to gender equality as a development goal and as a policy objective of digital financial inclusion.

Financial inclusion's digital turn

The G20 Principles for Innovative Financial Inclusion adopted in 2010, in the aftermath of the 2007–2008 financial crisis, supported the idea of financial innovation via new forms of financial service delivery that would be capable of reaching the financially excluded via mobile phones, banking agents and payment services provided by retail outlets at grocery stores, pharmacies, kiosks and petrol stations, among others (Principle 3, Innovation). The G20 Principles have been embraced by well-known international institutions such as the IMF, the World Bank, the UN and the World Economic Forum, by emerging actors in the field of financial inclusion such as the Alliance for Financial Inclusion (AFI), the Groupe Spéciale Mobile Association (GSMA) and the Better Than Cash Alliance, and by governmental and non-governmental organisations, financial institutions, corporations and philanthropic foundations such as the Bill and Melinda Gates Foundation, and research institutes such as the Institute for Money, Technology and Financial Inclusion (IMTFI) at the University of California, Irvine.

As well as the 2007–2008 financial crisis, the global financial inclusion agenda has been shaped by other factors. First, the development community's increasing interest in the financial methods used by people living in poverty or on a low income (Rutherford 2001; Collins *et al.* 2009) which also corresponded to the changing perception in mainstream development discourse of the 'poor' as actors (Sen 1999), entrepreneurs (de Soto 2000) and consumers (Prahalad 2004), rather than just as recipients of aid and development interventions. Second, the spread of information and communication technologies (ICTs) and particularly mobile phones in the Global South; and the consequent development of mobile phone-enabled financial services, namely 'mobile money', and forms of branchless banking. In this regard, Kenya's M-Pesa, the central case study in this book, has become a key example of the financial innovation envisaged in the G20 Principles due to its rapid growth in Kenya, where it has reached over 70 per cent of the local population.

Interest in the financial instruments used by the poor has increasingly grown beyond microcredit and microfinance. The book, *Portfolios of the Poor* (Collins *et al.* 2009), which followed *The Poor and Their Money* (Rutherford 2001), has been particularly acclaimed for bringing awareness of poor and low-income households' sophisticated money management practices to development and financial institutions and corporations (Rutherford 2001; Collins *et al.* 2009). It shows how people living on a low income, and particularly women, are competent financial subjects and how they rely on complex socio-financial mechanisms and use a mixture of informal and formal financial services to manage their everyday lives. These practices are often embedded in gendered structures and relations with family members, neighbours, moneylenders, and savings and credit groups (Collins *et al.* 2009: 14). The book is premised on the idea that '[n]ot having enough money is bad enough, [but] not being able to manage whatever money you have is worse' (ibid.: 184). While it recognises the complexity of poverty beyond financial exclusion, it also sees access to affordable and reliable financial services as instrumental in addressing this and improving peoples' livelihoods, at risk of legitimising the idea that poor people can live well on a low income if they have the instruments to manage their small amount of money efficiently.

Portfolios of the Poor generated a lot of interest within the development community and contributed to framing the global agenda for universal financial inclusion in line with the increasingly dominant approach to development that combines entrepreneurship and the production of profit for the private sector with the achievement of social objectives. The book introduced a methodological framework, the financial diaries, namely households' management of money within a defined timeframe, which has been adopted by various institutions researching financial inclusion.[11] It has also encouraged donors, corporations and financial inclusion professionals to think about 'latching onto people's existing networks' to provide a variety of financial services to those excluded from or under-served by mainstream finance (Maurer 2012: 417). ICTs are considered useful for facilitating this aim by producing information about people's networks as well as providing access to these networks. Among them, mobile phones are seen as one of the most accessible technologies because of their wide availability and affordability. Research has argued that mobile phones have low infrastructural costs compared to other technologies (Bar and Galperin 2007; Yonazi *et al.* 2012) and that mobile devices are marketed at a low price and can easily be shared, facilitating access (Aker and Mbiti 2010). Mobile phones have increasingly been promoted as instruments for social and economic inclusion and development, although it is important to highlight that the infrastructure for the mobile money network is private rather than public and so access to it involves a cost to users and a corresponding profit for providers. The Mobile for Development framework has been embraced by institutions such as the UN, World Bank, IMF and various private sector actors (Donner 2008). As part of this framework, mobile phones are often promoted as a pathway to overcoming the gender gap in technology, but also education, paid work and finance (Scott *et al.* 2004; Gurumurthy and Chami 2014).

The possibility of using the mobile phone network to expand access to formal financial services to the excluded and marginalised sections of the population was at the basis of the M-Pesa project and mobile money more generally. Consistent with the idea of innovative financial service delivery envisaged in the G20 Principles, mobile money has contributed to the process, started by microcredit, of eroding the mainstream banking infrastructure and has increased the number and types of financial service providers and financial circuits. This possibility is also addressed in the literature on branchless banking and financial technology more generally, broadly defined as Fintech.[12] The financial inclusion agenda and the institutions supporting it consider financial technology a key instrument of economic growth and the realisation of social goals such as poverty reduction and gender equality (UNCDF 2018). The agenda intends financial innovation to overcome infrastructural and regulatory barriers to facilitate access to formal finance and develop new financial products and services to help 'poor consumers' cope with their basic needs (Gabor and Brooks 2017). Similarly, the agenda supports gender equality, which, however, as will be discussed throughout this book, is mainly regarded as the measurable and even profitable goal of including women in the formal financial system. The agenda does not discuss how to address the gendered socio-economic disadvantages that determine financial exclusion, at the risk of repeating some of the negative patterns of microcredit and creating new ones.

Conclusion

This chapter has provided an overview of the relationship between gender equality and financial inclusion as two interrelated aspects of the international development project. While the disproportionate exclusion of women from formal finance is presented as a general assumption in development policies, the analysis conducted in this chapter has showed how financial exclusion derives from unequal gender roles and relations introduced with colonialism and shaped by development interventions. The introduction of monetary relations and rules governing the commodification of land, the wage economy and customary norms created a gendered socio-economic disadvantage that undermined women's status and entitlements and excluded them from economic development and access to financial services.

In addressing this exclusion, the mainstream development project, framed around Western liberal and neoliberal economic values, has increasingly promoted access to financial services as an opportunity for women to be included in the wage economy, gain equality and contribute to development. While financial inclusion measures are presented as possible solutions to gender inequality, they do not address the socio-economic disadvantage and structural inequalities that determined financial exclusion in the first place. Addressing these inequalities was central to the proposed but never implemented NIEO and to the Declaration on the Right to Development. Instead, development projects such as microcredit and microfinance have relied for their success on unequal gender relations such as women's responsibility for social provisioning and their positional vulnerability within and outside the household, often creating new forms of gender inequality. The digital turn in financial inclusion has created new avenues for extending financial markets and logics and producing profit for corporations, financial institutions and new development actors supporting the global financial inclusion agenda.

The core idea that women's access to finance can be used to overcome all barriers to equality is an understanding of gender equality that is more appealing to international donors, corporations and financial institutions than to the women affected by financial exclusion themselves. The problems of gender inequality reside not only in women, but also, and particularly, in the entanglement of global and local socio-economic and legal relations, structures and contexts through which they act. A main issue with the meaning and use of financial 'inclusion' in the mainstream development project is that inclusionary projects such as microcredit are built on existing inequalities without considering the responsibility of colonialism and of development interventions themselves for the production and reproduction of exclusions and disadvantages. Most development agents present themselves as external to rather than implicated in the production of the gendered inequalities that have caused financial exclusion: the responsibility for exclusion has increasingly been shifted from the countries and institutions that caused it onto those on whom it has been structurally imposed. This chapter argues that the rhetoric of financial inclusion has often served to reframe rather than challenge the inequalities produced by colonialism that have been reproduced by problematic development discourses and measures.

Notes

1 As Jean Robinson (1979: 86) argues, loans and aid tend to be accompanied by a package of technical assistance and organisation that contribute to the penetration of Western cultural and economic values, influencing markets and consumption patterns.

2 President Harry S. Truman's (1949) inaugural address, www.presidency.ucsb.edu/documents/inaugural-address-4 (accessed 20 July 2019).

3 International Covenant on Economic, Social and Cultural Rights, UNGA Res 2200 (XXI), 19 December 1966.

4 Robinson observes that under colonialism the unequal provision of essential social services was 'cemented into the class structure of developing countries' (1979: 141). For instance, colonisers built a few modern hospitals with all the latest sophisticated equipment despite the fact that the most elementary requirements for hygiene were not available in most households.

5 While the term 'NGO' was first used officially in 1949 by the UN, it was not until the 1990s that it became a popular way of designating new important local, national and international stakeholders in development.

6 The repugnancy clause was introduced as a method for filtering out any customary law deemed repugnant to British culture, which meant that anything found appalling, ridiculous or unhelpful to the inculcation of Western ideals could be banned. By introducing the repugnancy clause, the British became the arbiters of what was 'just' and 'moral' in African society.

7 Goal 3 of the MDGs was to 'promote gender equality and empower women', www.un.org/millenniumgoals/gender.shtml (accessed 15 August 2017). This has been

replaced by goal 5 of the SDGs: 'achieve gender equality and empower all women and girls', www.un.org/sustainabledevelopment/gender-equality/ (accessed 15 August 2017).

8 It is interesting that Grameen Bank Ordinance XLVI of 1983 does not mention lending to women, which became an official priority in 1985. According to the ordinance the Grameen Bank is recognised as an institution serving the poor and formally owned by the poor, and for this reason it was allowed to formulate its own policy.

9 'Programmatic success' of microcredit refers to quantitative indicators, that is the number of borrowers recruited to the programme and the amount lent to and recovered from them (Rahman 1999: 21).

10 G20 Financial Inclusion Experts Group, Innovative Financial Inclusion: Principles and Report on Innovative Financial Inclusion from the Access through Innovation Sub-Group of the G20 Financial Inclusion Experts Group, www.gpfi.org/sites/gpfi/files/documents/Principles%20and%20Report%20on%20Innovative%20Financial%20Inclusion_0.pdf (accessed 20 August 2019).

11 See for instance the studies conducted by Financial Sector Deepening Kenya, https://fsdkenya.org/financial-diaries/ (accessed 28 July 2019).

12 Branchless banking or finance refers to strategies aiming to extend the reach of financial services beyond physical bank branches to reduce providers' operational costs and facilitate customer access (Lyman, Pickens and Porteous 2008; Mas 2009). Branchless banking strategies come in a variety of forms and rely on different technical devices. There are two types of branchless banking: in the bank-led model the banking institution takes ownership and users have a pre-existing relationship with this institution; and in non-bank-led models a non-bank institution (for example the mobile network operator in the case of mobile money services) owns the account, even if a bank plays an important role facilitating the management of the cash float and storing the aggregate sum of cash to back the electronic value in virtual accounts. Correspondent banking in Brazil, for instance, uses POS (point of sale) terminals in retail and post office outlets to deliver bill payment, savings, credit, insurance and money transfer products in many municipalities across the country (Kumar *et al.* 2006).

References

Afonja, S. (1981) Changing Modes of Production and the Sexual Division of Labour Among the Yoruba. *Nigerian Journal of Economic and Social Studies* 22(1), 85–105.

Aker, J. C. and Mbiti, I. M. (2010) *Mobile Phones and Economic Development in Africa*, Working Paper 211. Washington, DC: Centre for Global Development.

Allon, F. (2014) The Feminisation of Finance. *Australian Feminist Studies* 29, 12–30.

Anghie, A. (2013) Whose Utopia? Human Rights, Development, and the Third World. *Qui Parle Special Issue: Human Rights between Past and Future*, 63–80.

Ardener, S. and Burman, S. (1995) *Money-go-rounds: The Importance of Rotating Saving and Credit Associations for Women*. London: Berg Publishers.

Armendariz, B. and Morduch, J. (2010) *The Economics of Microfinance*. London: Massachusetts Institute of Technology.

Austin, G. and Sugihara, K. (1993) *Local Suppliers of Credit in the Third World: 1750–1960*. New York: St Martin's Press.

Banda, F. (2003) Global Standards: Local Values. *International Journal of Law, Policy and the Family* 17(1), 1–27.

Bar, F. and Galperin, H. (2007) Wireless Communication and Development: Micro and Macro Linkages. *Information Technologies and International Development* 3(2), 73–86.

Basu, A. (1995) *The Challenge of Local Feminisms: Women's Movements in Global Perspective*. Boulder, CO: Westview Press.

Bedjaoui, M. (1979) *Towards a New International Economic Order*. Paris: UNESCO.

Benería, L. (2003) *Gender, Development and Globalisation: Economics as if All People Mattered*. New York: Routledge.

Bergeron, S. (2004) *Fragments of Development: Nation, Gender and the Space of Modernity*. Ann Arbor: University of Michigan Press.

Boserup, E. (1970) *Women's Role in Economic Development*. London: Allen and Unwin.

Bouman, F. J. A. and Houtman, R. (1988) Pawnbroking as an Instrument of Rural Banking in the Third World. *Economic Development and Cultural Change* 37(1), 69–89.

Breman, J. (2003) *The Labouring Poor: Patterns of Exploitation, Subordination and Exclusion*. Oxford: Oxford University Press.

Caufield, C. (1996) *Masters of Illusion: The World Bank and the Poverty of Nations*. New York: Henry Holt and Company.

Chanock, M. (1982) Making Customary Law: Men, Women and the Courts in Colonial Rhodesia, in M. J. Hay and M. Wright (eds) *African Women and the Law: Historical Perspectives*. Boston University papers on Africa, Boston, MA: African Studies Center.

Cheru, F. (2016) Developing Countries and the Right to Development: A Retrospective and Prospective African View. *Third World Quarterly* 37(7), 1268–1283.

Collins, D., Morduch, J., Rutherford, S. and Ruthven, O. (2009) *Portfolios of the Poor*. Princeton, NJ: Princeton University Press.

Conning, J. (1999) Outreach, Sustainability and Leverage in Monitored and Peer-Monitored Lending. *Journal of Development Economics* 60, 51–77.

Cornwall, A. (2005) *Readings in Gender in Africa*. London: The International African Institute and James Currey Ltd.

Cornwall, A. and Nyamu-Musembi, C. (2004) Putting the 'Rights-based Approach' to Development into Perspective. *Third World Quarterly* 25(8), 1415–1437.

Cornwall, A. and Rivas, M. (2015) From Gender Equality to Global Justice: Reclaiming a Transformative Agenda for Gender and Development. *Third World Quarterly* 36(2), 396–415.

Cornwall, A. and White, S. C. (2000) Men, Masculinities and Development Politics, Policies and Practice. *IDS Bulletin* 31(2), 1–6.

Cutrufelli, M. R. (1984) *Women of Africa: Roots of Oppression*. London: Zed Press.

De Soto, H. (2000) *The Mystery of Capital: Why Capitalism Triumphs in the West and Fails Everywhere Else*. London: Bantam Press.

Donner, J. (2008) Research Approaches to Mobile Use in the Developing World: A Review of the Literature. *The Information Society* 24(3), 140–159.

Eisenstein, H. (2005) A Dangerous Liaison? Feminism and Corporate Globalization. *Science and Society* 69(3), 487–518.

Elson, D. (1989) The Impact of Structural Adjustments on Women: Concepts and Issues, in B. Onimode (ed.) *The IMF, the World Bank and the African Debt, Volume 2: The Social and Political Impact*. London: Zed Press.

Elson, D. (1991) Structural Adjustment: Its Effect on Women, in T. Wallace and C. March (eds) *Changing Perceptions: Writings on Gender and Development*. Oxford: Oxfam.

Elson, D. (1992) Male Bias in Structural Adjustment, in H. Afshar and C. Dennis (eds) *Women and Adjustment Policies in the Third World*. London: Macmillan.

Elyachar, J. (2002) Empowerment Money: The World Bank, Non-governmental Organisations, and the Value of Culture in Egypt. *Public Culture* 14(3), 493–513.

Federici, S. (2011) Women, Land Struggles, and the Reconstruction of the Commons. *The Journal of Labour and Society* 14, 41–56.

Fukuyama, F. (1992) *The End of History and the Last Man.* New York: Avon Books.

Gabor, D. and Brooks, S. (2017) The Digital Revolution in Financial Inclusion: International Development in the Fintech Era. *New Political Economy* 22(4), 423–436.

Gaitskell, D. (1990) Devout Domesticity? A Century of African Women's Christianity in South Africa, in C. Walker (ed.) *Women and Gender in Southern Africa to 1945.* London: James Currey.

Geertz, C. (1962) The Rotating Credit Association: A 'Middle Rung' in Development. *Economic Development and Cultural Change* 19, 241–263.

Getachew, A. (2019) *Worldmaking After Empire.* Princeton, NJ: Princeton University Press.

Goetz, A. M. (1996) Who Takes Credit? Gender, Power and Control over Loan Use in Rural Credit Programs in Bangladesh. *World Development* 24(1), 45–63.

Gurumurthy, A. and Chami, N. (2014) *Gender Equality in the Information Society.* Brighton: Bridge Institute for Development Studies.

Guyer, J. I. (1991) Female Farming in Anthropology and African History, in M. Di Leonardo (ed.) *Gender at the Crossroads of Knowledge: Feminist Anthropology in the Postmodern Era.* Berkley: University of California Press, 257–277.

Guyer J. I. and Peters, P. E. (1987) Introduction, Special Issue on Conceptualising the Household: Issues of Theory, Method and Application. *Development and Change* 18(2), 197–214

Hay, M. J. and Wright, M. (1982) *African Women and the Law: Historical Perspectives.* Boston University Papers on Africa. Boston, MA: African Studies Centre.

Hermes, N. (2011) Microfinance: Its Impact, Outreach and Sustainability. *World Development* 39(6), 875–881.

Hodgson, D. (1999) 'Once Intrepid Warriors': Modernity and the Production of Maasai Masculinities. *Ethnology* 38(2), 121–150.

Jaquette, J. S. and Summerfield, G. (2006) *Women and Gender Equity in Development Theory and Practice: Institutions, Resources and Mobilization.* Durham, NC: Duke University Press.

Juma, L. (2002) Reconciling African Customary law and Human Rights in Kenya: Making a Case for Institutional Reformation and Revitalisation of Customary Adjudication Processes. *St. Thomas Law Review* 14, 459–512.

Kabeer, N. (2001) Conflicts over Credit: Re-evaluating the Empowerment Potential of Loans to Women in Rural Bangladesh. *World Development* 29(1), 63–84.

Kabeer, N. (2012) *Women's Economic Empowerment and Inclusive Growth: Labour Markets and Enterprise Development.* Supporting Inclusive Growth Working Paper 2012/1. UK Department for International Development and Canada International Development Research Centre, www.idrc.ca/sites/default/files/sp/Documents%20EN/NK-WEE-Concept-Paper.pdf (accessed 28 August 2019).

Kumar, A., Nair, A.., Parsons, A. and Urdapilleta, E. (2006) *Expanding Bank Outreach through Retail Partnership: Correspondent Banking in Brazil.* Washington, DC: World Bank.

Laesthaeghe, R. J. (1989) *Reproduction and Social Organization in Sub-Saharan Africa.* Berkeley: University of California Press.

Lairap-Fonderson, J. (2002) The Disciplinary Power of Microcredit: Examples from Kenya and Cameroon, in J. L. Parpart, S. M. Rai and K. A. Staudt (eds) *Rethinking Empowerment: Gender and Development in a Global/Local World.* London: Routledge.

Lewis, D. (2005) African Gender Research and Postcoloniality: Legacies and Challenges, in O. Oyèwùmí (ed.) *African Gender Studies.* New York: Palgrave Macmillan.

Lyman, T., Pickens, M. and Porteous, D. (2008) *Regulating Transformational Branchless Banking: Mobile Phones and Other Technology to Increase Access to Finance*. CGAP Focus, Washington, DC: CGAP.

Maathai, W. (2008) *Unbowed: One Woman's Story*. London: Arrow Books.

Maathai, W. (2010) *The Challenge for Africa*. London: Arrow Books.

Maclean, K. (2010) Capitalizing on Women's Social Capital? Women-Targeted Microfinance in Bolivia. *Development and Change* 42(3), 495–515.

Manji, A. (1999) Imagining Women's 'Legal World': Towards a Feminist Theory of Legal Pluralism in Africa. *Social and Legal Studies* 8, 435–455.

Manji, A. (2006) *The Politics of Land Reform in Africa*. London: Zed Books.

Manji, A. (2010) Eliminating Poverty? 'Financial Inclusion', Access to Land, and Gender Equality in International Development. *The Modern Law Review* 73(6), 985–1004.

Mas, I. (2009) The Economics of Branchless Banking. *Innovations: Technology, Governance, Globalisation* 4(2), 57–75.

Maurer, B. (2012) The Disunity of Finance: Alternative Practices to Western Finance, in K. K. Cetina and A. Preda (eds) *The Oxford Handbook of the Sociology of Finance*. Oxford: Oxford University Press.

Mayoux, L. (2002) *Women's Empowerment or Feminisation of Debt? Towards a New Agenda in African Microfinance*. Report based on One World Action Conference London March 2002, One World Action.

McKee, K. (1989) Microlevel Strategies for Supporting Livelihoods, Employment and Income Generation of Poor Women in the Third World: The Challenge of Significance. *World Development* 17(7), 993–1006.

Mikell, G. (1997) *African Feminism: The Politics of Survival in Sub-Saharan Africa*. Philadelphia: University of Pennsylvania Press.

Morduch, J. (2000) The Microfinance Schism. *World Development* 28(4), 617–629.

Mugo, M. G. (2012) *Writing and Speaking from the Heart of my Mind*. Trenton: Africa World Press.

Ngaruiya, W. and O'Brien, W. E. (2005) Revisiting Woman-Woman Marriage: Notes on Gikuyu Women, in O. Oyèwùmí (ed.) *African Gender Studies*. New York: Palgrave.

Nixon, R. (2013) *Slow Violence, Gender and the Environmentalism of the Poor*. Cambridge, MA: Harvard University Press.

Obeng, P. (2003) Gendered Nationalism: Forms of Masculinity in Former Asante of Ghana, in L. Lindsay and S. Miescher (eds) *Men and Masculinities in Modern Africa*. Portsmouth, NH: Heinemann.

Ocran, M. (2006) The Clash of Legal Cultures: The Treatment of Indigenous Law in Colonial and Post-Colonial Africa. *Akron Law Review* 39(2), 465–481.

Oduol, W. and Kabira, W. (1995) The Mother of Warriors and Her Daughters: The Women's Movement in Kenya, in A. Basu (ed.) *The Challenge of Local Feminisms: Women's Movements in Global Perspective*. Boulder, CO: Westview Press.

Okeyo, A. P. (2005) Definitions of Women and Development: An African Perspective, in O. Oyèwùmí (ed.) *African Gender Studies*, New York: Palgrave Macmillan.

Oyèwùmí, O. (1997) *The Invention of Women: Making an African Sense of Western Gender Discourses*. Minneapolis: University of Minnesota Press.

Oyèwùmí, O. (2005) *African Gender Studies*. New York: Palgrave.

Pahuja, S. (2011) *Decolonising International Law*. Cambridge: Cambridge University Press, 2011.

Prahalad, K. (2004) *The Fortune at the Bottom of the Pyramid: Eradicating Poverty through Profits*. State College, PA: Wharton School Publishing.

Rahman, A. (1999) *Women and Microcredit in Rural Bangladesh*. Boulder, CO: Westview Press.

Rankin, K. N. (2001) Governing Development: Neoliberalism, Microcredit and Rational Economic Woman. *Economy and Society* 30, 18–37.

Rankin, K. N. (2002) Social Capital, Microfinance, and the Politics of Development. *Feminist Economics* 8(1), 1–24.

Rankin, K. N. (2013) A Critical Geography of Poverty Finance. *Third World Quarterly* 34(4), 547–568.

Rittich, K. (2006) The Future of Law and Development: Second-Generation Reforms and the Incorporation of the Social, in D. M. Trubek and A. Santos (eds) *The New Law and Economic Development: A Critical Appraisal*. Cambridge: Cambridge University Press.

Robinson, J. (1979) *Aspects of Development and Underdevelopment*. Cambridge: Cambridge University Press.

Roodman, R. (2012) *Due Diligence: An Impertinent Enquiry into Microfinance*. Washington, DC: Centre for Global Development.

Roy, A. (2010) *Poverty Capital: Microfinance and the Making of Development*. New York: Routledge.

Rutherford, S. (2001) *The Poor and Their Money*. Oxford: Oxford University Press.

Scott, N., Mckemey, K. and Batchelor, S. J. (2004) The Uses of Telephones Amongst the Poor in Africa: Some Gender Implications. *Gender, Technology and Development* 8 (2004), 185–207.

Sen, A. (1999) *Development as Freedom*. Oxford: Oxford University Press.

Shakya, Y. B. and Rankin, K. N. (2008) The Politics of Subversion in Development Practice: An Exploration of Microfinance in Nepal and Vietnam. *Journal of Development Studies* 44(8), 1214–1235.

Slaughter, J. R. (2018) Hijacking Human Rights: Neoliberalism, the New Historiography, and the End of the Third World. *Human Rights Quarterly* 40(4), 735–775.

Soederberg, S. (2013) Universalising Financial Inclusion and the Securitisation of Development. *Third World Quarterly* 34(4), 593–612.

Stamp, P. (1991) Burying Otieno: The Politics of Gender and Ethnicity in Kenya. *Signs* 76(4), 808–845.

Tamale, S. (2011), *African Sexualities: A Reader*. Cape Town: Pambazuka Press.

Taylor, M. (2012) The Antinomies of Financial Inclusion: Debt, Distress and the Working of Indian Microfinance. *Journal of Agrarian Change* 12(4), 601–610.

Tripp, A. (2000) *Women and Politics in Uganda*. Oxford: James Currey.

UNCDF (United Nations Capital Development Fund) (2018) UNCDF and the SDGs: Financial Inclusion and the SDGs, www.uncdf.org/financial-inclusion-and-the-sdgs

Weber, E. (2017) Politics of 'Leaving No One Behind': Contesting the 2030 Sustainable Development Goals Agenda. *Globalizations* 14(3), 399–414.

White, H. and Black, R. (2004) *Targeting Development: Critical Perspectives on the MDGs*. New York: Routledge.

Whitehead, A. (1990) I'm Hungry Mum: The Politics of Domestic Budgeting, in K. Young, C. Wolkowitz and R. McCullagh (eds) *Of Marriage and the Market*. London: CSE Books.

Williams, T. (2001) Requiem for Microcredit? The Decline of a Romantic Ideal. *Banking and Finance Law Review* 19(2), 145–198.

World Bank (2006) *Gender Equality as Smart Economics: A World Bank Group Gender Action Plan*. Washington, DC: World Bank.

World Bank (2006) *Finance for All? Policies and Pitfalls in Expanding Access*. World Bank Policy Research Report. Washington, DC: World Bank.

World Bank (2012) *World Development Report 2012: Gender Equality and Development*. Washington, DC: World Bank.

Yonazi, E., Kelly, T., Halewood, N. and Blackman, C. (2012) *The Transformational Use of Information and Communication Technologies in Africa*. Washington, DC: World Bank.

Young, S. (2010) Gender, Mobility and the Financialisation of Development. *Geopolitics* 15(3), 606–627.

Yunus, M. (1999) *Banker to the Poor: Micro-lending and the Battle against Poverty*. New York: Public Affairs.

Zeitlin, M. F., Megawangi, R., Kramer, E. M., Colletta, N. D., Babatunde, E. D. and Garman, D. (1995) *Strengthening the Family: Implications for International Development*. Tokyo: United National University Press.

2 Theorising gender and financial inclusion

Opportunity v. redistribution

Gender, development and the rhetoric of inclusion

The term 'gender' emerged as a political category in feminist work in the early 1970s (Cornwall 2005: 5), and 'gender equality' has been used as a concept to denote the 'endless variety and monotonous similarities' of women's disadvantages across cultures and through history (Rubin 1975: 160). While the term 'gender equality' is often simplistically used to indicate hierarchical relations of power between women and men, it is also important to investigate the political, social, economic and legal processes and structures through which unequal relations are framed and reproduced. Considering the broader significance of gender relations also involves not taking a unitary and monolithic category of 'woman' for granted (Oyèwùmí 1997), and instead recognising and investigating the intersecting elements of gender equality and its different constituents including race, sexuality, indigeneity, religion, and socio-economic and poverty status, as well as family structures, markets, paid and unpaid work, physical and social infrastructure, legal protection, technological changes, and in postcolonial countries, the legacy of colonialism and international development governance.

While the struggle for women's rights and gender equality originated in local and global feminist movements (Basu 1995), debates on the topic have been internationalised and institutionalised within the framework of the United Nations (UN). In 1947 the UN created its Commission on the Status of Women, and in 1962 the UN General Assembly commissioned one of the first studies on the role of women in development. The report, compiled by Ester Boserup (1970), demonstrated the negative impact of colonialism on women's socio-economic status, their exclusion from agricultural and educational opportunities, their increased responsibility for unpaid work and the erosion of their rights. In response to growing interest in women's rights and the rise of women's movements worldwide, the UN established a Decade for Women from 1975–1985 and organised various World Conferences on Women, culminating in the adoption of the Beijing Declaration and Platform for Action in 1995.[1] In 1979 the UN also adopted the Convention on the Elimination of all Forms of Discrimination Against Women (CEDAW), which recognises women's universal right to equality. With its adoption of the Millennium Development Goals (MDGs) in 2000 the UN proclaimed gender equality and women's empowerment key development objectives, as reaffirmed in the Sustainable Development Goals (SDGs) in 2015.[2]

Debate on the status of women in former colonial countries was initially articulated as part of the Women in Development (WID) paradigm, and from the 1980s as part of the Gender and Development (GAD) framework. The WID approach, influenced by Western liberal feminism, found its key idea in Boserup's report and the argument that women's inclusion in economic development would improve their status but also contribute to the economy as a whole. GAD, which drew on postcolonial and Third World feminist critiques, challenged the WID access-based framework, or so-called 'add and stir approach', and was more concerned with the transformation of unequal gender relations and the social, economic and political structures in which women are located and act (Benería and Sen 1981; Mies 1986; Sen and Grown 1988; Moser 1993; Rai 2011).

Although GAD, unlike WID, paid attention to the contextual constructions of gender roles and differences among women, both frameworks have often been criticised for being based on Western categories and for embracing values and interests that fail to reflect women's different experiences, needs and priorities in postcolonial countries (Mohanty 1986; Basu 1992; Oyèwùmí 1997; Esteva and Prakash 1998). For instance, during the UN conferences a key area of debate between Western and African feminists concerned the different priorities in relation to the realisation of women's rights and gender equality. Western feminists labelled local practices such as female excision barbaric and patriarchal and considered them African women's primary problem (Oyèwùmí 2003; see also Thomas 2003). While African delegates recognised the necessity for ending the negative and dangerous aspects of these practices, they also highlighted how sufficient food and clean water were of greater and more urgent importance (Oyèwùmí 2003: 32). These decisions not only carry an ideological meaning but are also of key political importance and have relevant practical implications, as they influence international and national law and policy and the allocation of resources for gender equality via development programmes, foreign aid and even grants for projects and research (Steady 2005: 322).

Development measures to include women in development and tackle gender inequality have assumed a sameness in the forms of women's oppression and priorities and rarely consider the heterogeneity of women's struggles and the interaction of historical events, cultural factors, local realities and international influences when framing gender relations (Amos and Parmar 1984). For instance, as Mama (2011: e8) points out, feminist movements in African countries are extremely heterogeneous as they emerged in different colonial contexts before being further shaped by development interventions. These interventions have often eroded the political importance of women's independent initiatives and instrumentalised their work and activities to serve the needs of development. Examples include the use of existing self-help groups to facilitate the implementation of development programmes (Oduol and Kabira 1995: 189, 200) such as microcredit (Lairap-Fonderson 2002).

While women were portrayed as victims of African men and traditional culture and in need of liberation and support during the colonial and immediate postcolonial periods, throughout the implementation of the development project they have been increasingly presented as icons of change and invested with the responsibility for improving the livelihoods of their households, communities and countries (Elson 1998; Cornwall and Anyidoho 2010; Wilson 2011). The World Bank officially adopted this logic in 2006 in its development discourse 'gender equality as smart economics' (World Bank 2006, 2012), which was embraced by various development actors.

The progressive inclusion of women and gender issues in the development agenda marked a process of conflicting and converging interests among grassroots women, Western feminist groups, non-governmental organisations (NGOs), national governments, international organisations, donors, transnational networks, financial institutions and multinational corporations. This often ambiguous process was furthered by the adoption of the MDGs, later replaced by the SDGs, which contributed to expanding the development agenda to social objectives, including gender equality, and legitimised a variety of development actors to provide gender-related programmes, products and services without holding them accountable for the actual realisation of gender justice.

This is evident in the way development interventions privilege projects, products and services for the economic inclusion of women rather than, as initially envisaged by GAD, adopting measures to challenge the power structures and relations that determine women's oppression, exclusion and disadvantage. Oppression, exclusion and disadvantage have different dimensions and take different forms. The concept of intersectionality, which originated in Black feminist movements and scholarship, is used to illustrate overlapping grounds of discrimination based on social categorisations such as gender, race, class and other social relations (bell hooks 1982; Davis 1983; Lorde 1984; Crenshaw 1989; Hill Collins 1990). The concept of substantive equality is often used to acknowledge the unequal implications of so-called formal equality: treating people alike without considering the unequal structures and relations in which they are located and act (Fredman 2013, 2016; Albertyn, Fredman and Fudge 2014).[3] According to Strauss (2014), substantive equality is transformative in the sense that its purpose is to transform social and economic relations and the related political-legal mechanisms of distribution so that power and resources are no longer concentrated in the hands of a few people on grounds of their gender, race, class, and so on. The concept of social justice is also often used to indicate the process of transforming social structures, institutional contexts and relationships (Young 1990; Auchmuty 2008), and of satisfying marginalised groups' claims to recognition, redistribution and political participation (Fraser 2010: 365). These ideas are also framed around the broader concept of global justice, which situates such claims in the global history of the empire and its racialised and gendered distributive consequences (Bell 2019; Getachew 2019).

Although these theorisations have not gained enough traction to fundamentally shape the international development project, they provide useful tools for analysing the gender implications of particular development initiatives. This chapter draws on these feminist reflections and defines a conceptual framework for the analysis of digital financial inclusion as a development strategy for gender equality. The second section looks at the concept of social reproduction in the postcolonial context and examines financial inclusion within the nexus of finance, production, and social reproduction, drawing on the feminist political economy's claim that a gender-equitable system requires the spheres of finance and production to serve the needs of social reproduction (Elson 2010, 2014). The chapter then elaborates on this possibility by analysing the interrelated concepts of autonomy and solidarity, opportunity and redistribution. The third section deploys the concepts of autonomy and solidarity to show how the development narrative promoting autonomy through financial inclusion projects has not only contributed to shifting the responsibility for (under)development from governments and international institutions to vulnerable people, with significant gender implications, but has also instrumentalised and marketised gendered solidarity practices to ensure the functioning and profitability of such projects. The fourth section examines opportunity and redistribution as different ways of using financial inclusion to address gender inequality and shows the limits of a logic of opportunity and the transformative potential of a politics of redistribution in the use of digital financial platforms to redistribute power, resources and responsibilities.

Finance, production and social reproduction

As discussed in Chapter 1, the introduction of monetary relations, property rights and the wage economy under colonialism shaped gender roles and relations in line with Western capitalist economies and social structures. Colonial rules had differential impacts on women and men in Africa and affected the relationship between them (Okeyo 2005: 299): the repositioning of men as the family breadwinners and household heads (Obeng 2003) contributed to excluding women from paid work and access to formal finance and made them disproportionately responsible for unpaid work.[4] According to Lonsdale (1992), precolonial gender relations in Africa were based on the idea of gender asymmetry, as women's power was grounded in biological reproductive difference, but not in different responsibilities for paid and unpaid work. As Steady (1997: 7) explains, in precolonial African societies production was primarily for family use, and the question of the differential valuation of paid and unpaid work was not an issue. In her report for the UN, *Women's Role in Economic Development* (1970), Boserup states that the wage economy that targeted male workers disrupted earlier complementarity in food production and household management, resulting in the separation of women's unpaid work from waged labour and in turn undermining their social status. Women's exclusion from paid work and education resulted in the erosion of their rights and entitlements, and in financial exclusion (Etienne and Leacock 1980).

These dynamics contributed to creating a gendered dichotomy between the public and the private, categories that have framed Western feminist discourse.

According to Oyèwùmí (1997, 2003), in many precolonial African societies there was no distinction between public and private, and thus between work done within and outside the house. Rogers (1980: 25) explains that the division of labour in the modern economy

> is both cause and effect of the virtual monopoly of men of the important positions in the socio-economic hierarchy, and their associated control of the main institutions of modern society; law, politics, public administration, male clubs, the armed forces and police, commerce, industry and banking, trade unions, the media, and other major institutions.

Through this 'domestication' process women became fully responsible for managing the household resources, but had less authority on decisions regarding the use of such resources (Grueso and Arroyo 2005: 105). This was legitimised via law, which regulated the structures of landownership and property rights to women's detriment, affecting their ability to access formal financial services.

These factors resulted in women's socio-economic disadvantage, both compared to men and in relation to the resources available within their household (Sacks 1979). For instance, access to education for poor households is conditional on household resources, and research has shown how girls are often discriminated against because they are considered a less productive investment in the future wellbeing of the household than boys (Duggan 2005: 109), with relevant generational consequences in terms of gender inequality at the lower end of the income distribution. Research conducted in the late colonial and postcolonial period in Africa shows the dichotomy between women's responsibility for managing the household and their power to control resources. In 1974 the anthropologist Rosaldo argued that the fundamental inequality between men and women is structural and can be revealed by paying attention to women's contribution to and control and negotiations over resources. Robertson (1997), in her study of trade in postcolonial Nairobi, considers women's domestic work part of the productive realm on the basis that it generates profit for men and forms an arena for struggle between men and women.

Unpaid work, largely performed by women across space and time (Picchio 2003), has been increasingly recognised in development discourse. The final report of the UN's Third World Conference on Women, *Forward-looking Strategies for the Advancement of Women*, in Nairobi in 1985 recognised the importance of women's subsistence activities and recommended appropriate efforts to measure the contribution of their unpaid work to all aspects of development.[5] In 1995 the Declaration and Platform for Action adopted at the Fourth World Conference in Beijing called for women's 'contributions to the national economy including their contribution in the unremunerated and domestic sector' to be made visible, and for examination of 'the relationship of women's unremunerated work to the incidence of vulnerability to poverty'.[6] This commitment was confirmed in the report on the 20th anniversary of the

Declaration in concomitance with the adoption of the SDGs (UN Women 2015), which also recognise unpaid work.[7] However, these documents do not define or commit to a set of measures to support women's disproportionate burden of unpaid work, or to favour the fairer distribution of these responsibilities in society.

To better understand and possibly address the role of unpaid work in perpetuating gender inequalities, feminist political economy scholars coined the concept 'social reproduction' to refer to the social relations, processes and labour that go into the daily and generational maintenance of the population (Bakker and Gill 2008). It includes 'the provision of material resources (food, clothing, housing, transport) and the training of individual capabilities necessary for interaction in the social context of a particular time and place' (Picchio 2003: 2). Social reproduction can be organised by and through households, communities, self-help groups and non-profit organisations, and by the state through socio-economic rights and welfare policies. It can also be managed through markets, although it often responds to rules and norms other than market rationalities such as responsibility, reciprocity, altruism and solidarity.

Social reproduction largely depends on some form of income, which may be wages, earnings, arable land, informal-sector activities or money transfers from the government, organisations or private individuals such as family members and friends. The social reproduction sphere, as Kats explains, is vital for the functioning of society as it is made up of the 'fleshy, messy and indeterminate stuff of everyday life' and is 'a set of structured practices that unfold in dialectical relation with production, with which it is mutually constitutive and in tension' (Kats 2001: 711). Production, in fact, ultimately rests on social reproduction work (Bakker and Gill 2008: 22). However, as Rittich (2002: 129) points out 'there is nothing natural or inevitable about the boundaries between productive and reproductive activity'.

Although the work of social reproduction can be difficult to discern in practice, these theorisations have been useful for analysing the gendered implications of apparently gender-neutral development programmes and policies. The way in which development interventions have generally addressed women's burden of unpaid work has been to promote women's inclusion in the market economy by favouring their access to entrepreneurial opportunities while at the same time assuming the elasticity of their labour, time and 'natural' capacity for providing for their families and communities (Kabeer 1994). As a consequence, development initiatives have focused on providing support for women's economic activities through microcredit schemes and income-generating projects (Ardener and Burman 1995). The structural adjustment programmes (SAPs) are a key example of ostensibly gender-neutral development measures predominantly affecting women. While SAPs promoted productive opportunities and microcredit programmes for women, their focus on marketisation, cuts in public expenditure and the privatisation of social services disproportionately affected poorer women, increasing their burden of social reproduction work and forcing them into informal and insecure jobs (Elson 1989, 1991).

Although access to microcredit programmes, and financial inclusion more generally, is presented to women as a precondition for securing their emancipation and future wellbeing (Allon 2014), feminist scholarship has long questioned this assumption. As seen in Chapter 1, research on microcredit and microfinance has widely demonstrated how access to microcredit schemes can exacerbate gender inequality, reproducing and creating new forms of dependency and oppression for women both within and outside the household. Microcredit often creates a further burden of responsibility related to the strict rules about the repayment of loans and the risk of the debt trap, not only increasing the pressure on women to manage an income-generating activity to repay the loan but also risking affecting their ability to provide for their families, for instance by limiting the resources available within the household. Promoting financial inclusion without also supporting gendered responsibilities for social reproduction risks drawing more vulnerable people and households into market and financial circuits, mobilising unpaid work to support the profitability of corporations and financial institutions (Roberts 2015).

Diane Elson elaborates a framework for analysing the relationship between finance and gendered responsibilities for unpaid work, arguing that a gender-equitable system requires the fundamental reorganisation of the relations between the spheres of finance, production and social reproduction so that 'finance and production serve the needs of reproduction' (Elson 2014: 207). The sphere of finance comprises formal financial institutions such as banks and their regulators including central banks, finance ministries, retail agents, and in the case of mobile money, mobile network operators (MNO) and mobile money agents. This sphere also includes profit-oriented moneylenders and socially useful financial institutions such as rotating credit and savings associations (ROSCAs). Finance is considered important in terms of both developing financial markets (financial deepening) and universal access to affordable and convenient formal financial services such as credit, savings, payments, and insurance (financial inclusion). The sphere of production, where goods and services are produced for the market through activities such as farming, manufacturing and retailing, includes both formal and informal paid work, people working as employees, and those who are self-employed and contributing labour to small family farms and businesses. The sphere of social reproduction, as mentioned, is a non-market sphere of social provisioning supplying services directly concerned with the daily and intergenerational reproduction of people, especially through their care, socialisation and education. It also includes the important task of distribution, which Ferguson (2015: 117) defines as 'a pervasive process and a concrete set of activities'. This involves the distribution of resources such as goods, money, information and even emotional support among kin or community according to social rules and networks.

The spheres of finance, production and social reproduction are nationally and internationally linked through financial markets, international investment and trade, development assistance, law and policy measures, transnational partnerships, migration, information and communication technologies (ICTs) and other networks. They are coordinated through these links, and for this reason overlap in places; for instance social reproduction work such as care is often commodified, and it is difficult to distinguish between finance and production in some cases. These spheres are shaped by interactions between states, markets and societies, and are all gendered 'both in the ways they are populated and in the norms that structure their operation' (Elson 2014: 198, see also Elson 2010: 203).[8] They are also mediated by other relations such as those of race, class and poverty. Because of their gender roles and relations, men and women are not randomly distributed throughout these spheres: in the sphere of reproduction women's working time and the expectations of them are much greater than those of men, and women also predominate in the informal financial and economic sectors. This representation is affected by and also reinforces gender biases that have shaped and continue to influence the regulation of the three spheres.

Elson and Cagatay (2000) identify three key gender biases in policy: the male breadwinner bias, which excludes women or relegates them to the status of secondary workers in informal and precarious jobs with fewer rights, ignoring the fact that they play a key role in social reproduction; the commodification or privatisation bias, which has minimised the role of public provisioning on the assumption that the private sector is more effective than the public sector at delivering services, infrastructure and welfare benefits, while in reality the former excludes those who cannot afford to pay for services and results in an increased burden for poor and low-income women; and the deflationary bias, which refers to the prioritisation of low inflation and fiscal restraint over public spending and has had a negative impact on women's employment and their access to social services. Following the 2007–2008 financial crisis Young, Bakker and Elson (2011) added two further policy biases that negatively affect women: risk bias and creditor bias. They find that the increasing individualisation of risk and the asymmetrical relationship between creditor and debtor results in women being granted access to financial services, and credit in particular, on more disadvantageous terms than those offered to men (see in particular Schuberth and Young 2011). A similar asymmetrical relationship can be identified between the payer and the payee in payment systems and between the consumer and the provider of payment services (Angel and McCabe 2015). All these biases also affect access to financial services more generally.

While Elson applies this framework to analysing financial crises, it also provides useful insights into the gendered implications of digital financial inclusion, to examine whether digital financial platforms such as M-Pesa can contribute to rearranging the relations between finance, production and social reproduction and to what extent this can challenge gender inequalities at the lower end of the income distribution. The next two sections explore this possibility by analysing the interrelated concepts of autonomy and solidarity, and opportunity and redistribution.

Autonomy and solidarity

Autonomy and solidarity are two relevant aspects of the development discourse and key concepts via which the relationship between digital financial inclusion and gender equality can be investigated. The idea of autonomy, often associated with self-determination and independence, has acquired particular importance in the decolonisation process and through the various phases of the development project. However, autonomy in postcolonial countries has been conditional on the rules of Western governments, international development institutions and international law, and has also been mediated by different forms of solidarity at both the international level via aid and philanthropy, and at the national level through grassroots groups, social movements and government-sponsored solidarity. National solidarity emerged in many African countries during their struggle for independence and has been institutionalised as a political and legal principle. In Kenya, for instance, the idea of *harambee*, which means 'let's pull together', has been encouraged by the government since independence with a series of initiatives to stimulate economic growth and build resilience, some government-organised but generally provided by community members (Mbithi 1972; Ngau 1987).

Grassroots solidarity like that of women's self-help groups has often been necessary to cope with economic exclusion and provide reciprocal social and financial support following the dismantling of precolonial structures and the institutional changes introduced in the postcolonial period. These dynamics have influenced African scholars' theorisations of African feminisms rooted in cooperation between people in contrast to the individualism identified with Western feminism. For Nnaemeka (1998), for instance, terms used with reference to feminist engagement in Africa such as 'collaborate', 'negotiate', 'compromise', 'connectedness' and 'reciprocity' run counter to those used by Western feminist scholarship such as 'challenge', 'disrupt' and 'deconstruct'. However, the language of grassroots solidarity has been increasingly appropriated by development institutions targeting women with productive and financial opportunities to increase their autonomy, while at the same time portraying their survival strategies (also shared with men and the community) as forms of 'empowerment' rather than necessity.

The link between autonomy and solidarity in relation to gender equality was institutionalised in the MDGs framework together with the concept of empowerment, embedding some of the contradictions in the relationship between autonomy and solidarity. The MDGs contributed to the socialisation of development by adding to the aim of economic growth a series of social objectives including poverty reduction, gender equality and the empowerment of women (Kabeer 2015: 128). The intention was to expand development interventions to the values associated with the human dimension of development in addition to the mere economic one. This refocusing of development to include social goals drew upon and found its expression in Amartya Sen's theory of *Development as Freedom* (1999) and his capabilities approach, which supported a shift of attention from purely economic measures of development such as GDP to a more comprehensive index that includes social objectives, known as the Human Development Index (HDI).[9] Sen's normative framework centres on individuals' ability to realise their own goals and considers the main aim of development to be to provide people with basic freedoms in the form of intrinsic capacities, entitlements and opportunities that make them capable of shaping their lives and therefore empower them. In theorising this, Sen highlights the importance of autonomy but also values practices of solidarity. His approach has been adopted and revisited by feminist scholars to conceptualise gender equality in development theory and practice corresponding with the growth of the GAD approach, which, as mentioned, sought to reform gender relations in the Global South through a feminist reform project (see for example Nussbaum 2000; Fudge 2012).

In the MDGs empowerment, as also supported by Sen's theory, became a development goal together with gender equality. The concept of empowerment originated in feminist movements before it was appropriated by development and aid organisations, financial institutions and global corporations (Parpart, Rai and Staudt 2002; Cornwall and Rivas 2015: 404). Women's empowerment was articulated in the 1980s and 1990s as a grassroots approach mainly concerned with challenging power relations in favour of women's rights, social justice and the transformation of social, economic and political structures (Bisnath and Elson 2000; Kabeer 2005). This approach insisted that empowerment cannot be provided by others but is part of a process deriving from the recognition of all people being entitled to a rightful share of global power and wealth, and commitment to structural change in favour of greater equality and fairness. This narrative of empowerment emphasised the complex reciprocal relationship between women's self-understanding and self-expression, their access to and control of resources, and their potential for influencing discussions, discourses and agendas (Moser 1989; Rowlands 1997). In contrast to this approach, development measures related to empowerment mainly aim to increase women's autonomy and ability to access resources through microfinance and microenterprise. Access to finance together with various market-based measures acquires significance in this framework as a way of improving women's ability to cope with economic exclusion without paying attention to stereotyped local and global gender roles, power relations and structural inequalities. This is very important in understanding the relationship between financial inclusion and gender equality, and can be better explained through the concepts of 'freedom', 'choice' and 'resilience' as they are deployed in development interventions.

The first consideration is of the concept of 'freedom' adopted by development theory and practice following Sen's book *Development as Freedom* (1999). Although Sen defines freedom as enabling people to realise their own particular visions of wellbeing, development interventions have relied on assumptions about freedom grounded in longstanding Western traditions of liberal thought (Hickel 2014: 1359). These traditions focus on the importance of all individuals being free to shape their own lives, determine their own aims and fulfil their potential, and in this way to empower themselves. This logic has resulted in various market-based interventions with social objectives, supported on the one hand by the neoliberal idea that markets can liberate individuals, and on the other by the premise that free individuals are a precondition of well-functioning markets. These two sides of freedom allow for the convergence of the 'old' developmental purpose of economic growth with the 'new' notion of development as empowerment (Hickel 2014: 1359). Access to financial services has increasingly been seen as an instrument that bridges these two ideas of development.

While Sen's capabilities approach also considers the socio-economic and personal circumstances that can constrain the realisation of people's freedom, it places strong emphasis on choice: individuals' ability to do or be what they have reason to value (Sen 1999: 5). In terms of gender equality this has been linked to the concept of 'agency' as women's increased ability to make decisions under given circumstances (Hammings 2013). However, these given circumstances must be considered in relation not only to the global dynamics of inequality created since colonialism but also to stereotyped gender roles and power relations, and to women's increased responsibility for social reproduction work (Wilson 2011: 317–318, 2013). This demonstrates that decisions are not just an expression of choice but are embedded in socially constructed roles and economic structures. Some social reproduction work such as caring may be a matter not of choice but of responsibility, and also depends on socio-economic status and the availability of resources (Fredman 2013).

The link between responsibility and poverty has been investigated by Chant (2008), who renamed the 'feminisation of poverty programmes', namely the increasing number of poverty programmes that target women, the 'feminisation of responsibility and obligation' to reflect the increasing responsibilities and obligations of women in contributing to development. Chant argues that the emphasis of most development programmes aiming to alleviate simultaneously poverty and achieve gender equality, such as microcredit, is misguided, as poverty reduction and gender equality are distinct, even if overlapping, forms of disadvantage. While gender equality is promoted as a development goal in its own right, pursuing it as a means of reducing poverty is grounded in considerations of efficiency. The idea that focusing on women is one of the most efficient ways of ensuring all-round development benefits seems to have been translated into a generalised way of alleviating poverty primarily through gender equality (Razavi 1999: 419). This logic has been legitimised and institutionalised in the World Bank's (2006, 2012) 'gender equality as smart economics' framework, which advocates gender equality as a valuable instrument for economic efficiency and development, rather than recognising its intrinsic importance for social justice (Chant and Sweetman 2012; Roberts and Soederberg 2012; Prügl 2016). According to Chant the main problem with this 'feminisation of responsibility' is that it is usually not matched by any discernible increase in rewards or entitlements such as support for women's work in the form of social assistance, social infrastructure, policy or legislation protecting their rights and interests. Here we have the contradictory scenario where instead of development working for women, women end up working for development (Chant 2008).

This logic reiterates the argument of feminist political economy scholars concerning the intensification of women's labour in low-income households as a buffer against the consequences of the market-based initiatives that SAPs introduced (Elson 1989, 1991, 1992; Benería 2003). It also explains and shows the gendered implication of the use of discourses such as resilience, increasingly invoked in development policies in relation to the ability of vulnerable groups such as poor women to cope with difficult situations and emergencies.[10] Resilience, and the solidarity practices supporting it, can be considered social reproduction work: although they are generally assumed to be positive and even empowering, they often represent necessary survival practices. The positive promotion of resilience and solidarity shifts attention from structural problems and public responsibility for social provisioning, and can translate into over-reliance on women's unpaid work, in this way overlooking social reproduction as a critical and complex element of development that requires more than simple recognition in policy documents and development plans. The positive outlook of grassroots solidarity can also result in the instrumentalisation of solidarity practices for governance and market purposes while hiding the possible vulnerabilities that this generates. An example of this is provided in the literature on microcredit in relation to group lending and joint responsibility for repayments, and the social vulnerabilities deriving from the pressure and control that women experience in the microcredit mechanism (Rankin 2002).

The analysis conducted in this section shows how Sen's (1999) capabilities approach has been very influential in terms of reorienting the development project beyond utilitarian economic reasoning. However, international institutions have adopted a narrow and instrumental understanding of capabilities that pays little attention to support for social reproduction work, for instance through public services and social infrastructure (Kabeer 2015: 125). The progressive expansion of the development framework to include social goals such as gender equality has resulted in various development agents, organisations, corporations, donors and financial institutions being legitimised to provide 'socially relevant' products and services without being held accountable for the realisation of these goals (Blowfield and Dolan 2014). This is very important in thinking about the relationship between digital financial inclusion and gender equality, because the SDGs have contributed to creating a framework in which a variety of development agents, including powerful corporations and financial institutions, can participate in and influence the development agenda while hiding their role in reproducing rather than addressing problems related to gender inequality (Adams and Pingeot 2013).

Opportunity and redistribution

Opportunity and redistribution are two important perspectives from which to examine digital financial inclusion as a development strategy for gender equality, as creating opportunities, facilitating redistribution or a combination of the two are different ways of using access to finance to address gender inequalities. The idea of opportunity can be linked to the concepts of freedom and choice discussed in the previous section, and to the idea of creating an enabling environment for development interventions. The redistribution of resources and wealth, and also of power and responsibilities, is a key concern in thinking about substantive equality (Young 1990; Fraser 2003). Redistribution channels include wages and salaries, financial rewards, taxes, government subsidies and other forms of social protection (Benería 2003: 168), and reparations (Forrester 2019). The ways in which opportunities and/or redistributive measures are used depend on different assumptions about and understandings of development such as the causes of so-called underdevelopment, the means and aims of the development project and the local context and global relations that determine and regulate such measures.

Capitalist relations, introduced in Africa with colonialism, and the neoliberal idea of development realised in the postcolonial period were based on the premise that economic growth would result in a higher standard of living for everyone (Sachs 1990). In its basic formulation, neoliberal development entails providing conditions that enable the market sector and entrepreneurs to produce growth, accepting that this will result in inequality, and then creating new market opportunities while promoting development and aid programmes to help to rebalance the inequality (Harvey 2005; Ferguson 2006). Financial inclusion represents the necessary development of this neoliberal trend on one hand, on the other offers a useful framework for the expansion of opportunities for not only individuals, but also corporations and financial and development institutions to gain access to new markets and create new products and services. Tackling inequality *ex post* through market-enabled opportunities and without sufficient consideration of its historical, contextual and structural elements also affects the transformative potential of gender equality.

First of all, the logic of opportunity tends to ignore the political, economic and legal mechanisms that impoverished people in Africa in the first place. It obscures the roles of colonial exploitation and development interventions in the production and reproduction of poverty, the responsibility for which has increasingly been shifted from the countries and institutions that have caused and defined 'underdevelopment' to the people on whom it has been imposed. In terms of gender equality this means that approaches that seek to 'empower' women through market and financial opportunities without the necessary infrastructure, public services and market regulation to realise the socio-economic rights of women do not challenge unequal gender relations and can even result in greater gender inequality. This inequality is exacerbated in the case of poverty, as the politics of opportunity can add a further burden to the 'feminisation of responsibility' (Chant 2008) by expecting women to transform the opportunity into success. This expectation, and the possibility of challenging it, is complicated by the fact that the logic of opportunity relies on successful stories. Women, even if they are very few, who have succeeded in taking advantage of opportunities such as microcredit are exemplified as justification for developing new products and services (Roy 2010), reinforcing the idea that poverty is an individual responsibility. It also means that the small and often imperceptible changes that these women make every day via their social reproduction work are not captured in the definition of development 'success'.

Another important point is that in promoting a logic of opportunity, gender equality is not considered worthwhile in and for itself. An example of this is the fact that socio-economic rights are rarely treated as instruments for addressing gender inequality and women's disadvantages. Socio-economic rights, including the right to food, water, shelter, education, health and employment, are by definition more substantive and collective than political and civil rights and for this reason cannot simply be declared but require positive action, generally by governments; they must be embodied in social protection, infrastructure, services, and other measures that can have an actual impact on people's lives. Access to socio-economic rights is gendered, as it is shaped by the gendered nature of social institutions (Fredman 2013), including the legal and customary norms that have limited women's access to property, land and capital since colonialism. Measures related to the realisation of socio-economic rights as development interventions are usually framed as objectives rather than rights. They are often linked to conditions set by governments, international organisations and donors, or to other interests such as those of corporations. For instance, governments' inability to provide wage employment for poor people has often been addressed by promoting microcredit and micro-entrepreneurship in partnership with corporations and financial institutions, with more gain for the latter than for the poor. Depending on their purpose and realisation, socio-economic rights can represent a series of rights that are simply declaratory and even reinforce the status quo, or can genuinely advance substantive gender equality (Fredman 2007; Strauss 2014). Their realisation can address important aspects of women's disadvantage in unpaid and paid work, with particularly relevant implications for poor and low-income women. Socio-economic rights can favour a more equal distribution of gendered responsibilities for social reproduction work through public services and social assistance, contributing in this way to a broader redistribution of power and wealth (Klare 2015).

Money and finance, including digital finance, play a key role in the possible redistribution of responsibilities, power and wealth. Money is necessary to pay for the products and services needed for subsistence; public and private finances influence people's access to resources; and national and global financial governance affects the distribution of these resources. Major social problems such as poverty and inequality can be considered fundamentally distributive issues (Ferguson 2015). In his analysis of the 1974 famine in Bangladesh, Sen (1981) explains how it was caused by not the lack of the availability of food but the poor distribution of the food available. The same logic can be applied to the global distribution of wealth. The idea of the redistribution of wealth was central in anticolonial struggles and decolonial debate (Fanon 1963: 64). It was a key demand in the proposals for the New International Economic Order (NIEO) and the action plan for implementing the 'right to development' advanced by former colonial countries in the 1970s–1980s. Redistribution was considered a necessary condition of decolonial self-determination (Getachew 2019: 51) and essential for the achievement of decent living standards for the millions of people in former colonial countries (Anghie 2013).

Ferguson reflects on the distributive role of money in the context of digital cash transfers in South Africa and provides some useful insights on the politics of distribution in his book *Give a Man a Fish* (2015). The title of the book refers to the development cliché 'Give a man a fish and you feed him for a day; teach him to fish and you feed him for a lifetime'. Besides its clear gender bias (the assumption of the male worker and breadwinner) and imperialist approach to 'teaching', according to Ferguson this slogan encapsulates a certain developmental idea that recipients of development programmes or aid 'should get productive skills and the opportunity to work [ideally in waged employment, but more often self-employed as micro-entrepreneurs], not handouts and dependency' (Ferguson 2015: 35). The ability to fish here promises the opportunity to autonomously provide for oneself and one's family while contributing to a more structural transformation by altering one's relationship to the system of production. Besides assuming that only production, and not also finance and social reproduction, counts as structural, this claim considers poverty to be mainly a problem of production in the sense of not catching enough fish, and identifies the solution as bringing more people into productive labour by teaching them how to fish (Ferguson 2015: 36). Gender equality according to this logic would mean bringing women into the sphere of paid production just like men, at the same time making them potential consumers. This would not only ignore social reproduction work, but would also fail to give enough importance to the aspect of distribution to make sure that every person has fish.

According to Ferguson, to reduce inequality the world requires not the catching of more fish, but the redistribution of the fish it already has, and this should be regarded as the entitlement of all people to some specified share of the total global wealth (Ferguson 2015: 36). This supports the redistributive argument that development policies should target the wealth of the richest as well as focusing on improving the lives of the poorest. Ferguson's distributive claim is rooted in the idea that people in Third World countries are the rightful owners of a vast amount of wealth of which they have been unjustly deprived through a historic process of direct and indirect exploitation, dispossession and extraction.[11] This represents, as postcolonial scholars have long pointed out, a more politicised justification of money transfers than of aid or philanthropy (Nkrumah 1965; Manley 1991; Nyerere 2011; Ferguson 2015). Access to basic resources and welfare for all should not depend on charitable giving, which creates asymmetric power relations, but it should be a substantive entitlement with corresponding public obligation. While Ferguson does not deny the importance of production and the unequal structural conditions of the global economy, he questions the possibility of achieving full wage employment in the foreseeable future, and in particular of realising the distributive role usually devoted to productive work, especially in countries where there is extensive reliance on informal micro-entrepreneurship (Ferguson 2015: 192). For this reason, he reflects on making distribution central to political decisions and the potential of non-market distributive initiatives that give people choices without forcing them to conform to conditions imposed by the West or national political elites.

In more practical terms, Ferguson argues for a new form of social government based on digital money transfers with no or very limited conditions, representing a sort of '2.0 welfare state' that uses social assistance to achieve more substantive equality (Ferguson 2015: 26 and 38). The point on conditionality is very important, as it distinguishes social assistance from neoliberal development interventions that tie the receipt of cash to specific moralistic and disciplinary conditions such as lending to jointly liable groups and strict repayment schedules, as in the case of microcredit, and to a discretional or instrumental evaluation of who the 'deserving poor' are, for instance entrepreneurial/economically active subjects. Ferguson's proposal of money transfers as a distributive politics is based on decoupling paid job opportunities from consumption, with the intention of allowing poor people to buy basic goods and services independently of their paid activities. According to Ferguson, money transfers are about not replacing income lost through inactivity but rather supporting people whose economic activity is restricted due to poverty, poor health, or their relevant burden of unpaid work, without attaching conditions to the transfers (Ferguson 2015: 16). This can have important implications for gender relations in terms of alleviating women's burden of social reproduction work. It should be said that conditional money transfers have been strongly criticised by feminist scholars for relying on women as instruments of household management, reinforcing gender stereotypes and increasing their responsibilities (Molyneux 2006). While women are often the principal recipients of money in these schemes, they have to comply with various conditions, including for instance participating in workshops and agreeing to pass on the knowledge they acquire on subjects from health issues to money management to the community (Roberts 2015: 220).

Without the conditional aspect and the judgement on the 'deserving poor', money transfers have the potential to support women's unpaid work and contribute to more equal gender relations. However, even in the case of non-conditional money transfers it is important to consider possible gender conflict generated by money, such as male family members claiming control of the household's money, as demonstrated in the literature on microcredit (Goetz 1996; Kabeer 2001). Equally relevant, particularly to this research, is the analysis of the public and private infrastructure for the transfer and management of money. Importantly, redistribution involves different resources in addition to money such as land, natural resources, information and technology, local and global institutions and various dynamics of power that influence discourses, agendas and decisions. Ferguson's argument is significant in that it places a politics of distribution at the centre of the analysis of development and highlights its role in reframing the relationship between digital finance, production and social reproduction as part of the process towards substantive gender equality and global social justice. This research understands the political centrality of distribution as contributing to people's entitlement to redistribution and a decent livelihood, and not simply to the opportunity to gain a decent livelihood.

Conclusion

This chapter has provided a conceptual framework for the analysis of digital financial inclusion as a development strategy for gender equality conducted in this book. 'Gender, development and the rhetoric of inclusion' has defined the relationship between financial inclusion and gender equality in the context of international development and highlighted the multiple dimensions, contextual and conceptual differences and global influences that frame the idea of gender equality. 'Finance, production and social reproduction' has identified the unpaid work for which women have become largely responsible since the introduction of monetary relations and international trade during the colonial era, which is a key aspect of gender inequality. It has drawn on feminist political economy to define the gendered relations between finance, production and social reproduction, and the potential for financial inclusion to contribute to substantive equality and social justice. Exploring this potential further, the third and fourth sections have analysed the concepts of autonomy and solidarity, and opportunity and redistribution. 'Autonomy and solidarity' has demonstrated how the development discourse has increasingly encouraged the autonomy of women through their economic and financial inclusion while at the same time relying on and profiting from grassroots solidarity practices, often promoted as forms of resilience or even empowerment rather than of survival. Building on these reflections, 'Opportunity and redistribution' has examined how digital financial inclusion is based on a logic of opportunity that risks exacerbating gender inequality by imposing on women the further burden of transforming opportunities into success.

The chapter has introduced the complexity of gender equality as a political idea emerging from grassroots movements, as a principle in law and policy, and as a development objective. Gender equality has been increasingly deployed by development institutions, which have mainstreamed it into a plenitude of instruments and strategies within and beyond the UN framework. In the process gender equality has been deprived of its political meaning and has often been employed to support other interests, drawing attention away from the issues that motivated feminist struggles in the first place and resulting in what Narayan (2010) calls 'insane utilitarianism'. Development programmes, declarations, laws and policies may require governments and international and transnational institutions to realise certain social goals such as gender equality, but as Kabeer points out, there is little to hold them to account regarding achieving those goals or to prevent them from delivering development in ways that reproduce or exacerbate rather than challenge the disadvantages of more vulnerable groups (Kabeer 2015: 127). This is particularly the case when governments, corporations and financial institutions with interests other than or in contradiction to gender equality deliver these goals, legitimised by a development framework that privileges economic and financial growth over the realisation of substantive equality.

The chapter has illustrated how following the failure and criticism of SAPs and the adoption of the MDGs and SDGs, numerous commitments to gender equality have mainly resulted in the proliferation of opportunities related to market and financial inclusion. Real inclusiveness is not about giving people the opportunity to be included in spaces that others have created for them, but about recognising their entitlements with historical awareness and providing them with the power, structures and resources to fulfil them. These factors create a more substantive and just definition of equality in which digital financial inclusion can contribute to the process of changing gender relations only as part of a broader change in the approach to development. I argue that a radical rethinking of the development project according to a politics of redistribution can contribute to reorganising the relations between finance, production and social reproduction, resulting in the use of digital financial inclusion for more equal distribution of power, resources and gendered responsibilities for unpaid work, and thus more substantive gender equality.

Notes

1 The UN World Conferences on Women took place in Mexico in 1975, Nairobi in 1985, Vienna in 1993, Cairo in 1994 and Copenhagen in 1995.

2 UN, *Transforming our World: The 2030 Agenda for Sustainable Development*. Resolution A/RES/70/1, adopted by the General Assembly on 25 September 2015. New York: United Nations.

3 The concept of substantive equality has been used in various legal documents including the CEDAW, in whose Committee's General Recommendations it is described as *de facto* equality to distinguish it from formal equality, i.e. *de jure* equality.

4 According to Picchio (2003: 1), unpaid work consists of

> the labour involved in maintaining living spaces, buying and transforming the commodities used in the family, supplementing services provided to family members by the public and private sector and managing social and personal relationships. To this, which represents the great bulk of unpaid work, the care of people has to be added.

5 UN, Forward-looking Strategies for the Advancement of Women, 1985, http://www.un-documents.net/nflsaw.htm (accessed 1 July 2019).

6 UN, Beijing Declaration and Platform for Action, 1995, https://www.un.org/en/events/pastevents/pdfs/Beijing_Declaration_and_Platform_for_Action.pdf (accessed 20 July 2019).

7 The value of unpaid work has also been recognised in the SDGs (Goal 5 on gender equality): 'Recognise and value unpaid care and domestic work through the provision of public services, infrastructure and social protection policies and the promotion of shared responsibility within the household and the family as nationally appropriate.'

8 Elson (2010: 203) highlights the importance of distinguishing between quantitative and qualitative aspects of gender, namely gender numbers and gender norms. 'Gender numbers' refers to the numbers of men and women carrying out different activities as measured by sex-disaggregated statistics. 'Gender norms' refers to the constraints and choices that encourage stereotyped female and male behaviour that conform to the norm. Some gender numbers and norms are similar across countries, while others differ.

9 The HDI represents a new set of indicators which, rather than focusing on rates of economic growth, measures and maps the progress of human development goals relating to poverty reduction.

10 See for instance, V. Le Masson, A. Norton and E. Wilkinson (2015) *Gender and Resilience*, BRACED, www.braced.org/resources/i/gender-and-resilience/ (accessed 15 July 2019).

11 This distributive claim, in other words, considers colonialism and unfair economic relations and structures as the roots of inequality and poverty. However, we can make a distinction between redistributive demands advanced by the architects of the New International Economic Order, which were based on the claim that the structural conditions of the global economy transfer the gains of productivity to the Global North, and the *ex post* demand for historical redress and remedying of colonial exploitation in the form of reparations. In both cases the demand for redistribution is a political argument for entitlement and is not based on charity or a moral duty to assist. Other suggestions about tackling global inequality *ex post* include the development of a global method of taxation by the governments of rich states and the Tobin Tax, which is a tax on international financial transactions and currency exchange.

References

Adams, B. and Pingeot, L. (2013) *Whose Development, Whose UN? Reclaiming the UN's Values-Based Framework*. New York: Friedrich Ebert Stiftung.

Albertyn, C., Fredman, S. and Fudge, J. (2014) Introduction: Elusive Equalities: Sex, Gender and Women. *International Journal of Law in Context* 10(4), 421–426.

Allon, F. (2014) The Feminisation of Finance. *Australian Feminist Studies* 29, 12–30.

Amos, V. and Parmar, P. (1984) Challenging Imperial Feminism. *Feminist Review* 17(1), 3–19.

Angel, J. J. and McCabe, D. (2015) The Ethics of Payments: Paper, Plastic or Bitcoin? *Journal of Business Ethics* 123(3), 603–611.

Anghie, A. (2013) Whose Utopia? Human Rights, Development, and the Third World. *Qui Parle Special Issue: Human Rights between Past and Future*, 63–80.

Ardener, S. and Burman, S. (1995) *Money-go-rounds: The Importance of Rotating Saving and Credit Associations for Women*. London: Berg.

Auchmuty, R. (2008) The Married Women's Property Act: Equality was not the Issue, in R. Hunter (ed.) *Rethinking Equality Projects in Law*. Oregon: Hart Publishing, 13–29.

Bakker, I. and Gill, S. (2008) Introduction: Social Reproduction and Global Transformations – from the Everyday to the Global, in I. Bakker and R. Silvey (eds) *Beyond States and Markets: The Challenges of Social Reproduction*, New York: Routledge.

Basu, A. (1992) *Two Faces of Protest: Contrasting Modes of Women's Activism in India*. Berkley: University of California Press.

Basu, A. (1995) *The Challenge of Local Feminisms: Women's Movements in Global Perspective*. Boulder, CO: Westview Press.

Bell, D. (2019) *Empire, Race and Global Justice*. Cambridge: Cambridge University Press.

bell hooks (1982) *Ain't I a Woman? Black Women and Feminism*. London: Pluto Press.

Benería, L. (2003) *Gender, Development and Globalisation: Economics as if All People Mattered.* New York: Routledge.

Benería, L. and Sen, G. (1981) Accumulation, Reproduction and Women's Role in Economic Development: Boserup Revisited. *Signs* 7(2), 279–298.

Bisnath, S. and Elson, D. (2000) *Women's Empowerment Revisited.* New York: UNIFEM.

Blowfield, M. and Dolan, C. S. (2014) Business as a Development Agent: Evidence of Possibility and Improbability. *Third World Quarterly* 35(1), 22–42.

Boserup, E. (1970) *Women's Role in Economic Development*. London: Allen and Unwin.

Chant, S. (2008) The 'Feminisation of Poverty' and the 'Feminisation' of Anti-Poverty Programmes: Room for Revision? *Journal of Development Studies* 44(2), 165–197.

Chant, S. and Sweetman, C. (2012) Fixing Women or Fixing the World? 'Smart Economics', Efficiency Approaches, and Gender Equality in Development. *Gender and Development* 20(3), 517–529.

Cornwall, A. (2005) *Readings in Gender in Africa*. London: The International African Institute and James Currey Ltd.

Cornwall, A. and Anyidoho, N. A. (2010) Women's Empowerment: Contentions and Contestations. *Development* 53(2), 144–149.

Cornwall, A. and Rivas, A.-M. (2015) From Gender Equality to Global Justice: Reclaiming a Transformative Agenda for Gender and Development. *Third World Quarterly* 36(2), 396–415.

Crenshaw, K. (1989) Demarginalising the Intersection of Race and Sex: A Black Feminist Critique of Antidiscrimination Doctrine, Feminist Theory and Antiracist Politics. *University of Chicago Legal Forum* 1(8), 139–167.

Davis, A. (1983) *Women, Race and Class*. New York: Ballantine Books.

Duggan, L. (2005) Introduction to Households, Families and Work, in O. Oyèwùmí (ed.) *The Women, Gender and Development: A Reader*. London: Palgrave Macmillan.

Elson, D. (1989) The Impact of Structural Adjustments on Women: Concepts and Issues, in B Onimode (ed.) *The IMF, The World Bank and the African Debt, Volume 2: The Social and Political Impact*. London: Zed Press.

Elson, D. (1991) Structural Adjustment: Its Effect on Women, in T. Wallace and C. March (eds) *Changing Perceptions: Writings on Gender and Development*. Oxford: Oxfam, 1991.

Elson D. (1998) The Economic, the Political and the Domestic: Businesses, States and Households in the Organisation of Production. *New Political Economy* 3(2), 189–208.

Elson, D. (2010) Gender and the Global Economic Crisis in Developing Countries: A Framework for Analysis. *Gender and Development* 18(2), 201–212.

Elson, D. (2014) Economic Crises from the 1980s to the 2010s: A Gender Analysis, in S. M. Rai and G. Waylen (eds) *New Frontiers in Feminist Political Economy*. New York: Routledge, 189–212.

Elson, D. and Cagatay, N. (2000) The Social Content of Macroeconomic Policies. *World Development* 28(7), 1347–1364.

Esteva, G. and Prakash, M. S. (1998) *Grassroots Post-modernism: Remaking the Soil of Cultures*. London: Zed Books.

Etienne, M. and Leacock, E. (1980) *Women and Colonisation: Anthropological Perspectives*. New York: Praeger.

Fanon, F. (1963) *The Wretched of the Earth*. London: Penguin.

Ferguson, J. (2006) *Global Shadows: Africa in the Neoliberal World Order*. Durham, NC: Duke University Press.

Ferguson, J. (2007) Formalities of Poverty: Thinking about Social Assistance in Neoliberal South Africa. *African Studies Review* 50(2), 71–86.

Ferguson, J. (2015) *Give a Man a Fish: Reflections on the New Politics of Redistribution*. Durham, NC: Duke University Press.

Forrester, K. (2019) Reparations, History and the Origins of Global Justice, in D. Bell (ed.) *Empire, Race and Global Justice*. Cambridge: Cambridge University Press.

Fraser, N. (2003) Social Justice in the Age of Identity Politics: Redistribution, Recognition and Participation, in N. Fraser and A. Honneth (eds) *Redistribution or Recognition? A Political-Philosophical Exchange*. New York: Verso.

Fraser, N. (2010) Injustice at Intersecting Scales: On 'Social Exclusion' and the 'Global Poor'. *European Journal of Social Theory* 13(3), 363–371.

Fredman S. (2007) Redistribution and Recognition: Reconciling Inequalities, *South African Journal on Human Rights* 23(2), 214–234.

Fredman, S. (2013) Engendering Socio-economic Rights, in A. Hellum and H. S. Aasen (eds) *Women's Human Rights: CEDAW in International, Regional and National Law*. Cambridge: Cambridge University Press.

Fredman, S. (2016) Substantive Equality Revisited. *International Journal of Constitutional Law* 14(3), 712.

Fudge, J. (2012) Gender, Equality and Capabilities, in T. Novitz and D. Mangan (eds) *The Role of Labour Standards in Development*. Oxford: Oxford University Press.

Getachew, A. (2019) *Worldmaking After Empire*. Princeton, NJ: Princeton University Press.

Goetz, A. M. (1996) Who Takes Credit? Gender, Power and Control over Loan Use in Rural Credit Programs in Bangladesh. *World Development* 24(1), 45–63.

Grueso, L. and Arroyo, L. (2005) Women and the Defence of Place in Colombian Black Movement Struggles, in W. Harcourt and A. Escobar (eds) *Women and the Politics of Place*. Bloomfield: Kumarian Press.

Hammings, C. (ed.) (2013) *Gender, Agency and Coercion*, London: Palgrave Macmillan.

Harvey, D. (2005) *A Brief History of Neoliberalism*, Oxford: Oxford University Press.

Hickel, J. (2014) The 'Girl Effect': Liberalism, Empowerment and the Contradictions of Development. *Third World Quarterly* 35(8), 1355–1373.

Hill Collins, P. (1990) *Black Feminist Thought: Knowledge, Consciousness and the Politics of Empowerment*. London: Taylor and Francis, 1990.

Jaquette, J. S. and Summerfield, G. (2006) *Women and Gender Equity in Development Theory and Practice: Institutions, Resources and Mobilization*. Durham, NC: Duke University Press.

Kabeer, N. (1994) *Reversed Realities: Gender Hierarchies in Development Thought*. London: Verso.

Kabeer, N (2001) Conflicts over Credit: Re-evaluating the Empowerment Potential of Loans to Women in Rural Bangladesh. *World Development* 29(1), 63–84.

Kabeer, N. (2005) Gender Equality and Women's Empowerment: A Critical Analysis of the Third Millennium Development Goal. *Gender and Development* 13(2) 13.

Kabeer, N. (2015) Evolving Meanings of 'the Social' in the International Development Agenda. *Journal of International and Comparative Social Policy* 31(2), 114–131.

Katz, C. (2001) Vagabond Capitalism and the Necessity of Social Reproduction. *Antipode* 33(4), 709–728.

Klare, K. (2015) Critical Perspectives on Social and Economic Rights, Democracy and Separation of Powers, in H. Alviar Garcia, K. Klare and L. A. Williams (eds) *Social and Economic Rights and Theory and Practice: Critical Inquiries*. London: Routledge.

Lairap-Fonderson, J. (2002) The Disciplinary Power of Microcredit: Examples from Kenya and Cameroon, in J. L. Parpart, S. M. Rai and K. A. Staudt, *Rethinking Empowerment: Gender and Development in a Global/Local World*. London: Routledge.

Le Masson V., Norton, A. and Wilkinson, E. (2015) *Gender and Resilience*. London: DFID's Building Resilience to Climate Extremes and Disasters programme (BRACED).

Lonsdale, J. (1992) The Moral Economy of Mau Mau: Wealth, Poverty, and Civic Virtue in Kikuyu Political Thought, in B. Berman and J. Lonsdale, *Unhappy Valley: Conflict in Kenya and Africa, Book Two: Violence and Ethnicity*. London: James Currey.

Lorde, A. (1984). *Sister Outsider*. Berkeley, CA: The Crossing Press.

Mama A. (2011) What Does it Mean to Do Feminist Research in African Contexts? *Feminist Review* 98(1), e4–e20.

Manley, M. (1991) *The Poverty of Nations: Reflections on Underdevelopment and the World Economy*. London: Pluto.

Mbithi, P. M. (1972) Harambee Self-help: The Kenya Approach. *The African Review* 2(2), 147–166.

Mies, M. (1986) *Patriarchy and Accumulation on a World Scale: Women in the International Division of Labour*. London: Zed Books.

Mohanty, C. T. (1986) Under Western Eyes: Feminist Scholarship and Colonial Discourses. *Boundary 2* 12(3) 333–358.

Molyneux, M. (2006) Mothers at the Service of the New Poverty Agenda. *Social Policy and Administration* 40(4), 425–449.

Moser, C. (1989) The Impact of Recession and Structural Adjustment on Women: Ecuador. *Development* 31(1), 75–83.

Moser, C. (1993) *Gender, Planning and Development: Theory, Practice and Training*. London: Routledge.

Narayan, U. (2010) Global Gender Inequality and Empowerment of Women. *Perspectives on Politics* 8(1), 282–284.

Ngau, P. (1987) Tensions in Empowerment: The Experience of the 'Harambee' (Self-help) Movement in Kenya. *Economic Development and Cultural Change* 35(3), 523–538.

Nkrumah, K. (1965) *Neocolonialism: The Last Stage of Imperialism*. New York: International Publishers Co.

Nyerere, J. K. (2011) *Freedom and a New Economic Order: A Selection from Speeches, 1974–1999*. Dar es Salaam: Oxford University Press.

Nnaemeka, O. (1998) *Sisterhood, Feminism and Power: From Africa to the Diaspora*. Trenton: Africa World Press.

Nussbaum, M. (2000) *Women and Human Development: The Capabilities Approach*. Cambridge: Cambridge University Press.

Obeng P. (2003) Gendered Nationalism: Forms of Masculinity on Former Asante Ghana, in L. Linsday and S. Miescher (eds) *Men and Masculinities in Modern Africa*. Portsmouth, NH: Heinemann, 2003.

Oduol, W. and Kabira, W. (1995) The Mother of Warriors and Her Daughters: The Women's Movement in Kenya, in A. Basu (ed.), *The Challenge of Local Feminisms: Women's Movements in Global Perspective*. Oxford: Westview Press.

Okeyo, A. P. (2005) Definitions of Women and Development: An African Perspective, in O. Oyèwùmí (ed.) *African Gender Studies*. New York: Palgrave Macmillan, 299–311.

Oyèwùmí, O. (1997) *The Invention of Women: Making an African Sense of Western Gender Discourses*. Minneapolis: University of Minnesota Press.

Oyèwùmí, O. (ed.) (2003) *African Women and Feminism: Reflecting on the Politics of Sisterhood*. Trenton: Africa World Press.

Parpart, J. L., Rai, S. M. and Staudt, K. A. (2002) *Rethinking Empowerment: Gender and Development in a Global/Local World*. London: Routledge.

Picchio, A. (2003) *Unpaid Work and the Economy: A Gender Analysis of the Standards of Living*. London: Routledge.

Prügl, E. (2016) Neoliberalism with a Feminist Face. *Feminist Economics* 23(1), 30–53.

Rai, S. M. (2011) Gender and Development: Theoretical Perspectives, in N. Visvanathan, L. Duggan, N. Wiegersma and L. Nisonoff (eds) *The Women, Gender and Development Reader*. 2nd edition. London and New York: Zed Books, 28–37.

Rankin, K. N. (2002) Social Capital, Microfinance, and the Politics of Development. *Feminist Economics* 8(1), 1–24.

Razavi, S. (1999) Gendered Poverty and Wellbeing Introduction. *Development and Change* 30(3), 409–433.

Rittich, K. (2002) Feminisation and Contingency: Regulating the Stakes of Work for Women, in J. Conaghan, R. M. Fischl and K. Klare (eds) *Labour Law in an Era of Globalization: Transformative Practices and Possibilities*. Oxford: Oxford University Press.

Roberts, A. (2015) The Political Economy of Transnational Business Feminism. *International Feminist Journal of Politics* 17(2), 209–231.

Roberts, A. and Soederberg, S. (2012) Gender Equality as Smart Economics? A Critique of the 2012 World Development Report. *Third World Quarterly* 33(5), 949–968.

Robertson C. (1997) *Trouble Showed the Way: Women, Men and Trade in the Nairobi Area, 1890–1990*. Bloomington:Indiana University Press.

Rogers, B. (1980) *The Domestication of Women: Discrimination in Developing Societies*. London: Kogan Page.

Rosaldo, M. Z. (1974) Women, Culture and Society: A Theoretical Overview, in M. Z. Rosaldo and L. L. Lamphere (eds) *Women, Culture and Society*. Palo Alto, CA: Stanford University Press.

Rowlands, J. (1997) *Questioning Empowerment*. Oxford: Oxfam Publications.

Roy A. (2010) *Poverty Capital: Microfinance and the Making of Development*. New York: Routledge.

Rubin, G. (1975) The Traffic in Women: Notes on the 'Political Economy' of Sex, in R Reiter (ed.) *Towards an Anthropology of Women*. New York: Monthly Review Press.

Sachs, W. (1990) On the Archaeology of the Development Idea. *Ecologist* 20.

Sacks, K. (1979) *Sisters and Wives*. Westport, CT: Greenwood.

Schuberth, H. and Young, B. (2011) The Role of Gender in Governance of Financial Sector, in B. Young, I. Bakker and D. Elson (eds) *Questioning Financial Governance from a Feminist Perspective*. London: Routledge.

Sen, A. (1981) The Ingredients of Famine Analysis: Availability and Entitlements. *Quarterly Journal of Economics* 96(3).

Sen, A. (1999) *Development as Freedom*. Oxford: Oxford University Press.

Sen, G. and Grown, C. (1988) *Development, Crises and Alternative Visions: Third World Women's Perspective*, London: Earthscan,

Steady, F. C. (1997) African Feminism: A Worldwide Perspective, in R. Terborg-Penn, S. Harley and A. Benton Rushing (eds) *Women in Africa and the African Diaspora*. Washington, DC: Howard University Press.

Steady, F. C. (2005) An Investigative Framework for Gender Research in Africa in the New Millennium, in O. Oyèwùmí (ed.) *African Gender Studies*. New York: Palgrave.

Strauss, K. (2014) Accessing Pension Resources: The Right to Equality Inside and Out of the Labour Market. *International Journal of Law in Context* 10(4), 522–537.

Thomas, L. M. (2003) *Politics of the Womb: Women, Reproduction and the State in Kenya*. Berkeley: University of California Press.

UN Women (2015) *The Beijing Declaration and Platform Turns 20*. New York: UN Women.

Wilson, K. (2011) Race, Gender and Neoliberalism: Changing Visual Representations in Development. *Third World Quarterly* 32(2), 315–331.

Wilson, K. (2013) Agency as 'Smart Economics': Neoliberalism, Gender and Development, in C. Hammings (ed.) *Gender, Agency and Coercion*. London: Palgrave Macmillan.

World Bank (2006) *Gender Equality as Smart Economics: A World Bank Group Gender Action Plan*. Washington, DC: World Bank.

World Bank (2012) *World Development Report 2012: Gender Equality and Development*. Washington, DC: World Bank.

Young, I. M. (1990) *Justice and the Politics of Difference*. Princeton, NJ: Princeton University Press.

Young, B., Bakker, I. and Elson, D. (2011), *Questioning Financial Governance from a Feminist Perspective*. London: Routledge.

3 The story of M-Pesa in Kenya

A gender reading

Gender and financial exclusion in postcolonial Kenya

The republic of Kenya is an African country of about 50 million people.[1] It is one of the most varied countries in Africa, with coastline, forest, desert, mountains, Lake Victoria and the Rift Valley. Because of its coastal location and migration history, Kenya's population constitutes a multitude of ethnic communities or, as Wangari Maathai (2010: 185) calls them, micro-nations, including Kikuyu, Maasai, Luo, Basuba, Embu, Meru, Kalenjin, Luhya, Borana, and others. Kenya's capital, Nairobi, has long been the trading and financial capital of East Africa, which includes Tanzania, Uganda, Rwanda and Burundi. However, statistics for Kenya show high levels of inequality and a poverty rate of over 30 per cent.[2]

The rough boundaries of Kenya were defined more than a century ago following the division of East Africa into German and British administrations with the establishment of the East Protectorate in 1895 (Hornsby 2013: 21). Following the Mau Mau uprising, Kenya gained independence in 1963 after 60 years of British colonial rule (Gertzel 1970). Since then it has had four presidents: Jomo Kenyatta (1964–1978), Daniel arap Moi (1978–2002), Mwai Kibaki (2002–2013) and Uhuru Kenyatta (since 2013). Kenya began its transition towards independence under President Jomo Kenyatta.[3] The new political order, however, remained contingent upon the rules and institutions introduced by the colonial administration, including the idea of a modern nation state with a central government. As Maathai (2010: 184) explains, the modern Kenyan nation state is a collection of ethnic communities or micro-nations brought together by the colonisers as a single entity. Many Kenyans did not relate to the institution of the nation state created for them and remained attached to their micro-nations, hoping to access the resources of central government by electing someone from their micro-nation as a political leader (Maathai 2010: 184–185). This explains the propensity of those with the political power to do so for distributing resources on an ethno-regional basis (Klopp 2002; Branch 2011: 98; Hornsby 2013: 13).

Soon after independence the Kenyatta government promoted an 'Africanisation' agenda with the aim of providing all Kenyans with the resources and opportunities they had been deprived of during colonial rule (Mazrui 1967: 99;

Kenyatta 1968: 40). This was supported by principles such as *harambee*, which means 'let's pull together', and aimed to stimulate economic growth and build resilience (Mbithi 1972; Ngau 1987). The promise of Africanisation, however, often resulted in the allocation of resources in the interests of the political elite and their ethnic communities (Maathai 2010: 185). According to Kenyan feminist scholars, ideas related to Africanisation have also been used by the government to discriminate against women (Maathai 2010: 164; Oduol and Kabira 1995; Nzomo 1997). Despite women having played a key role in the struggle for independence (Otieno 1998), they were relegated to household work and denied political power and access to wealth: Moi, for instance, encouraged them to join the Maendeleo ya Wanawake Organisation (MYWO, 'Progress for Women' in Swahili) with the aim of educating them to become good mothers and housewives (Branch 2011: 187). MYWO was founded during the colonial era by a group of Western administrators and their wives, who sought to advance the status of Kenyan women according to Western values (Oduol and Kabira 1995: 196). They mobilised women's self-help groups to train them in childcare, cooking, hygiene and other traditional activities. During the Mau Mau uprising the MYWO maintained a close alliance with the colonial government in exchange for funding (Nzomo 1993). After independence the Kenyan government decided to maintain its connection with the MYWO, creating tensions with other women's organisations and activists. As Nzomo (1997: 232) explains, while post-independence governments often tried to co-opt women's organisations to gain political support, women were generally excluded from formal politics and centres of decision-making.

For a decade following its independence Kenya experienced a relatively stable economic environment, but the oil crisis of the 1970s damaged its economy and resulted in high import costs and budget deficit. In reaction to this the government began to seek external financial assistance from international institutions such as the World Bank and the International Monetary Foundation (IMF), and from donors (Kabubo-Mariara and Kiriti 2002). This assistance was provided via structural adjustment programmes (SAPs) implemented under Moi (Ngdungu 2003). As mentioned, the SAPs were loans provided by the Washington-based World Bank and IMF and were conditional on the adoption of neoliberal policies such as trade liberalisation, agricultural reforms, the privatisation of sectors such as telecommunications, increased taxes, and cuts in public spending on sectors such as education and healthcare (Hecox 1988).

SAPs in Kenya resulted in increasing not only the country's debt burden but also the proportion of its population living in poverty, which has been linked to the elimination of food subsidies, unfair terms of trade, policy instability and the introduction of fees for basic services such as healthcare and electricity (Kabubo-Mariara and Kiriti 2002; Ngdungu 2003). Cuts and privatisation also exacerbated gender inequality, affecting women's access to education and paid employment and increasing their responsibility for providing for the household, as documented by the Kenya Commission for the Status of Women (1994). The

1980s–1990s, however, also saw the proliferation and increased visibility of women's groups in Kenya. As Nzomo (1996) explains, in this period women's groups became more vocal and critical of the government. This growth in women's activism can be linked to two events: the impact of the UN Decade for Women, and in particular the World Conference on Women held in Nairobi in 1985; and the privatisations of public industries and services and weakening of the state that followed the introduction of SAPs, which resulted in new initiatives adopted under the framework of Women in Development (WID) and new institutions acting as development agents (Branch 2011: 186).

From the 1990s Western donors started directing aid outside the Kenyan government in the form of grants to non-governmental organisations (NGOs) and other local organisations that functioned as the donors' local gatekeepers (Hornsby 2013: 630–631). The donors could drive policy more directly in this way due to the NGOs' project-based approach. NGOs also contributed to disseminating the new language of inclusive development based on principles such as poverty reduction, gender equality and good governance. For some, NGOs represented both an alternative source of social provisioning and a possible way of weakening Moi's regime; others, such as corporations and financial institutions, saw NGOs and local organisations as business opportunities (Hornsby 2013: 630). Following this logic, SAPs replaced state-subsidised access to credit for agriculture with microcredit for micro-entrepreneurship. Microcredit was initially run by NGOs and has been increasingly offered by financial institutions. The first microcredit scheme for women in Kenya, the Kenya Women Finance Trust (KWFT), now renamed Kenya Women Microfinance Bank, was created in 1981 'to provide women with access to credit and technical assistance as a means of facilitating their integration into the economic development of Kenya' (World Bank 1997) in line with the WID approach.

In contrast to their focus on contributing to financial development via microcredit programmes, SAPs weakened Kenya's formal financial sector (Brownridge and Harvey 1998). Reforms aiming to stimulate competition in the market proved ineffective and affected local financial institutions negatively. The few larger banks began to focus on cost restructuring, resulting in a series of branch closures in less-profitable areas due to low demand and high operational costs (Brownridge and Harvey 1998). The low demand for financial services was due to several interrelated reasons, the first being people's lack of regular income and collateral, particularly in the case of women. Other reasons included the need for documentation such as an ID but also credit history, the required minimum balance, and the high transaction and maintenance fees. Those with an irregular income tend to find the minimum balance difficult to maintain and the fees high in proportion to their variable wages and savings, if any.[4] A main response to the exclusionary mainstream banking system has been the proliferation of informal finance and reliance on semi-formal and alternative financial services such as microfinance institutions, savings and credit co-operatives (SACCOs), and the creation of so-called 'friendly banks' such as the parastatal Post Office Savings Bank (PostBank) and Equity Bank.

Informal finance in Kenya includes moneylenders and shopkeepers, who provide credit; home banks and moneyguards, who look after savings;[5] middlemen and *hawala*,[6] who facilitate money transfers; and savings and credit clubs, usually referred to as *chamas*.[7] *Chamas* originated from the women's self-help groups that developed in rural areas before and during colonial rule (Oduol and Kabira 1995: 193; Lewa 2000: 74). Since then they have acquired a key socio-economic function and are used particularly by women to meet the needs of their households and communities.[8] The relationship between members is based on trust and solidarity, and peer pressure is applied if a participant does not comply with the rules set by the group itself. They take various forms such as rotating credit and saving associations (ROSCAs), accumulating savings and credit associations (ASCAs), table banking, social funds, and welfare groups. ROSCAs, also known as 'merry-go-round', are among the most important informal financial mechanisms in Kenya. Membership is usually based on pre-existing ties, and members meet at regular intervals and contribute the same amount of money to a common pot at every meeting. The whole pot is given to one member on a rotating basis so that each participant receives the pot over time.

ASCAs are similar to ROSCAs in that they require their members to meet regularly and contribute money to the pot, but they are governed by rules more like those of the Grameen Bank's microcredit model. Rather than being disbursed at each meeting, the massed contributions are lent to group members, and in some cases to outsiders, to be paid back with interest, enabling the central pot to grow. The money is kept by the group treasurer, with larger amounts kept in co-owned bank accounts that some banks offer specifically for *chamas*. The amount accumulated is used for further lending or investment such as buying land or starting a business. Women particularly perceive being able to buy land as the highest form of emancipation.[9] Table banking is similar to ASCAs and consists of self-help organisations that offer unsecured loans to women who are unable to access formal and semi-formal financial institutions.[10] Social funds are used for group savings and can take the form of ROSCAs or ASCAs. The money is collected for specific needs or events such as the education, sickness or death of a family or community member, and can act as a substitute for insurance and welfare products and services (Urdy 1994).

Where semi-formal and formal finance are concerned, microfinance institutions have proliferated in Kenya since the adoption of SAPs.[11] They provide deposit-taking or non-deposit-taking financial services: the first prudentially regulated like banks, and the second including a variety of non-prudentially regulated microfinance programmes. Microfinance institutions have progressively established a network of branches in rural areas which target the poor, particularly women, with the support of funds from development institutions. SACCOs are a key feature of Kenya's financial landscape, and are usually based on a common bond of employment or the production of a cash crop such as tea, coffee or dairy products. The so-called 'friendly banks' have increasingly targeted financially active segments of the population that are unable to access mainstream banks such as people owning informal businesses or microenterprises, agricultural workers and *chamas*. They have also widened their networks and adopted initiatives to extend financial services through retail providers. Equity Bank, for instance, is currently one of the largest commercial banks in terms of customers and has grown rapidly and extensively by focusing on providing financial products for low-income and rural consumers.[12] For example one of Equity Bank's projects, implemented to expand its reach, was the use of four-wheel-drive vehicles to provide microfinance services in rural Kenya on a weekly basis.[13] This project, funded by the UK Department for International Development (DFID), ran from January 2002 to August 2003 and involved vans carrying Equity Bank staff trained to offer financial products and guidance to smallholder farmers and agricultural workers in rural areas. This is one of the initiatives that contributed to the rapid growth of the number of rural Equity Bank clients in Kenya. With its strapline 'Taking banking services to the poor', this project is a clear example of development agencies and financial institutions' growing interest in providing financial services to the low-income market and of public-private collaborations aiming to realise this objective.

Kibaki succeeded Moi as president of Kenya in 2002 and was re-elected in 2007 in controversial circumstances following alleged election irregularities. His disputed victory resulted in revolts in early 2008 that had serious socio-economic consequences, such as the collapse of tourism, interrupted agricultural planting and exponential increases in food prices (Adam, Collier and Ndungd'u 2012). According to Maathai (2010: 195), the revolts were strongly motivated by demands for a more equitable distribution of resources and land rights. The post-election violence had a severe effect on the national economy and people's livelihoods, and contributed to weakening the financial system still further (Adam, Collier and Ndung'u 2012).

The Kibaki administration focused its policy reforms around a long-term neo-liberal development plan called Kenya Vision 2030, officially launched in 2008.[14] The Vision places particular emphasis on economic growth and financial development, but also seeks to contribute to the realisation of Sustainable Development Goals (SDGs) such as poverty reduction and gender equality, and to improve the country's political, social and economic governance. A main objective of the Vision's financial development strategy is to extend access to formal financial services to the excluded segments of the population. It supports the adoption of measures for strengthening alternative financial services such as microfinance institutions, encouraging the development of small and microenterprise and increasing the efficiency of the financial sector through institutional and legal reform (Atieno, Barako and Bokea 2012: 385). For this reason, Vision 2030 is considered the key policy framework for financial inclusion in Kenya. It was enthusiastically embraced by the current Uhuru Kenyatta government on its election in 2013 and has been defined by some commentators as 'the real Constitution of Kenya' in comparison to the Kenyan Constitution adopted by Parliament in 2010.[15] The latter is the first constitutional document since independence, following various attempts and referenda, and is characterised by the legal recognition of gender equality and socio-economic rights as will be discussed in Chapter 5.

This overview provides the necessary context for understanding the interaction of global and local factors that shaped the development of M-Pesa in Kenya, and its gender implications. The idea of M-Pesa originated from the grassroots practice of transferring prepaid mobile phone airtime and was institutionalised via a public-private partnership between DFID, Vodafone and its local partner Safaricom. This chapter examines the institutional arrangements that created the M-Pesa platform, contextualising them within Kenya's postcolonial history and the international development project. M-Pesa has been rapidly integrated into everyday gendered money-managing practices such as ROSCAs. However, the M-Pesa inclusionary infrastructure and regulations do not result in more equal gender roles and relations or greater social justice. Rather, I argue, it risks reproducing gender inequalities through the discourse that poor people can live well on a low income if they manage their small amount of money efficiently. In developing this argument, the second section investigates the background of M-Pesa by focusing on the influence of DFID on Kenya's financial sector and its role in linking mobile phones and access to finance. The third section illustrates the development of the M-Pesa infrastructure via the public-private partnership between DFID and Vodafone, with the involvement of various local and global institutions, and the fourth section examines the inclusionary regulation of mobile money.

Mobiles, airtime and finance

As mentioned, the idea of mobile money originated from the grassroots practice of transferring prepaid airtime following the rapid spread of mobile phones in Africa, and the M-Pesa service was created through a public-private partnership between DFID and Vodafone. This section investigates the background to the development of M-Pesa by looking at the role of DFID in the development of Kenya's financial sector and the origins and gender aspects of the links between the use of mobile phones and financial inclusion. DFID has played a key role in funding both financial development initiatives and research on mobile phones in African countries.

DFID is the UK government sector that manages aid and projects for international development. It was established in 1997, replacing the Ministry of Overseas Development at a time of change in thinking about development. This change was driven by the failure of SAPs and the debates surrounding the adoption of the UN MDGs, and involved a shift from aid policy to development policy with a particular focus on social objectives such as poverty reduction and gender equality (DFID 2000a, 2000b). The 2002 International Development Act replaced the 1980 Overseas Development and Cooperation Act, which itself had replaced the 1929 Colonial Development Act, and made poverty alleviation and the achievement of the MDGs central to DFID's policy.[16] A well-functioning financial sector is regarded in this policy as a prerequisite for economic growth and an instrument for the achievement of the MDGs. This focus on financial development encouraged donor countries to support financial sector development projects, often in partnership with the private sector.

In the late 1990s DFID designed the Financial Deepening Challenge Fund (FDCF) to contribute to the achievement of the MDGs. Defined as a 'business-focused challenge fund', the FDCF supported the belief that the MDGs could not be achieved without significant private sector participation in activities contributing to poverty reduction, including access to financial services (DFID 2005). Inherent in this belief was the expectation that the private sector is generally likely to commit to development projects where there is a strong commercial incentive to do so. The FDCF was an attempt to find new partnership-based mechanisms that would enable this type of commitment and was conceived to encourage commercial financial institutions to engage in risk-sharing partnerships with DFID (2004). Its main purpose was to develop innovative and commercially viable financial services that would benefit people living in poverty or on a low income, and in particular the 'economically active poor'. The innovation sought was seen as involving the development of a new product or service that would target specifically the poor, or the application of a technology that would reduce the costs of financial services, in this way increasing access to finance (Hughes and Lonie 2007: 67).

In April 2000 the FDCF was launched in East Africa (Kenya, Uganda and Tanzania) with a nine-month pilot phase. Due to the success of the pilot it was subsequently extended to Botswana, Lesotho, Malawi, Mozambique, Namibia, South Africa, Swaziland, Zambia and Zimbabwe in January 2001, and to India and Pakistan in July 2001. The FDCF made 15 million GBP available to encourage banks and other commercial entities to develop innovative approaches to extending sustainable financial services to excluded segments of the population (DFID 2004). It offered organisations registered in the 15 countries mentioned (12 in Sub-Saharan Africa plus India, Pakistan and the UK) the opportunity to secure grants of 500,000 GBP to one million GBP for financial development projects. DFID strongly supported the idea that engagement with the private sector was important to finding new business models with development potential, and in particular with the potential to provide poor and low-income people with affordable financial services.

At the beginning of the millennium DFID initiated another project to support the development of financial markets in Africa: the Financial Sector Deepening Trust (FSD). The FSD was designed to work directly with private sector institutions, governments and donors to address constraints to financial inclusion. The project aimed to develop the African financial sector by creating a long-term supportive institution that would contribute to building retail capacity and competition in the financial sector, develop various support services and address the institutional regulatory and supervisory environment, balancing financial inclusion and security concerns (Johnson and Williams 2013).

The FSD of Kenya was established in 2005 and attracted funding from not only DFID but also the World Bank,[17] Agence Française de Développement,[18] the Swedish International Development Agency and the Bill and Melinda Gates Foundation. It operates as an independent trust under the supervision of Klynveld Peat Marwick Goerdeler (KPMG) Kenya, and receives policy guidance from a programme investment committee coordinated by donors (Arora, Roe and Stone 2012).[19] The FSD's objective is to improve Kenya's financial sector and collaborate with public, private and non-profit institutions to provide marginalised groups with access to financial services.

Since 2005 the FSD has funded and supervised numerous qualitative and quantitative studies of financial practices among poor and low-income households in Kenya, contributed to policy discussions and monitored and supported the development of financial services.[20] It has also supported the financial inclusion of women and research projects on this topic (Johnson 2015), forming partnerships with NGOs such as Women's World Banking to develop new products and services towards this aim. The research and policy developed under FSD has international authority and influences the global agenda for financial inclusion. FSD has played a key role in the local development of M-Pesa and its promotion as an archetype of digital financial inclusion in the Global South. With the growing importance of FSD Kenya, in 2012 DFID invested 30 million GBP in the Skills and Innovation for Micro-Banking in Africa (SIMBA) Programme, also known as FSD Africa. This programme seeks to improve financial inclusion and financial sector development across Sub-Saharan Africa through collaboration with public sector organisations such as African central banks and finance ministries, the private sector – for instance banks, microfinance institutions and SACCOs – and donors.[21]

Besides these projects specifically focusing on financial inclusion, from 2001 DFID also funded a series of studies in Africa investigating the role of information and communication technologies (ICTs) in development and poverty reduction. The studies revealed the potential of the mobile phone network infrastructure for facilitating financial transactions (McKemey *et al.* 2003; Batchelor, 2005). The importance of ICTs in development discourse is related to their potential for reducing communication costs in countries where the infrastructure is often inadequate and unreliable, allowing quick and cheap information transfer and dissemination. The exchange of and access to information is seen as having strong political, social and economic relevance: difficulty in accessing information and information asymmetry can restrict people's participation in society (Stigler 1961). ITCs have the potential for reducing this inequality.

Mobile phones have been adopted in African countries more quickly and to a greater extent than any other ICT (Yonazi *et al.* 2012: 13). Researchers have attributed their rapid adoption to the low infrastructural requirements for setting up mobile services, with no need for cables or large-scale infrastructure, and the ease and low cost of reaching non-urban and remote areas (Bar and Galperin 2006: 10).[22] According to Aker and Mbiti (2010: 8), in Sub-Saharan Africa the first mobile phone adopters were primarily male, educated, young and wealthy urban-dwellers, as the initial cost of handsets and services was relatively high. But quite rapidly the users, and later the owners, of mobile phones included more females and less-educated, low-income and rural people. This has been related to various factors, and in particular to the low barrier to accessing a mobile phone, including the increasing availability of low-priced handsets manufactured in Asia, the practice of sharing phones or renting them for a small fee from informal local entrepreneurs, the intuitive and easily transmissible literacy required to use them, the introduction of low-denomination prepaid credit, and short message service (SMS) technology, a cheap and rapid form of communication (Aker and Mbiti 2010).

Researchers have observed that while discussions about mobile phones in the West have been framed around cultural discourses such as the rise of social networking, changing work patterns and work/life balance (Kats and Aakhu 2002; Tacchi, Kitner and Crawford 2012), narratives about their growing importance in countries of the Global South focus largely on their possible links to economic and social development (Ling and Horst 2011; Tacchi, Kitner and Crawford 2012). For instance, the use of mobile phones has been linked to entrepreneurial opportunities, the possibility to disseminate information and favour entrepreneurship. This has had important implications in terms of defining the relationship between gender and mobile phones in the Global South, as many projects related to mobile phones have focused on including women in economic and financial inclusion programmes and on creating entrepreneurial opportunities for them (Scott *et al.* 2004; Gurumurthy and Chami 2014).

In 2001 DFID funded a two-year research project called Innovative Demand Models for Telecommunications Services to investigate the use of ICTs, and in particular mobile phones, in three countries in Sub-Saharan Africa: Botswana, Ghana and Uganda. This research was conducted by the consultancy firm Gamos Ltd in collaboration with the Commonwealth Telecommunications Organisation and some local telecommunication organisations, and investigated the use of telecommunications services (fixed and mobile phones, fax, SMS, email and the Internet) in rural and low-income communities with the aim of informing governments, regulators, development agencies and the private sector, and to promote more inclusive measures.[23] This was the first of a series of DFID-funded studies investigating the relationship between new information technologies and poverty reduction. In 2003, for instance, DFID funded an ethnographic study investigating poor people's access to and use of ICTs in four countries of the Global South (Ghana, India, Jamaica and South Africa). The studies contributed to the now-consolidated research field of ICTs for Development and Mobiles for Development, which is characterised by collaboration between international organisations, donors, corporations, NGOs and civil society organisations (Donner 2008).

DFID's research in Sub-Saharan Africa found that even where ownership of mobile phones was low, people had embedded them into their communication behaviour and social and economic activities and the potential for expanding the use of mobile phones was already visible (Batchelor 2012). Interestingly, and contrary to researchers' expectations, the study revealed little gender bias in access to and attitudes towards the mobile phones (Scott and McKemey 2002). The research also found 'significant money transfer insight', as almost half of the respondents stated that they used mobile phones 'to discuss financial matters', involving not only discussing prices and negotiating sales with traders, but also arranging transfers of funds among family and community members (McKemey *et al.* 2003). This led the researchers and DFID to realise the potential of mobile phones for facilitating money transfers such as urban-rural remittances. The research also documented an innovative pattern of behaviour: in all three countries, people described how they were transferring and exchanging airtime as virtual currency (Batchelor 2005).

This practice was found to be common in African countries: people buy a prepaid scratch card and text the code to someone, for instance a trading partner, a family member or somebody they need to pay, who can choose to enter the code and use the airtime or sell the code to another person or a merchant for cash or some other commodity or service (Ray 2007; Maurer 2012). Here the cost of the text message represents a fixed fee for the transfer of value. As Maurer (2012: 600) also observes, if the recipient uses the airtime, the money initially used to purchase the prepaid card remains a means of exchange as it has been converted into airtime (a commodity) which the recipient has consumed; if the code sent to the recipient is sold to a vendor for cash, a money transfer has taken place. There is a variety of different ways of transferring airtime depending on people's creativity: for example the recipient may even repay a loan from a third party with airtime. As Bar and Riis argue (2000), users adapt technology such as mobile phones to their needs and it can evolve in ways its designers have not anticipated. In the case of prepaid airtime, people have found a way to facilitate the transfer of value across space and in real time using the mobile communications network. Airtime, which corresponds to the cost of the prepaid card, represents a form of electronic value issued by the mobile network operator (MNO) and not the state, and mobile phones offer the opportunity to circulate the value contained in the prepaid scratch card within a system free of significant barriers to access.

The practice of transferring airtime developed when prepaid cards became easily available. According to Aker and Mbiti (2010: 17), with the introduction of mobile phones in Sub-Saharan African countries, many local entrepreneurs started selling very small amounts of airtime in the street in exchange for a fee, and local entrepreneurs in rural areas purchased prepaid airtime from resellers in the cities to sell in rural villages (Ray 2007: 2). Similar practices had been already introduced by the Grameen Bank in Bangladesh with the Village Pay Phones project, which used the Bank's group-lending microcredit strategy to offer a micro-entrepreneurial opportunity to female microcredit customers, allowing them to rent mobile phones and sell telephone services in rural villages (Bayes, Von Braun and Akhter 1999; Bayes 2001). However, as Karim (2011: 100) observes, while the Grameen Bank had to invest in advance, the operational cost was borne by the borrowers, who paid more than the prevailing market rate. This meant that the Grameen Bank was the one profiting from the phone's wireless service. As had already happened with microcredit, the Grameen Village Pay Phone was exported beyond Bangladesh into Uganda, Rwanda and other African countries. However, its use declined and eventually disappeared altogether with the spread of affordable mobile phones in the Global South.

The example of the Grameen Village Pay Phone project, however, shows the potential profits for telephone service providers. MNOs started issuing small-denomination prepaid cards and building extensive phone-credit distribution networks in partnership with the formal (for example franchised phone shops) and informal (for example street sellers) sectors. In a number of Sub-Saharan countries including Kenya, small shops that traditionally sell groceries started selling airtime scratch cards and an increasing number of branded airtime resellers appeared in urban slums and rural areas (Aker and Mbiti 2010). Some MNOs introduced their own handsets onto the market; for instance Safaricom in Kenya released a series of low-cost handsets at 1,300 KES (about 10 GBP/13 USD, but still very expensive for many people, considering that even women owning small businesses have a monthly income of about 3,000–5,000 KES).[24] These practices contributed to mobile phones' rapid penetration of rural and slum areas.

A number of African MNOs such as MTN Nigeria launched prepaid cards in Nigeria and the UK, allowing Nigerians living in the UK to buy airtime for family members at home as a convenient alternative to sending small remittances (Ray 2007: 2). MNOs developed airtime transfer services in Mozambique (MCel), Kenya (Safaricom's Sambaza) and South Africa (MTN's Me2U), allowing customers to transfer a portion of their airtime to other users on the same network. Services such as Sambaza in Kenya were particularly used by people without access to financial services, who integrated them with informal finance such as *chamas* (Wandibba, Nangendo and Mulemi 2012). The characteristics of this service have led some commentators to suggest that airtime is a *de facto* form of electronic money or an alternative currency (Porteous 2006: 21). Even before airtime transfer services were launched in African countries, similar services, Smart Money and GCash, had been introduced in the Philippines to facilitate the transfer of remittances (Owens and Bantung-Herrera 2006; Alampay and Bala 2010; Mas and Radcliffe 2010).[25]

Prepaid airtime was seen as the precursor and conceptual foundation of mobile money transfer services and as a potential instrument for extending access to financial services to those excluded from mainstream banking (Maurer 2012: 589). This was the prelude to the development of M-Pesa in Kenya.

M-Pesa's inclusionary infrastructure

As discussed, the idea of using the mobile phone network to facilitate access to financial services originated from the grassroots practice of transferring small-denomination prepaid airtime from one mobile phone user to another. M-Pesa formalised this idea via a public-private partnership between DFID and Vodafone, its institutionalisation involving Vodafone's partner in Kenya, Safaricom, the Central Bank of Kenya (CBK), financial institutions, tech companies, regulators and local groups. This section illustrates how these institutional arrangements contributed to creating M-Pesa's inclusionary infrastructure.

According to Hughes and Lonie (2007: 66), debate about M-Pesa started at the 2003 World Summit for Sustainable Development in South Africa.[26] Nick

Hughes was the head of Social Enterprise at the UK-based multinational corporation Vodafone at the time, and one of his main roles was to understand how Vodafone could contribute to the achievement of the MDGs. At the beginning of the millennium there was growing interest among development institutions and donors in the role of the private sector in development, as also stated in numerous UN documents calling for 'global partnerships for development'.[27] Vodafone participated at the Summit as one of the world's larger ICT providers with a growing market in Kenya, Tanzania, Egypt and South Africa.[28]

In this role Hughes was invited to talk about the barriers that private sector organisations such as Vodafone face when engaging in development projects. He explained that private companies are legally bound to use their shareholders' capital to achieve immediate returns, and for this reason they tend not to involve themselves in long-term development projects whose gains are not assured (Hughes and Lonie 2007: 66). Usually development is the responsibility of company departments concerned with stakeholders' engagement, government relations, policy debate and corporate social responsibility. However, Hughes argued that the research and development departments of many technology-based companies such as Vodafone focus on developing the technology rather than expanding the market (ibid.). He pointed out how public-private partnerships could circumvent this issue and invest in long-term development projects that combine profit with social objectives.

At the summit Hughes discussed the Financial Deepening Challenge Fund (FDCF) with a DFID representative (ibid.) and suggested a project using the mobile phone infrastructure to facilitate and expand access to financial services in one of DFID's target areas in East Africa (Vaughan, Fengel and Joseph 2012). Vodafone already had a presence in both Kenya and Tanzania as the main partner of the dominant MNOs in the countries, Safaricom Kenya and Vodacom Tanzania. The rationale behind the project was to use the mobile network to move money faster and more cheaply and securely. This was seen as having potential for success in countries with limited infrastructure where a significant number of people have no bank account but have access to a mobile phone.

Despite some initial reservations about an MNO entering the financial services space to implement a development project, Vodafone was awarded one million GBP from the FDCF, matched by an equal combination of Vodafone's cash and staff time (Hughes and Lonie 2007: 67). The project aimed to fill a niche in the market by serving those with no access to formal financial services, and in this way to also contribute to the MDGs (ibid.). Besides a Vodafone team and consultants from Coffey International, which collaborated with DFID, Hughes engaged Hyperion, a consultancy firm specialising in micropayments, to develop the project. Following workshops in Kenya (Nairobi) and Tanzania (Dar es Salaam) attended by banks, microfinance institutions, NGOs with an interest in microcredit, MNOs, suppliers of technology services and financial sector regulators, Kenya was chosen for the experiment. Both DFID and Vodafone already had a relevant presence in the country. Vodafone's local partner

Safaricom, of which Vodafone owns 40 per cent, had a 75 per cent share of the mobile phone market at the time and a strong brand presence (Owino and Tanui 2011).[29] Since 2000, under its CEO Michael Joseph, Safaricom had started marketing pay-as-you-go products and had introduced billing in seconds and services such as Sambaza to facilitate the transfer of airtime.[30] Safaricom also rebranded and presented itself as distinctly Kenyan and the company that was bringing mobile phones to poor Kenyans. Local institutions and regulators, in particular the Central Bank of Kenya (CBK), expressed their willingness to collaborate on the project to develop innovative financial services. The presence of FSD in Kenya and the country's well-developed network of microfinance institutions were also influential reasons for choosing Kenya as target country for the project.

M-Pesa's infrastructure was developed on the ground and relied on institutional arrangements between local, UK and international institutions. Susie Lonie, a senior project manager at Vodafone with a background in Western-style mobile commerce, led its development in Kenya. First Vodafone commissioned Scientific Generics (now Sagentia), a consultancy firm based in Cambridge in the UK, to develop the M-Pesa software. Many of the available financial service platforms had been designed for integration with Western banking infrastructure and could only provide an additive banking approach, for example by adding new channels via which customers could access their bank accounts. However, because M-Pesa was not intended as a banking service but as an MNO-based mobile network service outside the banking infrastructure, its functionality needed to be integrated with MNO products and services (Wooder and Baker 2012).

The software was developed around SMS technology to allow the system to be used on the basic black-and-white mobile phones that were widely available on the Kenyan market (Wooder and Baker 2012). M-Pesa was situated on the SIM card and linked to the mobile number, and the system was designed in both English and Swahili to include people living in the rural areas who preferred to have the service in Swahili. The fact that the SMS works across different mobile networks meant that M-Pesa was available to all phone users, including those not registered with the M-Pesa service and those using mobile networks other than Safaricom. The use of SMS was seen as a new application of old technology in line with the idea of innovation required by the funding awarded by DFID. Interestingly, the main M-Pesa server was located in the UK and connected to Kenya via an Internet Protocol (IP) link, as the Internet in Kenya was not fast enough (Hughes and Lonie 2007: 72).

The M-Pesa service aimed to facilitate the transfer of money outside the banking infrastructure by allowing the conversion of cash into electronic money (e-money); the transfer of e-money to other users, whether people or institutions, for which the payer would pay a fee proportionate to the amount transferred; and the conversion of e-money back into cash, for which the payee would pay a fee. Customers deposit cash with an M-Pesa agent and receive the equivalent value of e-money in their mobile money account (the 'cash in' transaction, or deposit).

They then use their mobile phone to give secure PIN-protected instructions to the service provider to transfer funds in the form of e-money to any other phone number, which the recipient can withdraw as cash from an M-Pesa agent (the 'cash out' transaction, or withdrawal). To develop the system DFID and Vodafone relied on Safaricom's well-established network of airtime dealer outlets, using them as mobile money agents where consumers could open an M-Pesa account and convert cash into e-money and vice versa.

M-Pesa agents are provided with a mobile phone which has an M-Pesa agent's menu, different from customers, which enables them to register customers and manage their own M-Pesa agent account. They act as cash merchants and are responsible for managing liquidity and meeting customers' requests. When customers deposit money the agent's cash balance increased and the agent has to deposit the same amount of cash in the M-Pesa bank account; when customers withdraw money the amount of cash available to the agent's decrease and the agent has to withdraw cash from the M-Pesa bank account to rebalance liquidity. The team, in consultation with CBK, decided to hold M-Pesa money in a pulled trust account at the Commercial Bank of Africa under the custody of the non-profit M-Pesa Holding Company.[31] As the M-Pesa project specifically targeted the 'unbanked', the service needed to be able to operate without the need for customers to have a bank account. For this reason, while the Commercial Bank of Africa would provide the banking services necessary to store M-Pesa funds, those funds must be managed on the customers' behalf by a trustee. This meant that M-Pesa customers would not be paid the interest on money kept in the M-Pesa account, which instead would be used for the benefit of all Kenyans. The M-Pesa Foundation was created in 2010 as an independent charitable trust for this purpose. To support the functioning of M-Pesa two divisions of Safaricom were created: the customer services division, which took calls from customers and agents with problems, and the finance division, which supervised the flow of cash to and from M-Pesa bank accounts and guaranteed that e-money was always matched by real money (Hughes and Lonie 2007: 73).

A pilot test of the functionality of the M-Pesa service was carried out in October 2005. It involved about 500 customers of a local microfinance institution, Faulu Kenya, from three areas: Nairobi's central business district, the informal settlement of Mathare and the market town of Thika. These were provided with mobile phones and instructed on how to use M-Pesa to repay their microfinance loans. M-Pesa was initially conceived as a system mainly for facilitating microfinance transactions, allowing customers to receive and repay microcredit loans using their mobile phones and the MNO's distribution network. The service was expected to help microfinance institutions extend their reach to more remote locations, run their businesses more efficiently and offer more competitive loans due to the reduced cost of dealing with cash and sending agents to rural areas to disburse or collect money (Hughes and Lonie 2007: 68). However, the pilot demonstrated that M-Pesa was more useful as a platform for micropayments than for improving the efficiency of microfinance institutions. Participants in the pilot were mainly using the service for person-to-person transfers, storing money on the M-Pesa electronic wallet and sending money to their families in the rural areas (ibid.: 76). They integrated the service into their everyday financial practices, including gendered forms of informal finance such as *chamas* and the practice of sending national remittances from urban to rural areas. 'Sending money home' became a main proposition at the launch of M-Pesa in March 2007, reflecting Vodafone's aspiration to create a low-cost international remittance service with much lower transaction fees than those of banks, post offices and Western Union (ibid.: 77).[32] M-Pesa was launched a few months before the 2007 post-election revolts, when it was used by NGOs and international organisations to implement cash transfer programmes and by the population to transfer money to family and friends, bypassing blocked streets and the closure of financial institutions caused by the revolt (Morawcznski 2009).

The progressive integration of M-Pesa in everyday life and the consequent expansion of the service was facilitated by two aspects of its infrastructure: the agent network and the fee structure. The agent network has grown rapidly from 2,500 in its first year of operation to over 10,000 in 2009 and 156,000 in 2018. Agents are organised hierarchically: Safaricom signs an agency agreement with a master agent, who then recruits a number of M-Pesa retail agents, airtime resellers and shops that offer a cash in/cash out service, register new customers and provide customer support. Retail agents receive a percentage of the commission for cash in/cash out transactions and a commission for each new customer signed up. This enabled agents to penetrate areas under-served by financial institutions, contributing to the mobile money's expansion into urban slums and rural areas.

Second, although M-Pesa is a development project set up to benefit poor and marginalised groups by providing them with access to finance, the mobile network infrastructure is privately owned and charges a fee for its use. The fee has an important regulatory role in defining access to and use of M-Pesa. The fee for each transaction is taken directly from the customer's account as a fixed amount rather than a percentage of the transaction, making each transaction profitable for the MNO on a stand-alone basis (Mas and Radcliffe 2010). There is no charge for signing up or for converting cash into e-money (i.e. depositing money in the e-wallet), and the charge for transferring e-money and reconverting it into cash (i.e. withdrawing money) is determined by the amount and whether the recipient is registered with M-Pesa. The different fees for registered and unregistered customers contributed to expanding the reach of the service. SMS technology, as mentioned, allows M-Pesa customers to send money to any person with a mobile phone in Kenya, whether or not they subscribe to M-Pesa. However, when M-Pesa was launched the fee for transferring money to unregistered customers was much higher than that for registered users.[33] Research shows that M-Pesa users persuaded their relatives and friends to sign up to M-Pesa to avoid the higher transfer fee, contributing to the rapid expansion of the service (Mas and Radcliffe 2010: 15).

Like the mobile phone, M-Pesa has been rapidly integrated into people's everyday financial practices, facilitated by collaboration with local institutions and the business logic of scaling up its network (Vaughan, Fengel and Joseph 2012). These practices are grounded in Kenya's colonial and postcolonial history, and they are gendered. For instance, the practice of sending and receiving remittances was a consequence of the introduction of the wage economy during the colonial era, targeting men as the paid workers and breadwinners and women as responsible for the household and dependent on men. The creation of informal credit and savings and support groups such as *chamas* was driven by women's exclusion from paid work and financial services, discussed in Chapter 1. Similarly, the introduction of microfinance and mobile phones and the presence of Vodafone in the country owning 40 per cent of Safaricom is linked to the privatisation of telecom companies imposed by SAPs. This means that the M-Pesa infrastructure is embedded in existing unequal gender roles and relations, and facilitating inclusion does not necessarily involve challenging these inequalities.

M-Pesa's inclusionary regulation

The development of the M-Pesa platform required the involvement of the Central Bank of Kenya (CBK), the regulatory body for banking and payment services in Kenya.[34] At the time of the pilot there was no regulation of mobile phone-enabled money transfer services and so no examples on which to draw. The CBK decided that the Kenya Banking Act did not provide a legal basis for either M-Pesa or the regulation of mobile money products offered by MNOs. Mobile money providers were not considered financial intermediaries, and mobile money services could not be classified as banking businesses as specified in the Kenyan Banking Act. A banking business involves not only accepting money from the public, but also 'the employing of money held on deposit on current accounts, or any part of the money, by lending, investment or in any manner for the account and at the risk of the person so employing the money'.[35] The M-Pesa system was designed to provide a money transfer service outside the banking infrastructure, converting cash into e-money and e-money into cash through mobile money agents acting as cash merchants. For this reason, the CBK collaborated with Safaricom as the MNO, the UK Financial Services Authority (FSA), the consultancy firm Consult Hyperion and FSD Kenya to provide a regulatory framework for M-Pesa.

The CBK opted for a 'test and learn' approach to the regulation of mobile money.[36] While legal and risk assessments and audits were conducted to ensure that M-Pesa had embedded all necessary security procedures (AFI 2010),[37] the CBK supervised the service in partnership with the MNO, maintaining an openness to new financial services and providers (AFI 2010). The security procedures included international anti-money laundering (AML) rules and counter-terrorist financing (CTF), limits to the amount that could be held in the M-Pesa account and to the size of transactions, and 'know your customer' (KYC) and customer due diligence (CDD) procedures to be implemented by M-Pesa agents,[38] which required customers to show official identification when signing up to the service and conducting transactions.[39] Following a first successful audit by FSA and Consult Hyperion, the CBK authorised the launch of M-Pesa in March 2007 and issued Safaricom with a Letter of No Objection on condition that it complied with the security rules above (Muthiora 2015). The letter permitted M-Pesa to function under the oversight of the CBK until the adoption of the National Payments System (NPS) Act 2011 and the related Regulations 2014.[40] Safaricom was permitted to operate under special licence from the Communications Commission of Kenya without the need for a banking licence, and the Communications Act 1998 was amended in 2009 to recognise electronic transactions.[41] In this way M-Pesa was created at the intersection between telecommunications and finance, with the CBK and the Communications Commission of Kenya collaborating on its regulation (Houpis and Bellis 2007).

The formalisation of mobile money regulatory practices was accomplished in several steps. In 2008/2009 a second audit was conducted by Consult Hyperion, following complaints from banks and MNOs other than Safaricom that the CBK was operating to a double standard by allowing a non-bank to conduct financial services without the regulatory burden imposed on the banking industry (Omwansa and Sullivan 2012: 57). In January 2009 the Treasury concluded that M-Pesa was both 'safe and reliable'. With the aim of creating a clearer legal framework for mobile money, in 2010 the CBK proposed a draft regulation for national and international electronic retail payments, and in 2011 the Kenyan Parliament adopted the National Payment System (NPS) Act. The Act provided the legal basis for the adoption of the NPS Regulations 2014, which codified the regulatory practices adopted by the CBK since the launch of M-Pesa in 2007, ensuring the system's integrity and security but also favouring its expansion (Muthiora 2015: 20). The Regulations allow both banks and non-banks to provide mobile money services, and mobile money providers to offer a variety of e-money products and services.

Safaricom has concluded partnerships with a variety of public and private sector institutions to provide opportunities to access financial services for the financially excluded. They also provide financial institutions and corporations with opportunities to offer their products to M-Pesa users while creating profits for the MNO. Agreements with microfinance institutions, SACCOs and banks have allowed them to use the M-Pesa platform to facilitate access to formal financial services. For instance, microfinance institutions such as the Kenya Women Finance Trust (KWFT), now named the Kenya Women Microfinance Bank, have integrated their credit, savings and insurance products with M-Pesa. Among other attempts to facilitate access to formal financial services such as credit and savings, in 2012 Safaricom and the Commercial Bank of Africa (CBA) launched M-Shwari (*shwari* is the Swahili word for calm), an M-Pesa banking service that has developed savings and credit products emulating the use of M-Pesa. It allows M-Pesa users to open a free savings account directly from their mobile phone without a minimum deposit or a credit history, and offers low-value (100–50,000 KES) 30-day short-term loans for a 7.5 per cent facilitation fee (Cook and McKay 2015). Loan approval is an automated procedure based on credit-scoring rules that use the applicant's airtime and M-Pesa transaction records. Following the launch of M-Shwari, Safaricom partnered with other banks such as the Commercial Bank of Kenya to establish similar mobile banking products. Besides financial institutions, Safaricom has also partnered with corporations, philanthropic foundations, development organisations and NGOs to develop M-Pesa-enabled products and services enabling access to water, electricity, healthcare and education, as discussed in Chapter 4.

The CBK's test and learn approach to the regulation of M-Pesa, allowing the system to grow, has been internationally acclaimed and has influenced the global financial inclusion agenda, in which FSD Kenya also played a key role. Just before the launch of M-Pesa, FSD conducted the 2006 FinAccess survey (FSD 2007) highlighting the low level of access to financial services throughout the country: 26.4 per cent of the adult population were included in the formal financial system, of which 18.9 per cent had access to formal financial services such as banks or Postbank, and 7.5 per cent to semi-formal financial services such as deposit-taking microfinance institutions and SACCOs; 35.2 per cent used informal financial services such as ASCAs and ROSCAs, of which 58.2 per cent were female; and about 38.4 per cent did not use any type of institutionalised financial service and were categorised as 'financially excluded'. The FSD survey also investigated the use of and familiarity with mobile technology, finding that 54.4 per cent of the adult population had access to a mobile phone, with 20.6 per cent regularly sending airtime credit to someone else. After the release of this survey the CBK was persuaded that using mobile phones to facilitate the transfer of money could open up many opportunities for increasing financial inclusion in Kenya. The CBK saw this document as important evidence justifying the lenient regulation of M-Pesa and contributing to creating an enabling environment for the development of mobile money services (AFI 2010).

The FinAccess survey has been repeated regularly since 2006. The number of people with access to formal and semi-formal finance, which since 2007 includes also mobile money, increased from 19 per cent in 2006 to 36.4 per cent in 2009, 66 per cent in 2013, 75 per cent in 2016 and 82.5 in 2019 (FSD 2007, 2009, 2012, 2016, 2019). The number of women using formal financial services has increased from 20.5 in 2006, of which 14.3 per cent used formal and 5.9 per cent semi-formal finance, to 70.7 per cent in 2016 (34.6 formal, 36.1 semi-formal finance including mobile money). The number of men increased from 33.2 in 2006, of which 23.8 per cent used formal and 9.2 per cent semi-formal finance, to 79.7 per cent in 2016 (50.4 formal, 28.9 semi-formal). These surveys show that the percentage of women and men with access to formal finance has grown evenly, and how mobile money has become a formal financial instrument used particularly by women. If on the one hand the increase in women's use of mobile money has contributed to promoting M-Pesa as a successful digital financial inclusion project for gender equality (Suri and Jack 2016), on the other the results have encouraged measures to close the persistent gap between women and men. Here gender equality is treated mainly as a measurable outcome which can be achieved with more mobile money products and services targeting women.[42]

What have not received as much attention, however, are the gendered causes of financial exclusion. These causes, as seen in Chapter 1, can be traced back to the colonial period and the introduction of property rights, the wage economy, and customary norms and gender stereotypes that have excluded women from the economic system, increased their social reproduction work and portrayed them as dependent. The causes of financial exclusion are briefly mentioned in the FinAccess survey 2006 (FSD 2007), which gives the two primary reasons as lack of income (58.9 per cent) and lack of regular income (31.6 per cent), and reports that the main reason for stopping using a bank account was loss of income source. These data, however, do not provide information about gender for an understanding of the intersection of gender and socio-economic disadvantage.

The regulation of mobile money has been considered instrumental in eliminating barriers to accessing and using M-Pesa, but has focused on its expansion without recognising the causes of exclusion. Although M-Pesa's regulatory framework has allowed many people from both sides of the gender divide to access the service, not paying attention to the socio-economic disadvantage that causes financial exclusion risks reproducing, or even exacerbating, gender inequality. The fact that M-Pesa has contributed to lowering the regulatory barriers to accessing formal financial services without any ostensible gender discrimination does not automatically make it a successful financial inclusion project in terms of gender equality and particularly substantive gender equality.

Conclusion

This chapter has provided a detailed account of the institutional arrangements that have contributed to the development of M-Pesa as a financial inclusion project, highlighting its gender aspects. The story of M-Pesa is not a linear one, and the chapter has sought to unravel and reveal the different political, socio-economic and legal dynamics that frame M-Pesa, paying particular attention to the interaction between the Kenyan and global contexts. The first section has provided an overview of Kenya's postcolonial political economy and its gender implications, and has analysed its financial sector and the increasing centrality of financial inclusion policies. The second section has explored the background of M-Pesa, in particular the spread and grassroots uses of mobile phones and the role of DFID in supporting initiatives, research and policy on financial inclusion in Africa. The third section has illustrated the development of the M-Pesa platform and the infrastructural and technological elements that contributed to its rapid expansion; and the fourth section has examined the regulatory decisions made by the CBK in collaboration with the MNO and other regulatory entities that have facilitated access to M-Pesa and the proliferation of mobile money services and providers.

The origins and institutionalisation of M-Pesa are grounded in Kenya's colonial and postcolonial history, and have been influenced by development interventions such as the introduction of microfinance and the privatisation of the telecommunication sector under SAPs, the adoption of the MDGs in 2000 now replaced by the SDGs, the increasing focus on public-private partnerships to fund and implement development projects and the growing importance of financial inclusion as a development tool. M-Pesa, unlike microcredit, did not specifically target women, but its platform is embedded in the unequal gender roles and relations shaped by colonialism and development. Informal finance practices such as *chamas* derive from women's economic and financial exclusion since colonialism and their responsibility for social provisioning. This responsibility was disproportionately increased by the privatisation of social services under SAPs and created the need for more private finance, often only available in the form of microcredit schemes.

M-Pesa provided a new instrument for managing money and accessing financial services with low infrastructural and regulatory barriers. However, despite the low barriers, M-Pesa is a privately owned institution that can be accessed by paying a fee, so financial inclusion makes profit for the MNO. M-Pesa's inclusionary arrangements have contributed to increasing the number of women able to access semi-formal finance, particularly in the form of mobile money. This inclusion, however, does not challenge the gendered structural and socio-economic disadvantages that determine financial exclusion and can reproduce and even exacerbate gender inequalities. Promoting the narrative that poor people can live well on a small and irregular income if they have access to a financial instrument such as M-Pesa with which to manage and distribute their small amount of money efficiently is particularly dangerous in this regard. This narrative risks creating even more gendered responsibility for social reproduction work, and can be used to market more mobile money products and services rather than addressing the causes of financial exclusion.

Notes

1 UN Data Kenya http://data.un.org/CountryProfile.aspx?crName=kenya#Economic (accessed 20 August 2016).

2 According to the World Bank, the population living below the national poverty line is 36.1 per cent, http://data.worldbank.org/country/kenya (accessed 8 August 2019).

3 Jomo Kenyatta was a Kikuyu, one of Kenya's largest ethnic groups. The Mau Mau movement that fought for Kenya's independence from Britain, consisted largely of Kikuyu (Berman and Lonsdale 1992).

4 This information also emerged consistently in focus groups conducted in Nairobi at Kawangware, 28 November 2012 and 2 December 2012, and Ngando, 8 and 9 December 2012.

5 Home banking refers to money kept hidden at home, for instance in a small tin box or under a mattress. This method of saving is considered accessible and inexpensive, and does not involve the need to maintain a balance or pay maintenance fees, but the money is subject to theft or damage and can create controversy in the household. Money-guards are individuals, often female, who are paid a fee to keep money safe for those who cannot afford formal savings accounts and for this reason pay a form of negative interest rate for savings.

6 *Hawala* is an Arabic term for a particular form of informal value transfer.

7 While the plural of *chama* in Swahili is *vyama* (see Kinyanjui 2012), I use *chamas* here as this is the term that I used colloquially in my fieldwork. *Chamas* can be registered as community-based organisations (CBOs) with the Ministry of Gender, Children

and Social Development by paying a fee and complying with certain requirements such as having a constitution that clearly states the objectives of the group. The aim of the registration is legal recognition which, for instance, allows the group to receive funds from donors, open a bank account or take out loans, for which they are jointly liable (interview with the Kenya National Commission for Gender Equality, Nairobi, Kenya, 10 December 2012).

8 According to Johnson's (2004) study in Kenya, men tend to control large and periodic incomes while women tend to manage smaller but more frequent amounts of money, and for this reason ROSCAs fit women's money management needs better. This evidence obviously relies on structural inequalities in access to employment, on the disproportionate responsibility of women for social reproduction work and on gender biases such as the male breadwinner bias. However, although females predominate in ROSCAs, they are also used by men. For a more detailed account of the current use of *chamas* see FSD Kenya, 'Kenya Financial Diaries: Shilingi Kwa Shilingi: The Financial Lives of the Poor', Nairobi: FSD Kenya, August 2014.

9 This point was mentioned in all the focus groups I conducted in Nairobi, and it was presented as the primary purpose of the Kawangware Jitahidi Women Group, Kawangware, Nairobi.

10 Table banking was mentioned to me for the first time during an interview with the Women Enterprise Fund in Nairobi, Kenya, on 30 November 2012.

11 Formal financial services and products are prudentially regulated by an independent statutory government agency such as the Central Bank of Kenya, the Capital Markets Authority, the Insurance Regulatory Authority, the Retirement Benefits Authority and, since 2010, the SACCO Societies Regulatory Authority. Semi-formal financial services and products are subject to non-prudential regulation (oversight) by government ministries/departments.

12 Equity Bank Limited is a Kenyan commercial bank licenced under the Kenyan Banking Act that has expanded to Uganda, South Sudan, Rwanda and Tanzania. Equity Bank originated from Equity Building Society, which initially provided mortgage financing, particularly for low-income customers. This Society was declared technically insolvent in 1993 and turned itself around to become a microfinance institution focusing on the low-income market. It started to grow very quickly, resulting in its transformation into a bank in 2005 and flotation on the stock market in 2006. In the past few years it has seen huge growth and is now the bank with the most customers in Kenya.

13 The Remote Village Mobile Banking project was co-financed by the UK Department for International Development and Equity Bank; see DFID (2003) *Remote Village Mobile Banking: Project Completion Report*, London-Nairobi: DFID and Equity Building Society.

14 Government of the Republic of Kenya, *Kenya Vision 2030*, 2007, www.vision2030.go.ke/ (accessed 8 May 2019).

15 Mentioned in Manji (2015: 3), referring to David Malombe of Kenya's Human Rights Commission at a panel discussion marking the third anniversary of the promulgation of the Constitution of Kenya 2010, 'Taking Back Gains: Marching Towards Constitutionalism', at the Mazingira Institute on 27 August 2013.

16 Office of Public Sector Information, International Development Act 2002, 8 April 2002, www.legislation.gov.uk/ukpga/2002/1/enacted (accessed 10 June 2019).

17 Specifically from the Kenya Ministry of Trade and Industry through the Micro, Small and Medium Enterprise Competitiveness project funded by the World Bank.

18 Specifically from the Kenya Ministry of Finance under the Micro-Finance Sector Support Credit Programme financed by the Agence Française de Développement.

19 KPMG Kenya is a company affiliated with KPMG international, a Swiss cooperative which operates as a network of member firms offering audit, tax and advisory services.

20 In 2009 Oxford Policy Management (OPM) conducted an evaluation of the impact of FSD Kenya's programme which concluded that the cost of the FSD to DFID from 2005 to the end of 2010 was 29.4 million GBP, while the value of its benefits was 103.9 million GBP. For this reason, as DFID is accountable to UK taxpayers, this was overall considered a successful project (Stone, Johnson Hayes 2010; Arora, Roe and Stone 2012).
21 FSD Africa is based in Nairobi and provides technical support to a network of eight FSD Trusts: AFR in Rwanda, EFInA in Nigeria, FSD Kenya, FSD Tanzania, the FinMark Trust in South Africa, FSD Uganda, FSD Zambia and MAFiP in Mozambique. DFID, Skills and Innovation for Micro Banking in Africa (SIMBA), http://devtracker.dfid.gov.uk/projects/GB–1–201394/ (accessed 5 August 2019).
22 Research in Sub-Saharan Africa has shown that landlines require the installation of lines along every road and with smaller lines into every household, and this can be expensive, especially in countries with poor roads, vast distances and low population density. Mobile phone coverage, on the other hand, is primarily provided via a network of specialised base stations which can provide service within a 5–10-kilometre radius (Aker and Mbiti 2010: 4–5). Other problems related to landline phones are the cost of the rental and the complexity of the monthly bills, which can create tension in the household and put pressure on older women, who according to research are often held responsible for the landline while mobile phones may force each individual to be responsible for his/her own bill (Host and Mill 2006: 75).
23 The local telecommunication organisations were the Botswana Telecommunication Authority, the Commonwealth Telecommunications Organisation, the National Communications Authority Ghana and the Uganda Communications Commission.
24 Focus group in Kawangware, Nairobi, 28 November 2012.
25 Smart Money was launched in December 2000 as the result of a partnership between a telecom company (SMART Telecom), a bank (Banco de Oro) and MasterCard. It was designed to enable airtime distribution: users could transfer funds from their bank account to a Smart Money account, which allowed them to send airtime from their account to another account via SMS technology. GCash was introduced in 2004 as an electronic money transfer facility for payments, and in particular for remittances.
26 Nick Hughes and Susie Lonie are also among the owners of the M-Pesa patent. World Intellectual Property Organisation, International Bureau, International Publication Date 22 February 2007. Inventors/applicants: Murdoch T. N. S., Bowley C., Vaughan L., W. D. Carew (Scientific Generics Limited, Cambridge); N. Hughes and S. Lonie (Vodafone).
27 MDG 8 addressed Global Partnerships for Development.
28 MDG target 8f stated that the benefits of new technologies should be made available to all, including poor and low-income people, in collaboration with the private sector.
29 The liberalisation and privatisation of the telecommunications sector was required by the SAPs and involved the Kenyan government's sale of the Kenya Posts and Telecommunications Corporation. The first step towards liberalisation was taken in the late 1990s with a split in functions: the Postal Corporation of Kenya operated email services, and Telekom Kenya, voice and data communications. The Communication Commission of Kenya was established to regulate Telekom and future entrants to the market. Two mobile communication companies entered the market: Safaricom, which began to offer services in 1997 as a subsidiary of Telekom Kenya and was privatised in 2000 after a substantial portion (40 per cent) was acquired by Vodafone; and Kencell, a partnership between a French communications and entertainment consortium and the Kenyan Sameer Group, which also began to offer services in 1997 and was bought by Celtel in 2004, by Zain in 2008 and by Airtel in 2010. In 2008 the government released new licences to two telecommunication companies, Orange, and Yu, a subsidiary of India's Essar Communication Holding. In 2008, after the rapid growth of M-Pesa the Kenyan government sold 25 per cent of Safaricom shares, now held in small tranches by a range of investors.

30 Interview with Safaricom, Nairobi 30 November 2012.

31 Declaration of Trust, M-Pesa Holding Co Limited, 23 February 2007. As the size of the M-Pesa Trust account grew, the trustee in consultation with CBK decided to spread the funds across several banks to reduce the risk of single custodial bank or corruption (Muthiora 2015: 11).

32 The first M-Pesa advert reproduced the gendered narrative of male workers in urban areas sending money to female family members in rural areas. It featured a businessman working in a Nairobi office using the M-Pesa service to send money to his mother in a rural part of Kenya. She hears a beep and sees a text message confirming that she has received money on her M-Pesa account. She walks to an M-Pesa agent, shows her ID card and picks up the cash. Before M-Pesa remittances were usually sent as cash by bus via friends and family, or by travelling home in person. Formal financial services such as banks and Post Bank were generally expensive and had very few branches in rural areas.

33 When M-Pesa was launched it cost 30 KES to send 20,000 KES to a registered user and 350 KES to send the same amount if the user was not registered; now it costs 102 KES to send 20,000 KES to a registered user and 288 KES to send the same amount to an unregistered user, increasing to 309 KES to send 20,001–25,001 KES to an unregistered user.

Fees for money transfers currently range from 11 KES to send 101–500 KES (45 KES to unregistered users); 77 KES to send 5,001–7,500 KES (166 KES to unregistered users); and 105 to send 20,001–70,000 KES, the maximum amount transferable (309 KES to unregistered users, with a maximum amount sent of 35,000). With the latest changes to the fees structure there is no fee for transferring 1–100 KES to users, but it costs 10 KES to withdraw 50–100 KES, with a minimum withdrawal of 50 KES. 1 KES=0,0099 USD/0,0076 GBP. The full list of M-Pesa charges is available at www.safaricom.co.ke/personal/m-pesa/getting-started/m-pesa-rates (accessed 2 May 2019).

34 The Central Bank of Kenya Act was amended in 2003 to give the CBK a broad oversight mandate over payment systems. Under Section 4A(i)d of the Central Bank of Kenya Act, the CBK must formulate and implement policies to best promote the establishment, regulation and supervision of efficient and effective payment, clearing and settlement systems.

35 Laws of Kenya, Banking Act 1989 (amended 15 September 2015), Nairobi: Central Bank of Kenya. Part I section 2(C).

36 This term was used by Njuguna Ngundu, Governor of the Central Bank of Kenya from 2007 to 2015 (see Muthiora 2015).

37 Consult Hyperion conducted various security tests including checking the functionality of the encryption of the SIM card, which holds the confidential customer data, and reviewing the use of hardware security modules on the M-Pesa servers. The consultants also ensured that the M-Pesa system allowed for comprehensive reporting and management to make sure that transactions could be monitored both individually and en masse. This meant that the CBK could request accurate information about the system from Safaricom. See Makin, Regulatory Issues Around Mobile Banking, OECD, www.oecd.org/ict/4d/43631885.pdf (accessed 3 August 2019).

38 Before a new agent is authorised to provide the M-Pesa service, Safaricom provides training on anti-money laundering (AML), counter-terrorist financing and know-your-customer procedures. Similarly, Safaricom staff members are given formal web-based AML awareness training. The program, adapted from the AML policy instituted by the Vodafone Group, encompasses all aspects of the M-Pesa service and is audited annually by Vodafone Group Money Laundering Reporting Office (Buku and Meredith 2013).

39 All M-Pesa transactions are PIN-protected and are recorded not just electronically but also in a paper logbook containing the balance, date, agent ID, transaction ID, transaction type, value, customer phone number, customer name and ID number. Customers are

asked to sign the log of each transaction, to discourage fraud. Each entry in the log is written in triplicate with a copy for the retail agent, a copy for the master agent and a third copy sent to Safaricom. Considering that all information is recorded electronically, the logbook played a key role in building customers' trust, reassuring them that the transactions are recorded (Zollman and Collins 2010). Kenya has an established national ID card scheme, however showing an ID card could still be a barrier to accessing the service for some people (Alexandre, Mas and Radcliffe 2010).

40 Laws of Kenya, National Payment System Act, N. 39 of 2011. Laws of Kenya, National Payment System Regulations 2014, *Kenya Gazette* Supplement no. 119, Legislative Supplement no. 43.

41 Laws of Kenya, The Kenya Information and Communication Act 1998, Chapter 411 A. Rev. 2011. Electronic transactions Part VI A.

42 GSMA, Mobile for Development, Connected Women Programme, www.gsma.com/mobilefordevelopment/connected-women/ (accessed 4 August 2019).

References

Adam, C. S., Collier, P. and Ndung'u, N. S. (2012) *Kenya: Policies for Prosperity*. Oxford: Oxford University Press.

Aker, J. C. and Mbiti, I. M. (2010) *Mobile Phones and Economic Development in Africa*. Working Paper 211. Washington, DC: Centre for Global Development.

Alampay, E. and Bala, G. (2010) Mobile 2.0: M-money for the BoP in the Philippines. *Information Technologies and International Development* 6(4), 77–92.

Alexandre, C., Mas, I. and Radcliffe, D. (2010) *Regulating New Banking Models That Can Bring Financial Services to All*. Seattle, WA: Bill and Melinda Gates Foundation.

Alliance for Financial Inclusion (2010) *Case Study: Enabling Mobile Money Transfer: The Central Bank of Kenya's Treatment of M-Pesa*. Bangkok: Alliance for Financial Inclusion.

Arora, S., Roe, A. and Stone, R. (2012) *Assessing Value for Money: The Case of Donor Support to FSD Kenya*. Oxford: Oxford Policy Management.

Atieno, R., Barako, D. and Bokea C. (2012) Policies for Prosperity, Innovation, and Financial Access: The Role of M-Pesa, in C. S. Adam, P. Collier and N. S. Ndung'u (eds) *Kenya: Policies for Prosperity*. Oxford: Oxford University Press.

Bar, F. and Galperin, H. (2006) Wireless Communication and Development: Micro and Macro Linkages. *Information Technologies and International Development* 3(2), 1–2.

Bar F. and Riis A. M. (2000) Tapping User-driven Innovation: A New Rationale for Universal Service. *The Information Society* 16(2), 99–108.

Batchelor, S. (2005) Sending Money Outside the Envelope. *Development Magazines* 31, London: UK Department for International Development.

Batchelor, S. (2012) Changing the Financial Landscape of Africa: An Unusual Story of Evidence-informed Innovation, Intentional Policy Influence and Private Sector Engagement. *IDS Bulletin* 43(5), 84–90.

Bayes, A. (2001) Infrastructure and Rural Development: Insights from Grameen Bank Village Phone Initiative in Bangladesh. *Agricultural Economics* 25, 261–272.

Bayes, A., Von Braun, J. and Akhter, R. (1999) *Village Pay Phones and Poverty Reduction: Insights from Grameen Bank Initiative in Bangladesh*. ZEF Discussion Paper on Development Policy, ZEF: Bonn.

Berman, B. and Lonsdale, J. (1992) *Unhappy Valley, Book Two: Violence and Ethnicity*. London: James Currey.

Branch, D. (2011) *Kenya: Between Hope and Despair*, 1963–2011. New Haven, CT: Yale University Press.

Brownridge, M. and Harvey, C. (1998) *Banking in Africa: The Impact of Financial Sector Reforms Since Independence*. Oxford: James Currey Ltd.

Buku, M. W. and Meredith, M. W. (2013) Safaricom and M-Pesa in Kenya: Financial Inclusion and Financial Integrity, *Washington Journal of Law, Technology and Arts* 8(3), 376–400.

Cook, T. and McKay, C. (2015) *How M-Shwari Works: The Story so Far*. Washington: CGAP and FSD Kenya.

DFID (2000a) *Eliminating World Poverty: A Challenge for the 21st Century*. Cm 3789. London: The Stationery Office.

DFID (2000b) *Eliminating World Poverty: Making Globalisation Work for the Poor*. Cm. 5006. London: The Stationery Office.

DFID (2004) *Discussion Document FDCF: Assessing its Achievements and Possible Future Directions*. London: The Stationery Office.

DFID Financial Sector Team, Policy Division (December 2005) *Financial Deepening Challenge Fund: Strategic Project Review*. London: The Stationery Office.

Donner, J. (2008) Research Approaches to Mobile Use in the Developing World: A Review of the Literature. *The Information Society* 24(3), 140–159.

FSD Kenya and The Steadman Group Research Division (2007) *Financial Access in Kenya: Results of the 2006 National Survey*. Nairobi: FSD Kenya.

FSD Kenya and Central Bank of Kenya (2009) *FinAccess National Survey 2009: Dynamics of Kenya's Changing Financial Landscape*. Nairobi: FSD Kenya.

FSD Kenya and Central Bank of Kenya (2013) *FinAccess National Survey 2013: Profiling Developments in Financial Access and Usage in Kenya*. Nairobi: FSD Kenya.

FSD Kenya and Central Bank of Kenya, Kenya National Bureau of Statistics (2016) *The 2016 FinAccess Household Survey on Financial Inclusion*. Nairobi: FSD Kenya.

FSD Kenya, Central Bank of Kenya, National Bureau of Statistics (2019) *2019 FinAccess Household Survey*. Nairobi: FSD Kenya.

Gertzel, C. (1970) *The Politics of Independent Kenya*. Nairobi: Heinemann Educational Books.

Gurumurthy, A. and Chami, N. (2014) *Gender Equality in the Information Society*, Brighton: Bridge IDS, 2014.

Hecox, W. (1988) Structural Adjustment, Donor Conditionality and Industrialisation in Kenya, in P. Coughlin and G. Ikiara (eds) *Industrialisation in Kenya: In Search of a Strategy*. Nairobi: Heinemann.

Hornsby, C. (2013) *Kenya: A History Since Independence*. London: I. B. Tauris.

Host, H. A. and Mill, D. (2006) *The Cell Phone: An Anthropology of Communication*. New York: Berg Publications.

Houpis, G. and Bellis, J. (2007) The Regulatory Implications of Mobile and Financial Services Convergence, in *The Transformational Potential of M-Transactions: Moving the Debate Forward*, Policy Paper Series No. 6. London: Vodafone Group PLC.

Hughes, N. and Lonie, S. (2007) M-Pesa: Mobile Money for the 'Unbanked': Turning Cellphones into 24-Hour Tellers in Kenya. *Innovations* 2(1–2), 63–81.

International Development Act 2002. London: The Stationery Office. Available at www.legislation.gov.uk/ukpga/2002/1 (accessed 10 August 2019).

Johnson, S. (2004) Gender Norms in Financial Markets: Evidence from Kenya. *World Development* 32(8), 1355–1374.

Johnson, S. (2015) *Capacities to Aspire and Capacities to Save: A Gendered Analysis of Motivations for Liquidity Management*. Nairobi: FSD Kenya.

Johnson, S. and Williams, R. (2013) The Political Economy of Financial Inclusion: Working with Governments on Market Development. *Bath Papers in International Development and Well-being*, Working Paper 23. Bath: Centre for Development Studies.

Kabubo-Mariara, J. and Kiriti, T. W. (2002) Structural Adjustment, Poverty and Economic Growth: An Analysis for Kenya, *AERC Research Paper* 124. Nairobi: African Economic Research Consortium.

Karim, L. (2011) *Microfinance and its Discontent: Women in Debt in Bangladesh*. Minneapolis: University of Minnesota Press.

Kats, J. and Aakhu, M. (2002) *Perpetual Contact: Mobile Communication, Private Talk, Public Performance*. Cambridge: Cambridge University Press.

Kenyatta, J. (1968) *Suffering Without Bitterness*. Nairobi: East African Publishing House.

Kinyanjui, Njeri M. (2012) *Vyama: Institutions of Hope*. Oakville, CA: Nsemia.

Klopp, J. M. (2002) Can Moral Ethnicity Trump Political Tribalism? The Struggle for Land and Nation in Kenya. *African Studies* 61(2), 269–294.

Laws of Kenya, Central Bank of Kenya Act 1966 (amended 1 January 2014) and Banking Act 1995 (amended 15 September 2015), Nairobi: Central Bank of Kenya.

Lewa M. R. (2000) Women's Groups and the Law in Kenya, in K. Kibwana and L. M. Mute (eds) *Law and the Quest for Gender Equality in Kenya*. Nairobi: Claripress.

Ling, R. and Horst, H. A. (2011) Mobile Communication in the Global South. *New Media and Society* 13(3), 363–374.

Maathai, W. (2010) *The Challenge of Africa*. London: Arrow Books.

Makin, P. (2019) Regulatory Issues Around Mobile Banking, OECD, www.oecd.org/ict/4d/43631885.pdf (accessed 3 August 2019).

Manji, A. (2015) Bulldozers, Homes and Highways: Nairobi and the Right to the City. *Review of African Political Economy* 42(144), 206–224.

Mas, I. and Radcliffe, D. (2010) *Mobile Payments go Viral: M-Pesa in Kenya*. Seattle, WA: Bill and Melinda Gates Foundation.

Maurer, M. (2012) Mobile Money: Communication, Consumption and Change in the Payment Space, *Journal of Development Studies* 48(5), 589–604.

Mazrui, A. (1967) *Towards a Pax Africana*. Chicago, IL: University of Chicago Press.

Mbithi, P. M. (1972) Harambee Self-help: The Kenya Approach. *The African Review* 2(2), 47–166.

McKemey, K., Scott, N., Souter, D., Afullo, T., KIbombo, R. and Sakyi-Dawson, O. (2003) *Innovative Demand for Models for Telecommunications Services: Final Report*. London: Commonwealth Telecommunications Organisation.

Morawcznski, O. (2009) Exploring the Usage and Impact of 'Transformational' Mobile Financial Services: The Case of M-Pesa in Kenya. *Journal of Eastern African Studies* 3(3), 509–525.

Muthiora, B. (2015) *Enabling Mobile Money Policies in Kenya: Fostering a Digital Financial Revolution*. London: GSMA.

Ngau, P. (1987) Tensions in Empowerment: The Experience of the 'Harambee' (Self- help) Movement in Kenya. *Economic Development and Cultural Change* 35(3), 523–538.

Ngdungu, N. (2003) Kenya Macroeconomic Management, in M. S. Kimenyi, J. Mbaku, Mukum John and N. Mwaniki (eds) *Restarting and Sustaining Economic Growth and Development in Africa: The Case of Kenya*. Aldershot: Ashgate.

Nzomo, J. (1993) The Kenya's Women Movement in a Changing Political Context, in S. Khasiani and E. Njiro (eds) *The Women's Movement in Kenya*. Nairobi: Association of African Women for Research and Development.

Nzomo, M. (1997) Kenyan Woman in Politics and Public Decision Making, in G. Mikell (ed.) *African Feminism: The Politics of Survival in Sub-Saharan Africa*. Philadelphia: University of Pennsylvania Press.

Nzomo, M. (1996) The Political Economy of the African Crisis: Gender Impacts and Responses. *International Journal* 51, 78–102.

Oduol, W. and Kabira, W. (1995) The Mother of Warriors and Her Daughters: The Women's Movement in Kenya, in A. Basu (ed.) *The Challenge of Local Feminisms: Women's Movements in Global Perspective*. Boulder, CO: Westview Press.

Omwansa, T. K. and Sullivan, N. P. (2012) *Money, Real Quick: Kenya's Disruptive Mobile Money Innovation*. Appledore: Balloonview.

Otieno, W. W. (1998) *Mau Mau's Daughter: A Life History*. Boulder, CO: Lynne Rienner Publishers.

Owens, J. and Bantung-Herrera, A. (2006) *Catching the Technology Wave: Mobile Phone Banking and Text-a-Payment in the Philippines*. Washington, DC: Chemonics International.

Owino, D. and Tanui, J. (2011) *The State of Competition Report: Mobile Money Transfer, Agricultural Bulk Storage and Milling, and the Media Sectors in Kenya*. Nairobi: Institute of Economic Affairs.

Porteous, D. (2006) *The Enabling Environment for Mobile Banking in Africa*. London: DFID.

Ray, M. (2007) Africa's 'Cyber' Currency, *iafrica.com*, 2 March 2007.

Scott, N. and McKemey, K. (2002) *The Use of Telephones in Rural and Low-income Communities in Africa*, 42nd Meeting of CTO Council, London.

Scott, N., McKemey, K. and Batchelor, S. J. (2004) The Uses of Telephones Amongst the Poor in Africa: Some Gender Implications. *Gender, Technology and Development* 8(2), 185–207.

Stone, R., Johnson, S. and Hayes, J. (2010) *FSD Kenya Impact Assessment: Summary*. Oxford: OPM.

Stigler, G. J. (1961) The Economics of Information. *Journal of Political Economy* LXIX(3), 213–235.

Suri, T. and Jack, W. (2016) The Long-run Poverty and Gender Impacts of Mobile Money. *Science* 354(6317), 1288–1292.

Tacchi, J., Kitner, K. R. and Crawford, K. (2012) Meaningful Mobility: Gender, Development and Mobile Phones. *Feminist Media Studies* 12(4), 528–537.

Urdy, C. (1994) Risk and Insurance in a Rural Credit Market: An Empirical Investigation in Northern Nigeria. *Review of Economic Studies* 61(3), 495–526.

Vaughan, P., Fengel, W. and Joseph, M. (2012) Scaling up Through Disruptive Business Models: The Inside Story of Mobile Money in Kenya, in L. Chandy, A. Hosono, H. Kharas and J. F. Linn (eds) *Getting to Scale: How to Bring Development Solutions to Millions of Poor People*. Washington, DC: Brookings Institution Press.

Wandibba, S., Nangendo, S. M. and Mulemi, B. A. (2012) *Gender Empowerment and Access to Financial Services in Machakos County, Eastern Kenya*. Nairobi: IMTFI and Institute of Anthropology, Gender and African Studies.

Wooder, S. and Baker, S. (2012) Extracting Key Lessons in Service Innovation. *Journal of Product Innovation Management* 29(1), 13–20.

World Bank (1997) *Kenya Women Finance Trust: A Case Study of a Micro-finance Scheme*. Washington, DC: World Bank.

Yonazi, E., Kelly, T., Halewood, N. and Blackman, C. (2012) *The Transformational Use of Information and Communication Technologies in Africa*. Washington, DC: World Bank.

Zollman, J. and Collins, D. (2010) *Financial Capability and the Poor: Are We Missing the Mark?* Nairobi: FSD Kenya.

4 The gendered narratives of mobile money

From social entrepreneurship to philanthrocapitalism

Gender, entrepreneurship and financial inclusion

Entrepreneurship has become an increasingly important idea in mainstream development discourse and a key concept in analyses of the relationship between gender and financial inclusion. The focus on entrepreneurship reflects a shift in development thinking from seeing the poor as beneficiaries of aid and development expertise to seeing them as actors, consumers and entrepreneurs responsible for their own development (Rankin 2001; Elyachar 2005, 2012). As discussed in Chapter 2, the conceptual premises of this idea can be found in Sen's *Development as Freedom*, which claims that development should be evaluated in terms of 'the "capabilities" of persons to lead the kind of lives they value – and have reason to value' (Sen 1999: 18). According to this idea, development interventions need to focus on providing people living in poverty with opportunities to become the architects of their own development. This shift is particularly evident in the area of gender equality. Women, initially excluded from the development project, have become the target of development interventions and are increasingly considered icons of change with untapped entrepreneurial capacity, able to lift their households, communities and countries out of poverty and to contribute to their development. This approach, legitimised by international policies such as 'gender equality as smart economics' (World Bank 2006, 2012), embraces the idea of inclusive markets while promoting a more social approach to development (Rittich 2006) that characterised the adoption of the Millennium Development Goals (MDGs), now replaced by the Sustainable Development Goals (SDGs). These policies promote entrepreneurship as a tool for achieving both economic growth and social goals (Blowfield 2010; Blowfield and Dolan 2014).

The emphasis on entrepreneurship began to gain traction under a neoliberal privatisation policy agenda introduced with the structural adjustment programmes (SAPs), and assumed a more social connotation with the adoption of the MDGs and later the SDGs. Research on SAPs has shown how the privatisation of common property resources, public utilities and services had a negative impact on people living on a low income, even exacerbating poverty (Elson 1989, 1991, 1992; Benería and Feldman 1992; Bakker 1994). Charging fees for healthcare and education, ending food subsidies and replacing state-subsidised access to credit for agriculture with microcredit for micro-entrepreneurship forced families to rely on their own insufficient resources and on moneylenders and microcredit schemes. These dynamics had important consequences in terms of gender relations, increasing women's responsibility for social reproduction work (Benería 2003: 131; Eisenstein 2005: 507). The failure and the criticism of SAPs and the increasing pressure to reframe the nexus between development and economic growth and realign it in terms of poverty reduction under the MDGs resulted in a focus on social objectives, including gender equality in the development agenda (Rittich 2006: 203).

This emphasis on social goals, together with reliance on entrepreneurship as a development strategy, extended not only the scope of development discourse and interventions but also the involvement of development actors such as NGOs, the private sector and philanthropic foundations, and led to the creation of new forms of development funding. The focus on social objectives also entailed the restructuring of the relationship between the state, as public provider, and its citizens, raising questions about development actors' accountability regarding the realisation of social goals. The expanded agenda has increasingly resulted in programmes and policies to facilitate access to markets, income and affordable products and services, and often included attempts to formalise informal segments of the economy (Ferguson 2007). While these programmes and policies are informed by neoliberal values such as efficiency and profitability, they are also premised on a rhetoric of social, economic and financial inclusion (Blowfield and Dolan 2014: 28).

Microcredit and microfinance are examples of this idea of entrepreneurial inclusion. The initial microcredit schemes represented entrepreneurship as an opportunity for women living in poverty, who had previously not been considered creditworthy due to their lack of assets and regular wages. Microcredit schemes enabled women to access an extremely structured form of loan for entrepreneurial profit-making activities approved by the microfinance institutions. Women could only access loans for the production of goods and services for sale in the market, and their success was attributed to their talent and ability as entrepreneurs (Rankin 2001). While entrepreneurship was considered necessary to ensure the repayment of microcredit, it was promoted primarily as a way of providing women with an employment opportunity and a source of income to support their household. For these reasons, microcredit was, and to some extent still is, seen as a means of including, empowering and promoting women's equality. As Lairap-Fonderson (2002: 185) argues, while Western research in the 1970s often exaggerated African women's subordination, in the new millennium research and international organisations have often exaggerated the increased equality, empowerment and autonomy of sub-Saharan women resulting from initiatives such as microcredit. Autonomy in this discourse refers to the entrepreneurial capacity that women are called upon to develop in order to improve their own situation and negotiate their livelihood.

Research has widely demonstrated how the autonomy that microcredit offers is often illusory due to the strict repayment schedules and meetings, peer pressure and potential social stigma attached to failing to make repayments (Rahman 1999; Williams 2001; Rankin 2002), as well as forms of oppression within the household due to conflict about the use of the loan (Goetz 1996; Kabeer 2001). While most women need a loan to cope with unexpected events and provide basic resources and services for the household, micro-entrepreneurship is unlikely to serve this end and is even more unlikely to change their position. Microcredit adds to women's unpaid work the responsibility for managing their often unproductive micro-business and repaying the loan. Moreover, research has consistently demonstrated that micro-entrepreneurship does not provide the same possibilities as regularly-paid wage employment, particularly as it does not guarantee an adequate income to meet basic needs and can thus create even greater precarity in poor women's lives (Kabeer 2012). Micro-entrepreneurship promotes the idea that poor households can be productive by developing and taking responsibility for their own entrepreneurial capacity.

The entrepreneurship promoted by microcredit manifests primarily in the 'micro-informal' small-scale and informal sectors of the economy (Elyachar 2002). The only option for many women is to invest in common familial activities such as hairdressing or selling fish, flowers or unprocessed food, however saturated the market. These informal businesses require only small amounts of money to get started and can often be combined with household work (Lairap-Fonderson 2002: 192). The blurring of household and informal workspaces is typical of informal entrepreneurship. Microcredit only enables women to sell goods in their locality, where there are often too many competing micro-entrepreneurs relative to market demand. For instance, a Kenya Women Finance Trust survey (World Bank 1997: 25) conducted a few years after microfinance was introduced in Kenya showed that about 90 per cent of microcredit loans supported the sale of second-hand clothes and unprocessed food, while the rest was spread between manufacturing and services such as hairdressing and food kiosks. If selling vegetables and second-hand clothes are some of women's most popular income-generating activities, they involve low productivity and low returns and often have to compete with cheap imports (Lairap-Fonderson 2002: 192). In other words, while providing women with some income, microcredit makes many women and their ability to support themselves and their households dependent on the success of a micro-business that is unlikely to succeed.

The other side of the entrepreneurship discourse in relation to gender and financial inclusion concerns how financial services such as microcredit and microfinance represent a business opportunity for Western corporations and financial institutions, and often involve intricate relations between the private sector and donors. For instance, while the entrepreneurship discourse supports the idea that microcredit institutions should not be dependent on aid and should become self-sustaining, in reality they have remained largely reliant on donors while increasingly becoming the domain of the private sector (Armendariz and Morduch 2010: 15). Various scholars such as the Zambian-born economist Dambisa Moyo (2009) have argued that aid has a negative role in development. She highlights the need to break the dependency and free Africa from Western aid and bureaucracy, but also maintains that the market is important if this aim is to be achieved.

As discussed in Chapter 1, financial inclusion policies have moved from donor-supported microcredit programmes for poverty reduction and women's empowerment to commercially oriented, self-sustaining and regulated micro-finance institutions that function according to financial markets. The focus on creating market-led financial institution is defined as the 'microfinance revolution' by Marguerite Robinson (2001) in her study for the World Bank. She argues that state-led financial development is corrupted by local elites, and that development via financial markets is more egalitarian. Looking at gender relations, however, demonstrates the limits of this claim. Women at the lower end of the income distribution remain largely excluded from financial markets for various reasons, ranging from insufficient assets and irregular income due to their lack of stable employment to a disproportionate amount of unpaid work. Without considering the contextual socio-economic disadvantage and the structural inequalities shaped by colonial rule and development interventions, Robinson draws a line between the economically active/entrepreneurial poor and the economically inactive poor, separating the 'bankable' from the so-called 'unbankable'. In these terms, being bankable represents the ultimate means of autonomy, freedom, economic capacity and choice for women living in poverty.

Like microcredit, M-Pesa is a donor-funded, market-based solution to financial inclusion, a mechanism favouring access to formal financial services and deepening financial sector liberalisation while simultaneously ensuring social legitimacy. It is premised on the narrative of social entrepreneurship, which is increasingly influential in mainstream development discourse. According to this narrative, business models can address social problems while simultaneously making a profit (Nicholls 2006), and poverty reduction and social goals such as gender equality can be achieved by encouraging entrepreneurship among the poor and those on a low income (Dolan 2012). M-Pesa's business value is represented by the fees that customers pay to use the service, the interest earned on M-Pesa bank accounts and managed by the M-Pesa Holding Company, and the monetary and reputational gain for Safaricom and Vodafone. Its social value is seen as financial inclusion and the potential economic and social gains that mobile money projects promise. While M-Pesa is potentially a payment service for all Kenyans, its social impact is primarily related to the benefits it can bring to the 'unbanked poor' and its possible contribution to the achievement of the SDGs, for instance through access to clean water, healthcare, affordable energy and employment opportunities. These benefits are considered achievable via a mix of entrepreneurship, philanthropy and partnerships seeking to extend opportunities that allow poor consumers to access financial capital, goods and services.

This chapter examines the gender aspects of the social entrepreneurship narrative underpinning the development of M-Pesa. It shows how social entrepreneurship and its various articulations promote a particular approach to gender equality based more on the proliferation of commercially oriented opportunities than on redistributive measures. Such opportunities include access to necessary products and services and to employment as mobile money agents. Although women have contributed greatly to the expansion of the M-Pesa platform, the profits, funding and investments deriving from M-Pesa are not redistributed to address the socio-economic disadvantages that cause gendered financial exclusion, for instance through the public provision of resources, services and social infrastructure. The M-Pesa system offers entrepreneurial opportunities but leaves the responsibility and risks inherent in taking advantage of them to the designed beneficiaries, the unbanked poor, in this way increasing their gendered responsibility for social reproduction work.

The second section investigates the gender aspects of the narrative of social entrepreneurship and its various articulations such as 'social business', 'shared value', 'creative capitalism' and 'bottom-of-the-pyramid capitalism' and traces the shift from social entrepreneurship to philanthrocapitalism, a type of philanthropy that emulates for-profit business in the capitalist world. In doing so it shows how financial inclusion is seen as a key development tool across these narratives. The following two sections illustrate the operation of these narratives within the M-Pesa system, focusing on their gender implications. The third section looks at some key products and services built on the M-Pesa infrastructure that constitute what can be called the M-Pesa ecosystem. Many of these products and services providing opportunities to access basic resources such as water, electricity, healthcare and education indirectly target women because of their major role in social provisioning. The fourth section analyses the M-Pesa agent network and how it provides women with the opportunity to start or manage microenterprises and to work as mobile money agents.

Financial inclusion: from social entrepreneurship to philanthrocapitalism

This chapter argues that M-Pesa is premised on a narrative of social entrepreneurship, namely the idea that business models can both address social problems and produce profits (Nicholls 2006). According to McGoey (2015: 65), the term originated in the US and was popularised in the 1980s by Bill Drayton, the founder of the American non-profit organisation Ashoka, to fund Changemakers, a group of individuals working for social gain. The concept was later embraced by Klaus Schwab, the founder of the World Economic Forum (WEF) who in 1998 set up the Schwab Foundation for Social Entrepreneurship, and since then it has been increasingly used to define socially motivated business initiatives in the Global North as well as development projects in the South.

Interestingly, the World Social Forum (WSF), set up in 2001, promotes a different idea of 'social'. This forum represents a site for the articulation of a series of proposals and initiatives for transnational exchange among social movements and NGOs with the aim of global economic solidarity, in contrast to what Sousa Santos (2006) calls 'hegemonic globalisation'. The institutional framework of hegemonic globalisation represents the economic and social model based on privatisation, liberalisation, market relations and entrepreneurship established with the Washington Consensus in the 1980s and embraced by the WEF. The WSF, on the other hand, recognises economic restructuring and the redistribution of resources and power as guiding principles for social justice, as proclaimed by the supporters of the New International Economic Order (NIEO).

The definition of social entrepreneurship is often contested and unclear because it is a multi-dimensional construct that includes a variety of possible models, dynamics and interests (Nicholls 2006: 12). In general terms the aim of social entrepreneurship is to achieve social objectives, usually more vaguely defined as 'missions', by adopting novel, effective and efficient business logic and methods (ibid.: 2–3). This can consist, for instance, of new partnerships across the public, private and social sectors, the creation of new ventures to deliver goods and services not yet supplied by existing markets, or new modes of finance, perhaps combined with development assistance (Elkington and Hartigan 2008; Richey and Ponte 2011). M-Pesa, for instance, used the mobile technology in an innovative way, relying on the existing airtime reseller network and on public-private partnerships to expand the use of M-Pesa and its infrastructure. This section looks at the gender aspects of the narrative of social entrepreneurship, which has acquired increasing importance in mainstream development discourse in parallel with the focus on financial inclusion policies. It examines the different articulations of social entrepreneurship including social business, shared value, creative and bottom-of-the-pyramid (BoP) capitalism and Africapitalism, and illustrates how they have contributed to framing M-Pesa as an archetype of digital financial inclusion.

In the postcolonial period, economic liberalisation policies adopted by the International Monetary Fund (IMF) and the World Bank led multinational corporations to seek to establish free trade zones in developing countries where tariffs, taxes and regulations were reduced or eliminated (Eisenstein 2005: 503). Following the failure and criticism of SAPs and the debate on poverty reduction that preceded the adoption of the MDGs, the role of corporations in labour and human rights abuses came under public scrutiny. They responded by adopting voluntary codes of practice governing the socio-economic impact of their activities. Corporate social responsibility (CSR), defined by the World Business Council as 'the commitment of business to contribute to sustainable economic development working with employees, their families, the local community and society at large to improve their quality of life', is probably the most evident example of these codes of practice (Banerjee 2008: 60). CSR also emerged from the feminist political economy's critique of multinationals, particularly their labour standards and employment conditions and their implications for gender inequality (Pearson and Seyfang 2001; Pearson 2007). However, CSR is a voluntary, discretionary and self-regulatory mechanism and is more often used as a marketing and branding expedient to attract customers and funding than to address serious concern about social issues (Banerjee 2008: 60). For instance, CSR sees gender equality as instrumental in enhancing a company's image and boosting its reputation, retaining staff, attracting media interest and public attention and securing customer loyalty (Roberts and Soederberg 2012).

The role of business and corporations in development has increasingly become more incisive, with the creation of new business models, partnerships and financial instruments to contribute to social goals such as poverty reduction, education, healthcare and gender equality.[1] Following the adoption of the MDGs, although development policies recognised the importance of the private sector they did not clearly define the role of business as a development tool and/or actor.[2] Kofi Annan, as Secretary General of the UN, constituted a special Commission on the Private Sector and Development under the auspices of the UNDP in 2003. In its final report the Commission concluded that the private sector could alleviate poverty and contribute to human development in different ways, including increasing domestic wealth and employment, for instance by 'unleashing the capacity of local entrepreneurs' (UNDP 2004: ii). This report was followed in 2006 by the UN's *Growing Inclusive Market Initiative: Business Works for Development and Development Works for Business*, confirming its belief that the private sector is a strong resource for development. Inclusive business as a development strategy was adopted by the World Bank through the International Financial Corporation and by private sector-centred institutions such as the WEF.

The private sector's involvement in development relates to its potential for creating jobs, introducing innovation and efficiency and attracting funds in the form of investment and donations. Banerjee (2008: 69), however, argues that the impact of business, and in particular multinational corporations, on countries of the Global South can be even more powerful, as they can be perceived as 'carriers of democratic value'. While colonisation brought Western legal structures and values to the colonies, the rise of a liberal economic order signalled by the Washington Consensus and the end of the Cold War exported the norms and institutions associated with global capitalism and liberal democracy (Tamanaha 2011: 9). Multinational corporations played a key role in this process, even acting as substitutes for governments by providing employment and access to necessary products and services, but without the accountability to citizens that states generally provide (Banerjee 2008).

As Blowfield and Dolan (2014) explain, business has increasingly acquired a role as development agent, thus becoming an integral part of the development agenda. In their terms this means not only social consideration beyond the business objective, as in CSR, but also consciously seeking to deliver outcomes that contribute to international development goals (ibid.: 23). This renewed role for business can result in the ambiguous solution promoted by institutions such as the WEF (2009: 6) of reframing problems related to poverty as business opportunities, redefining, for instance, concerns about clean water and healthcare as market opportunities, for example by selling products such as soap and mosquito nets (Blowfield and Dolan 2014: 30). This often requires partnership with 'development experts' and donors and aid agencies, but also with market research consultancies, local entrepreneurs and NGOs for a better understanding of the habits and behaviours of the beneficiaries/consumers (ibid.: 32). The relevance of business and collaborative partnerships in social development is also embraced by the UN's 2030 Agenda for Sustainable Development.

That gender equality is a relevant aspect of the inclusive business project emerges from documents adopted by development institutions, in particular the World Bank, composing the so-called 'business case for gender equality'. Since the adoption of the MDGs gender equality, together with women's empowerment, has increasingly been regarded as a development goal that makes economic sense, or in the World Bank's (2006) words, 'smart economics'. The World Bank's 'gender equality as smart economics' framework presents gender equality as a way of tackling inequalities in access to economic opportunities and as an instrument for enhancing economic efficiency without reforming the institutions whose decisions and resource distribution shape women's lives (Chant and Sweetman 2012: 524). According to the 2012 *World Development Report: Gender Equality and Development*, for instance, 'greater control over household resources by women leads to more investment in children's human capital, with dynamic positive effects on economic growth' (World Bank 2012: 5). This framework sees access to financial services as a main instrument for realising inclusive markets and creating opportunities for the poor. Along these lines the World Bank report *Women, Business and the Law 2016: Getting to Equal* (2015) considers gender inequality in access to credit and financial services a main impediment to business and to development, prosperity and national competitiveness.

Yunus developed the concept of social business in relation to microcredit. In his terms, social business is a broader concept that includes microcredit and aims to make the capitalist economy more inclusive and beneficial for all (Yunus and Weber 2010: xiv). Central to this idea is access to credit as a human right, suggesting that microcredit is not only a development tool but also a form of ethical economics: a 'business built on the selfless part of human nature' (ibid.: xvii). He assumes a link between microcredit and poverty reduction and considers the involvement of the private sector necessary to generate enough income to cover the cost of lending money to the poor. However, this income should be used with a philanthropic aim and not for personal profit. His approach to gender equality is very much in line with the framework of gender equality as smart economics, presenting female microcredit borrowers as more able to benefit their families and communities through its use than male borrowers (ibid.: x, xiii).

The link between philanthropy and business has also been theorised by the Harvard business scholar Porter and the corporate lawyer Kramer (Porter and Kramer 1999, 2006, 2011), who coined the concept of 'shared value', namely pursuing a philanthropic strategy that aligns with a corporation's commercial interests. They see the potential of commercial activities with a social purpose to increase not only economic but also social value. Unlike Yunus's approach, creating shared value means making a profit for the business owners and in so doing, contributing to social objectives such as creating jobs, providing goods and services and helping to fund social projects. In this model financial access for the poor should not be seen as a mere social obligation but as 'win-win logic' (Porter and Kramer 2011). They also, in resonance with the smart economics approach, see gender equality as both a goal and an instrument favouring economic and financial efficiency.[3]

The idea of combining business with philanthropy also defines Bill Gates's concept of 'creative capitalism' (Gates and Kiviat 2008), which focuses on how consumer-based technology can facilitate innovation and how philanthropic foundations can offer incentives to companies to create and deliver new products and services for people living in poverty. Creative capitalism legitimises the idea that the poor constitute a potential market for corporations, echoing Prahalad's BoP argument, to which Bill Gates alludes in his explanation of creative capitalism. The BoP approach refers to how poor and marginalised groups represent a potential market that is under-served or not served at all by the private sector, and he aims to bring them into the global economy via new models of financial inclusion, entrepreneurship and consumption.

In his book *The Fortune at the Bottom of the Pyramid* (2004: 5), Prahalad argues that people living in poverty should be seen not as victims, but as resilient and creative entrepreneurs and value-conscious consumers. This focus on the entrepreneurial capacities of people at the lower end of the income distribution evokes De Soto's (2000) definition of 'the poor' as 'heroic entrepreneurs'. However, unlike De Soto, Prahalad's model sees the solution to poverty not in the formalisation of informal segments of the economy, but in the involvement of corporations to provide products and services for the BoP market. In his view these products and services should be small and affordable, adapting to the consumers' irregular income and using new purchase schemes such as providing products and services on credit to be repaid in small and flexible instalments. According to the BoP framework financial services should be provided by innovative and cost-conscious lenders that use economies of scale to offer affordable, mass-produced financial services. According to Prahalad this approach opens up a new world of opportunities both for the poor and for companies. In gender terms, he argues that the entrepreneurial capacities of women are particularly important, as women have a leading role in 'building a new society at the BoP' (Prahalad 2004: 108).

More recently these ideas surrounding the narrative of creative capitalism have found expression in the concept of 'philanthrocapitalism', a method of philanthropy that emulates for-profit business in the capitalist world. According to McGoey (2014, 2015), this term was coined in 2006 in *The Economist* and later developed by Bishop, *The Economist*'s US Business Editor, and Green, a former policymaker at the UK Department for International Development (DFID) (Bishop and Green 2008). They define philanthrocapitalism in two main ways: at the micro level it means applying a business method to philanthropic activities, while at the macro level it describes how capitalism itself can be philanthropic, driving innovation in a way that can, at least potentially, benefit everyone through new products and services and lower prices. This logic is based on the assumption that poverty, inequality and other world problems cannot be solved through charity or political action alone: they also need business, which can provide innovation and efficiency (Guilhot 2007; McGoey 2015).

As McGoey (2015: 16) explains, the idea of organising philanthropy in the same way as corporations was originally of American businessman John Davison Rockefeller. However, while Rockefeller and similar philanthropists decided to run their philanthropic trusts in an efficient and business-like way in line with the operating principles that applied to their business practice, they never openly admitted that their giving was aimed at directly increasing their corporate profits (McGoey 2014: 111). Philanthrocapitalism is more impact-oriented and, unlike previous models and practices, is characterised by an explicit spirit of profit-making considered necessary for reinvesting in new projects and contributing to creating more development opportunities. Philanthrocapitalists are predominantly entrepreneurs, such as Bill Gates, Mark Zuckerberg, Jeffrey Skoll, Marcus Goldman and Samuel Sachs, who have made fortunes in the tech or finance industries and are driven by the aim of bringing innovative financing models and new performance metrics to philanthropy, making it more efficient and lucrative (ibid.). Foundations combining philanthropy with entrepreneurship have also been established by political figures such as the Clinton Foundation, which features in the foreword to Bishop and Green's mentioned book (2008), and the Cherie Blair Foundation for Women with its specific focus on supporting women entrepreneurs in line with the framework of gender equality as smart economics.

Among philanthrocapitalist foundations, the Bill and Melinda Gates Foundation stands out with its wealth and public support from governments, international organisations, corporations and celebrities (McGoey 2015). The majority of the fortune that Gates has accumulated via his business at Microsoft is used to fund projects and research, and in so doing it influences the development agenda. The Foundation collaborates with governments and the private sector, offering companies incentives to create and deliver new products and services for the poor. Financial inclusion is one of its current priorities, and in 2006 it partnered with a variety of institutions to launch the Financial Services for the poor initiative. Following the success of M-Pesa in Kenya, the Foundation has invested in mobile money projects and digital financial inclusion more generally. It has also been indirectly involved in shaping the global agenda and policy frameworks for digital financial inclusion by funding the institutions leading this debate, such as the Alliance for Financial Inclusion and the mobile money programme at Groupe Spéciale Mobile Association (GSMA).

Besides developing digital financial services and an enabling regulatory environment for digital financial inclusion, another key focus of the Foundation is gender equality. While the Gates Foundation emphasises the importance of mobile money for creating new opportunities for women, it simplistically considers the increasing number of women able to access formal finance as evidence of their successful financial inclusion.[4] On its website the Foundation highlights how the digitalisation of social protection programmes could contribute to the financial inclusion of women by providing them with incentives to use digital payment, but does not address how digital platforms and philanthropic foundations could contribute to funding such programmes.

Philanthrocapitalist foundations can even have negative implications for gender equality deriving from the opening up of new markets for Western multinational corporations, the use of philanthropic foundations to obtain tax reductions, and the direct and indirect roles of philanthrocapitalism in protecting and expanding assets rather than redistributing wealth to address the socio-economic disadvantages of women living on a low income. Philanthrocapitalism after all has corresponded to the rise in private wealth of what Oxfam calls 'the richer 1 per cent'.[5]

The narrative of philanthrocapitalism has also been embraced by African political leaders and entrepreneurs supporting the idea of Africapitalism. This term, coined by the Nigerian economist and philanthropist Tony Elumelu (2014), unlike the Western idea of philanthrocapitalism, recognises colonialism as one of the causes of poverty, but it also considers private investment in social entrepreneurship the solution to creating economic and social wealth as well as political transformation. Africapitalism is linked to the idea of 'Africa Rising' (*The Economist* 2012), to which the rapid growth of M-Pesa has contributed. M-Pesa has been influenced by the ideas of social entrepreneurship, shared values, BoP, philanthrocapitalism and Africapitalism. As discussed in Chapter 3, it started by identifying a potential market, targeting the 'unbanked poor', and a social objective, namely financial inclusion and the social gains that this can bring. M-Pesa was developed through a public-private partnership between DFID and Vodafone's Social Enterprise department, sharing the costs and risks of a long-term project combining profit with social objectives. The partnership with Safaricom provided a doorway to local markets and revealed poor people's financial practices to Vodafone. Consideration of consumers' needs and the potential for different mobile money products and services have found further validation in the various partnerships between Safaricom and philanthropic foundations, corporations, governments, NGOs, development experts, consultants, regulators and international organisations, all of which are committed to development, poverty reduction and gender equality via digital financial inclusion.

Since the launch of M-Pesa Safaricom has become Kenya's largest and most profitable company, producing a revenue of almost 240.3 billion KES and making net profits of about 63 billion KES (619 million USD) in 2019, of which M-Pesa accounts for about 31 per cent.[6] While Safaricom brands itself as distinctly Kenyan and the company that brought first the mobile phone and then financial services to all Kenyans, it is important to consider that only 35 per cent of it is owned by the Kenyan government, with 40 per cent owned by Vodafone and the remaining 25 per cent of shares, sold by the government in 2008 for 52 billion KES (*The Economist* 2008), held in small tranches by a range of mainly foreign investors. As Bateman, Duvendack and Loubere (2019: 7–8) observe, this means that a significant portion of the revenue produced by M-Pesa is not locally redistributed but repatriated back to shareholders in the UK and other countries in a form of neo-colonial digital extraction. The interest on funds held in customers' M-Pesa trust accounts is paid to the M-Pesa Holding Company and managed by the M-Pesa Foundation, created in 2010 for this purpose as an independent charitable trust.[7] Projects funded by the M-Pesa Foundation use the mobile money platform to combine entrepreneurial education, technological innovation and social objectives. Similar projects are also funded by the Safaricom Foundation, one of the largest corporate foundations in Kenya.

Gender equality is an important social objective of these projects, although framed as a simple, measurable and profitable goal, achievable via mechanisms of market inclusion and instrumental to economic growth, in line with gender equality as smart economics framework. M-Pesa has created opportunities for entrepreneurship, philanthropy and wealth, but its contribution to challenging unequal social relations, including gender inequality, is questionable. To illustrate this point, the next two sections examine the gender implications of the social entrepreneurship narrative underpinning M-Pesa by looking at the products, services and job opportunities built on the M-Pesa infrastructure.

Mobile money ecosystems

As discussed, M-Pesa is premised on a narrative of social entrepreneurship that combines social and business value. The business value is represented by the fees paid by customers, the interest earned on M-Pesa trust accounts and Safaricom and Vodafone's monetary and reputational gain. The social value is represented by financial inclusion and its possible social gains. Social gains include the opportunity to use the M-Pesa infrastructure to facilitate access to needed resources and services such as water, healthcare and electricity, in this way contributing to the SDGs. To this end Safaricom has collaborated with financial institutions, corporations, philanthropic foundations, community groups and NGOs. As the mobile network operator (MNO), it provides the channel through which money moves, for a fee, while philanthropic foundations and corporations provide funding and expertise to develop the projects, products and services to be distributed or sold through the M-Pesa infrastructure (Maurer 2015: 22).

The purpose of these products and services is to facilitate access to finance for the unbanked poor while also offering them the opportunity to access basic resources for which they pay via the M-Pesa platform in small and flexible instalments suitable for people with a small and irregular income. Besides relying on mobile data to develop new products and services (Maurer 2015; Gabor and Brooks 2016), Safaricom has also created platforms such as Zindua Café to encourage their customers to share ideas and proposals for new mobile money products and services.[8] While echoing Escobar's (2010) criticism that the voices of the poor are not evident in developing discourse, the purpose of considering people's voices in digital financial inclusion acquires a different entrepreneurial aim. Mobile money-enabled projects, products and services have contributed to expanding M-Pesa across a variety of formal and informal sectors such as finance, commerce, healthcare and education, constituting the so-called mobile money ecosystem (Kendall *et al.* 2012). There are countless possibilities for combining mobile technology and retail finance so that mobile money becomes part of everyday socio-economic relations (Yenkey, Doering and Aceves 2015).

The projects supported by the M-Pesa Foundation are developed around the idea of social entrepreneurship. For instance one of the largest projects, the M-Pesa Academy, driven by the principles of entrepreneurship, technology and innovation, provides educational opportunities for 'talented but economically disadvantaged students with demonstrable leadership potential'.[9] Other projects supported by the M-Pesa Foundation use mobile money services to improve healthcare, with a number targeting women's reproductive role. Uzazi Salama (Safe Motherhood), for example, is a programme realised through a partnership between the M-Pesa Foundation, Amref Health Africa, the PharmAccess Foundation and the Samburu County Government to create a more efficient transport and referral system for maternal healthcare. A similar scheme, the Health Enablement and Learning Platform (HELP), is an M-learning programme based on a partnership between the M-Pesa Foundation, Amref Health Africa, Kenya's Ministry of Health, and Accenture Development Partnerships in three areas of Kenya: Nairobi's Kibera slum, the rural district of Mwingi and the Samburu pastoralist region. It provides mobile phone-based training to volunteers who are then made responsible for passing on health-related information to community members and providing support in health emergencies.[10]

Similar projects are also provided outside the M-Pesa Foundation framework in partnership with other philanthropic foundations and local institutions. FistulaCare, for instance, provided by the Freedom from Fistula Foundation (FFF) founded by the millionaire businesswoman and philanthropist Ann Gloag in 2008, facilitates the free treatment of women with fistula. Women can call the FFF hotline and receive treatment at the Jamaa Mission Hospital in Nairobi. If a woman cannot afford transport to the hospital FFF sends their fare via M-Pesa with an additional 25 KES to cover the transaction fee to withdraw the money and other expenses.[11] However, the Fistula Foundation advertises only the free fistula treatment and not the support for the fare to the hospital, preventing some women contacting and benefiting from FFF.[12] A similar project has been implemented in Tanzania via a collaboration between the Comprehensive Community-Based Rehabilitation Hospital and the UN Population Fund (UNFPA). The project works through community ambassadors, intermediaries who receive a small payment for identifying women with fistula and then liaise with the hospital and send them money to travel to hospital via M-Pesa.[13]

Other projects developed in partnership with enterprises, financial institutions and philanthropic foundations use the mobile money platform to offer fee-based products and services to facilitate access to basic resources such as electricity and water. These products and services, which target poor households and women in particular as those who are largely responsible for social provisioning, are bought on credit and repaid in small and flexible instalments via M-Pesa. M-Kopa (*kopa* means 'to borrow' in Swahili), for example, was founded in 2011 by the same Nick Hugh who had been head of social enterprise at Vodafone and had started M-Pesa. It is a micro-solar power product consisting of a base station with a solar panel, three lamps and a charging kit for mobile phones. It was developed via a partnership between Safaricom, entrepreneurs, developers and donors which initially included the Bill and Melinda Gates Foundation, DFID and the Shell Foundation, later joined by other multinational corporations including Mitsui. The donors and companies provide resources for the development of the system, which is offered on credit to be repaid via the mobile money platform. Customers pay about 18,999 KES for the product, which includes a deposit of 2,999 KES and daily payments of 50 KES for a year via M-Pesa or, more recently, other mobile money services.[14] Customers can use the system as long as they keep up their payments, and after a year, when the repayment is complete, they own the micro-solar power system. M-Kopa relies on the mobile money infrastructure to sell micro-solar power products to low-income households, allowing them to pay on a flexible instalment plan, and promoting access to solar power as instrumental in increasing opportunities for work and for children's education.

Grundfos-Lifelink is a project developed by the Danish water pump manufacturing company Grundfos to deliver water systems and associated infrastructure to low-income markets and combines existing water-service technology with innovative business models and payment methods. The project was piloted in 2009 in the rural semi-arid community of Katitika and relied on the M-Pesa payment system.[15] As Patricia Kameri-Mbote (Kameri-Mbote and Cullet 1997: 23) points out, to understand water constraints in countries like Kenya requires recognising how colonial rule, attempts at modernisation and development programmes such as SAPs have affected access to water, particularly in rural communities. K'Akumu (2004: 213) explains that after independence the process of privatising water had begun with the adoption of the 2002 Water Act under the IMF's conditions, which particularly affected people with low incomes living in urban slums and rural areas, who could not afford to pay for clean water following privatisation. The Grundfos-Lifelink project aims to address the problem of access to clean water by adopting the logic of social entrepreneurship. Grundfos established the company Grundfos-Lifelink Kenya, a joint venture between Grundfos and Denmark's Investment Fund for Developing Countries that concluded a partnership with Safaricom to provide villagers with the opportunity to buy clean water from a community water pump via M-Pesa. Villagers pay for their water consumption through M-Pesa to a smart key bob that can be used to draw water from solar-powered water pumps. The business model of the project is that the upfront cost of the system is paid by the company via a corporate social responsibility programme and/or supported by philanthropic foundations and development organisations, while everyday water consumption repays for the system, which then becomes community-owned. According to Haas and Nagarajan (2011) the upfront cost of the Katitika project to be repaid was 1,780,000 KES. As stated in the report on the pilot, one of the system's main objectives was to help villagers to start micro-businesses such as making bricks, cultivating kitchen gardens and tree nurseries and selling bottled water from jerry cans in other villages (Haas and Nagarajan 2011).

These examples represent a very small part of the complex mobile money ecosystem in Kenya: there are numerous other mobile money projects, developed via

M-Pesa or more recently other providers, and apparently infinite possibilities for new ones (Kendall *et al.* 2012). As M-Pesa started as a financial inclusion project, all such products and services are tied to this main objective, underlining the idea that access to finance is necessary for the achievement of social objectives such as poverty reduction and gender equality. As many mobile money projects and products target women directly in their biological reproductive role or indirectly in their social reproductive role, this has automatically contributed to increasing the number of women 'included' in the financial system by offering them products and services that they and their household desperately need and which are not publicly provided. While these projects are appealing and can be considered useful for supporting social reproduction work in the absence of other forms of access, not all poor people can access or successfully use them, not only because they need a mobile phone and an M-Pesa account but also due to other limitations.

In the case of maternal health programmes provided with the support of the M-Pesa Foundation and other donors, for instance, there is often a lack of information about eligibility for participation. Such programmes, as well as projects including Grundfos-Lifelink, are often limited to particular geographical areas depending on the partnership concerned and the partners' interests. In the case of fee-based products and services the main obstacle is the initial deposit and the daily or weekly commitment to pay. Most people who are financially excluded do not have a regular income, and commitment to a mobile money opportunity with the expectation that it will result in an improved livelihood tends to increase gendered responsibility for social reproduction work. Such projects also provide limited and conditional access to electricity and water, and for this reason their long-term benefits to poor people are often questionable. While different mobile money projects can have a different impact on particular local groups and in particular areas, overall consideration of the gendered implications of mobile money-based products and services is important.

First, the proliferation of mobile money projects with social relevance has affected the relationship between the government and its citizens. In Kenya, as in other former colonial countries, the state has been often considered a shadow entity, weakened first by colonial power and later by bureaucracy and criticised for the corruption of the ruling elite and their ambiguous relations with international financial institutions (Sandbrook and Barker 1985; Ferguson 1994). As discussed in Chapter 3, in the SAPs era Moi's regime supported the privatisation processes imposed by the IMF and the World Bank, which however resulted in the state's failure to provide for the welfare of its people, placing particular burdens on the shoulders of women with a low income and affecting their ability to provide for themselves and their households. Many social services, not publicly available, became informally provided by local community groups, churches and later, NGOs.

According to Maurer (2012), banks' failure to reach rural communities and poorer people living in slums can also be considered a failure of the state which highlighted the need for new financial infrastructure. As discussed, M-Pesa relies on the mobile network to reach the financially excluded, bypassing the traditional banking infrastructure with a system for transferring money that does not involve excessive fees and intermediaries. In the same way, the M-Pesa infrastructure has been used to provide access to mobile-money-based privately provided resources and services such as water, electricity and healthcare. The extension of M-Pesa's role beyond financial services was made possible by partnerships between Safaricom and other corporations, financial institutions, NGOs, local communities, philanthropic foundations and governments, as mentioned above. While this resembles a privatisation process, it is different from the modes of privatisation seen since the imposition of SAPs.

As McGoey (2014), drawing on Mazzucato's (2013) work on the entrepreneurial state, points out, despite the frequent portrayal of M-Pesa as a non-governmental cashless system, government support has been vital to ensuring the sustainability and profitability of its services. This is due not only to the UK government providing Vodafone with a grant of about one million GBP to establish M-Pesa via DFID, but also to the involvement of the Kenyan government itself. The Central Bank of Kenya (CBK) and the Telecommunications and Finance ministries have played a central role in allowing M-Pesa to function and develop. The Kenyan government also partnered with Safaricom to digitise government payments, increase revenue collection and allow citizens to make and receive payments for services including land registration, driving licences, visas, voluntary contributions to the National Health Insurance Fund, and payments to public institutions such as the National Social Security Fund using mobile money, all of which create a profit for the MNO (GSMA 2017). The main focus of the state's involvement in the creation and development of M-Pesa, however, is on providing an affordable money transfer service for the financially excluded, rather than fairer redistribution of resources such as water, necessary services such as healthcare and electricity and social welfare more generally.

Second, the use of a business model based on transaction fees and transaction data with the involvement of governments and philanthropic foundations has led to a complex scenario with a different set of priorities and power relations. M-Pesa-integrated projects such as M-Kopa are promoted as a way of formalising and facilitating access to resources and services by creating a new system of governance that is recognised by the state but goes beyond it, with the MNO as its fulcrum and the involvement of various global and local partners. These M-Pesa partnerships are meant to assist or substitute for some of the state's key functions by giving people the opportunity and responsibility for improving their lives, while representing a secure source of revenue for the MNO. For instance, the M-Kopa solar power kit is promoted as giving the poor the opportunity to study and work, with their own responsibility for their success.

While the products and services offered through the M-Pesa infrastructure seek to facilitate the achievement of social goals and guarantee access to basic resources via the use of mobile money, in fact they reconceptualise key resources as for-profit enterprises, transforming basic needs into market opportunities purchasable via mobile financial services. As basic resources and services are sold through the M-Pesa infrastructure they become formalised, marketised and financialised. As the number of 'financially included' people increases, more livelihoods become dependent on the market and integrated into financial circuits. While this may provide poor people with more opportunity to access clean water and energy, they also become the target of private profit. The financialisaton of resources puts profit ahead of social welfare and basic needs (Fraser 2014: 546). In the M-Pesa ecosystem resources are often bought on credit or through savings schemes, repaid in small and/or flexible instalments that include a fee to the MNO for most transaction, creating a secure source of profit for Safaricom (Maurer 2012: 425). As Ribot and Peluso argue in *A Theory of Access* (2003: 165), fees regulate forms of decentralised and marketised access and often impede the realisation of decent standards of living for all people.

Mobile money products and services can appear to generate emancipatory effects by creating opportunities for greater financial inclusion, helping poor households to access material input for social provisioning and access to social services. These individualised and marketised forms of access, however, reproduce division and inequality among the population and impose new burdens on poorer women, who are disproportionately responsible for social reproduction work (Molyneux 2006; Roberts 2014b). The opportunity to gain autonomy, independence and equality via mobile money platforms is limited by the gendered structural inequalities that originated in colonial history and postcolonial development policies. These inequalities expose a general problem of financial inclusion as a development strategy for gender equality: the potential benefits can very easily become a burden when strategies to include women in development simply increase the load that women bear and the number of demands they face (Kabeer 2015). Mobile money projects create opportunities for women at the lower end of the income distribution without providing them with the resources and social infrastructure they need to take advantage of the opportunities offered.

While the public money and support that allowed the development of M-Pesa have contributed to facilitating the movement of money within the country and created a secure source of profit for the MNO, it has not secured social benefits for citizens, and particularly not for M-Pesa's target beneficiaries, the unbanked poor. Following the rapid growth of M-Pesa, philanthropic foundations, international organisations and private institutions have increasingly addressed funding financial inclusion and a plurality of mobile money products and services rather than directly supporting access to basic resources, services and social infrastructure. The increasing number of women with access to M-Pesa and mobile money programmes has become a measure of the success of the project and influences funding and investment. The institutions involved see investing in mobile money as a way of favouring sustainable economic growth and contributing to the achievement of social objectives such as gender equality while they themselves gain a profit. In this way, targeting women has become the justification for and instrument of mobile money initiatives. As Roberts and Soederberg (2012: 965) argue, since the adoption of SAPs, approaches, measures and policies that advance the argument for gender equality through market and financial participation have constrained governments' ability to finance public and redistributive forms of social provisioning which are necessary for substantive gender equality.

M-Pesa has not challenged the pattern initiated by the SAPs and continues to promote gender equality simply by increasing the availability of market and financial opportunities for women. This section has shown how M-Pesa has contributed to reconceptualising access to basic resources and services as entrepreneurial and financial opportunities, resulting in partnerships and funding addressing the mobile money market rather than the public provision of social infrastructure and assistance. The funds and new sources of revenue that have followed the rapid development of M-Pesa have not been redistributed, and possible rewards offered based on a logic of opportunity leave the responsibility for and risks inherent in taking advantage of them to the users themselves, often increasing gender-based responsibility rather than contributing to challenging unequal gender relations.

Mobile money agents

Besides providing opportunities for poor and low-income consumers to access basic resources and services, other social benefits associated with M-Pesa are linked to the possibility to use mobile money services to facilitate the management of micro-entrepreneurship and the opportunity to work as an M-Pesa agent. As seen in Chapter 3, during the M-Pesa pilot it emerged that the platform could also be used to encourage micro-entrepreneurship and facilitate both informal and registered microenterprises.[16] The majority of informal entrepreneurs, known in Kenya as *jua kali*, are women (Muiruri 2010; UN Women 2015) and informal entrepreneurship is often the only employment available to allow them to provide for themselves and their household (Mbithi 2014: 114).

Many informal and casual workers have integrated M-Pesa into their microbusinesses. According to a Financial Sector Deepening (FSD) study (Mas and Ng'weno 2012), informal entrepreneurs find M-Pesa a useful financial tool for both transferring and storing money, as many do not earn enough to be eligible for a bank account. During my fieldwork in Nairobi it emerged that women selling vegetables, fruit, flowers, second-hand clothes and similar products used mobile phones to call different markets and negotiate prices and M-Pesa to pay their suppliers in advance, rather than going from one market to another.[17] They also purchased goods from distant locations via M-Pesa to save travelling time, arranging for *matatu* drivers to deliver the products to them.[18] Other women, working as casual workers, preferred their pay to go directly into their M-Pesa account to avoid carrying cash. Women working in hairdressing, selling chapatis or involved in community, social and personal services found M-Pesa useful for making payments and for storing money safely on their mobile phones. M-Pesa is seen as an instrument that facilitates transactions and increases efficiency in balancing paid and unpaid work. It has also been integrated into government programmes to allow women entrepreneurs to manage the microfinance schemes offered by the Women Enterprise Fund established by Kenya Vision 2030.[19]

A major entrepreneurial opportunity created by M-Pesa and linked to gender equality is the possibility for poor and low-income women to work as mobile money agents. M-Pesa agents provide the infrastructure and mechanism by which electronic money moves and have played a key role in the expansion of the service (Maurer *et al.* 2013: 54). They are organised hierarchically, with master or super agents and retail agents. The master agents have a contractual relationship with Safaricom and are responsible for recruiting retail agents and managing the agent's liquidity so that they can meet customers' requests for cash.[20] M-Pesa retail agents, also called sub-agents, operate under the master agents and are responsible for opening accounts, registering new customers, handling deposits and withdrawals and customer support. The opportunity to work as a mobile money agent is supported as a development strategy by international organisations and philanthropic foundations in line with the social entrepreneurship narrative and the framework of gender equality as smart economics (World Bank 2006, 2012).

In 2010, for instance, the Cherie Blair Foundation for Women established a mobile technology programme in partnership with various mobile network operators (MNOs), corporations and local NGOs and groups that includes among its objectives 'increasing the participation and capacity of women in mobile and banking agent networks'. This programme followed a report in collaboration with GSMA, *Women and Mobile: A Global Opportunity. A Study on the Mobile Phone Gender Gap in Low and Middle-Income Countries* (2010), which emphasised that the inclusion of women in the mobile money business would bring social benefits to them and their families as well as a 12 billion USD revenue opportunity for MNOs. This report was followed by two other studies: *Mobile Retail Channels* (Cherie Blair Foundation 2011) concludes that female agents contribute to higher revenue potential, stronger brand image and access to untapped markets while gaining skills training and economic opportunities, and *Mobile Value Added Services* (Cherie Blair Foundation 2012) resulted in the development of a mobile learning tool that is used to deliver business training and tips to businesswomen in Nigeria, Tanzania and Indonesia.

The ideas promoted in these reports encourage women to participate in the mobile money market not only as consumers but also as providers. By framing the mobile money market as social business and gender equality as smart economics, they argue that women and MNOs both benefit with training, economic opportunities and possibly increased autonomy and wellbeing for women, and more profits for MNOs. However, two key factors must be considered to understand the gender implications of these ideas. The first is that like microcredit programmes, mobile money agents tend to replicate rather than challenge women's positional vulnerability and socio-economic disadvantage. The second is that poor and low-income women working as mobile money agents contribute to the aim of financial inclusion without receiving commensurate rewards for their additional unpaid work.

While there are various surveys on M-Pesa users, it is more difficult to find data on M-Pesa agents. During my fieldwork in 2012, 24 of the 28 retail or sub-agents interviewed in the Kawangware and Ngando districts were women.[21] Working as a money agent requires a high level of flexibility in terms of time and willingness to help customers. Research on informal finance has long emphasised the role of women as money agents in both the Global South and the Global North. In her work on moneylenders in the UK in the 1990s, Rowlingson (1994: 8) found that 'female agents had close relationships with women customers' and that the money-lending industry can be considered part of 'women's economy'. Reporting on her fieldwork on microfinance in India, Karim (2011: 106) explains how a locally famous female moneylender considered school education for her daughter less important than teaching her about the practice of money-lending.

As the literature on microcredit discussed in Chapter 1 shows, women are considered more responsible and reliable than men in their management of money (Rahman 1999). During my fieldwork in Nairobi women were defined as reliable and to be trusted with money. Some customers recalled that when M-Pesa was launched they particularly did not trust male agents, feeling that they were cheating them. For instance retail agents receive a commission for each new customer registered and for each withdrawal and deposit, with 70 per cent going to the retail agent and 30 per cent to the master agent, rather than a payment based on the amount transacted, and some agents invented strategies to increase the number of transactions per day, for example by capping the amount that could be withdrawn so that customers had to make more transactions. Women were also considered more patient with customers and more willing to take the time to explain how M-Pesa works and to help with transactions. Elderly people with less experience of mobile phones affirmed that they trusted female agents to the extent of revealing their M-Pesa PIN number to them so that the agent could make the transaction on their behalf. These dynamics have also helped to build trust in the system, which has been an important element of the development of M-Pesa. Master agents prefer to hire women because they perceive them as trustworthy and more precise when concluding transactions, and more efficient than men at serving customers and working longer hours.

If women want to open their own M-Pesa retail agency this requires approaching a master agent and signing an agreement costing about 20,000–50,000 KES. As mentioned, the retail agent's contractual relationship is not with Safaricom but with the master agent. While some women own their M-Pesa agent, many work for family members or master agents for low remuneration that is often a combination of salary and commission (about 2,000–3,000 KES per month). While in the last couple of years more women have succeeded in opening an M-Pesa business by themselves or via a savings and credit group, this is not necessarily a remunerative business. There are currently about 167,000 M-Pesa retail agencies in Kenya (Safaricom 2019: 6) and they are becoming increasingly less profitable as the business begins to saturate the market, depending on the location and number of agents in the area. According to research by the Helix Institute for Digital Finance (2015), an agent's average monthly profit is about 7,000 KES and, already in 2015, 17 per cent of agencies were no longer profitable. The main risks in setting up a mobile money agency are not being able to cover the costs of the business, fraud and robbery. Failure is seen as the responsibility of the agent, and Safaricom, its Foundation and the government offer no programmes to support these entrepreneurs. Instead, recent developments in the regulation of mobile money and the adoption of the National Payment System Regulations 2014 discussed in Chapter 5 have allowed M-Pesa agents to offer mobile money services from different providers and MNOs other than Safaricom.

The opportunity to work as an M-Pesa agent is clearly an alternative to the lack of wage employment and maintains many of the elements of informal micro-entrepreneurship. For women this represents an income or additional income and it is flexible enough to allow them to juggle paid and unpaid work. It is common, for instance, to see women working as agents accompanied by their small children, or opening an agency close to their homes. To start an M-Pesa agency requires only training from the master agent, the employer or Safaricom, and no certification is needed. Informal micro-entrepreneurship is often a necessity rather than a choice, and this is important in the evaluation of the opportunities that mobile money projects offer. A study by the University of Nairobi and Plymouth University (Kaijage and Wjeeler 2013), funded by DFID, found that more than three-quarters of Kenya graduates would prefer to work for the public sector or a large domestic or multinational company: self-employment and entrepreneurial work was the least desirable career choice, with only 3 per cent expressing a preference for this option. Despite this outcome the study concludes that 'it is essential to develop a new paradigm for entrepreneurship education that is grounded in the economic and social context of the entrepreneurs' (ibid.: 22).

The M-Pesa agents seem to reproduce gender stereotypes about women (i.e. being responsible), the kind of work they do (i.e. customer services) and the circumscribed spatiality of their work (i.e. in agency kiosks). Working as agents allows them to combine paid and unpaid work. As Kabeer (2012) explains, this kind of work does not eliminate the social and economic impediments to women's integration into the labour market, and certainly does not contribute to reducing the precarity of poor women's lives. However, if working as a mobile money agent does not integrate women into the labour market, it does integrate them into the financial system. According to Roberts (2014a: 110), training women as mobile money agents 'serves to deepen the reach of finance by linking women entrepreneurs to mobile money retail chains'.

This inclusion, however, relegates women to a particular form of finance, a kind of second-class banking that defines the conditions on which women can be included in the financial system. This is the result of financial inclusion policies focusing on developing inclusionary techniques rather than addressing the socio-economic disadvantage and marginalisation of women that cause financial exclusion in the first place. The same idea of 'banking on women' promoted by the International Finance Corporation (IFC) seeks to extend formal financial logics to women's informal finance to include them in a profitable financial market. In the case of M-Pesa, the FSD's FinAccess surveys show that since the introduction of M-Pesa the percentage of people in Kenya using informal finance has decreased from 32 per cent – the majority of whom were women – in 2006 to 6 per cent in 2019, while the number of people with access to formal and semi-formal finance such as mobile money has increased from 20 per cent in 2006 to 83 per cent in 2019 (FSD 2007, 2019). Including women in the financial system not just as consumers but also as financial providers has contributed to the expansion of mobile money. However, while working as mobile money agents is presented to women as an opportunity to improve their status and the livelihood of their household, they are also charged with the responsibility and risks inherent in taking advantage of this opportunity without receiving a commensurate reward for their work.

This section has shown how the social entrepreneurship narrative has been used to promote the mobile money agency as an entrepreneurial opportunity for women and has been instrumental in contributing to financial inclusion via M-Pesa. Consistent with the framework of gender equality as smart economics, women agents are used as evidence that digital financial inclusion can contribute to the social goal of gender equality while also contributing to economic development. However, this viewpoint, powered by gendered assumptions about the reliability and solidarity of women, risks reproducing and creating new gender inequalities in access to and in taking advantage of economic and financial opportunities. It also risks increasing women's responsibilities for social reproduction work without providing them with adequate economic reward and social support, and undermining the potential for using digital financial inclusion to contribute to substantive gender equality.

Conclusion

This chapter has located the development of M-Pesa within the narrative of social entrepreneurship in development discourse and has analysed its gender implications. The narrative has evolved in parallel with the private sector's involvement in development and the increasing focus on financial inclusion as an instrument for economic growth while simultaneously contributing to social objectives such as gender equality. 'Gender, entrepreneurship and financial inclusion' has introduced the role of entrepreneurship in development discourse and its role in framing the relationship between financial inclusion and gender equality. 'Financial inclusion: from social entrepreneurship to philanthrocapitalism' has analysed the gender aspects of the narrative of social entrepreneurship and its articulations such as social business, shared value, creative and bottom-of-the-pyramid capitalism, and traced the shift from social entrepreneurship to philanthrocapitalism, a type of philanthropy that emulates for-profit business in the capitalist world. The third and fourth sections have examined how these narratives have influenced and legitimised the conceptualisation and evolution of M-Pesa and the various opportunities built on its infrastructure. 'Mobile money ecosystems' has investigated the opportunities for poor households and consumers to access basic resources and services via privately provided, fee-based products and services built on M-Pesa's infrastructure. 'Mobile money agents' has explored the entrepreneurial and employment opportunities created via M-Pesa, focusing on the potential for poor women to work as M-Pesa agents. The analysis shows how M-Pesa-enabled products, services and employment are presented as entrepreneurial opportunities, leaving the responsibility for and risks inherent in taking advantage of them to the unbanked poor, often reproducing gender inequalities and increasing gender-based responsibility.

Some considerations emerge from this analysis. The first is the centrality of business or, using Fisher's (2009) words, 'business ontology' typical of Western capitalism, according to which everything in society from access to finance, healthcare and education should be run on a business model and the expectation that financial development and technology will bring profits for business, benefits for people and prosperity for the country. Such business logic, however, is increasingly including the word 'social', as demonstrated by the concept of social entrepreneurship. While 'social' in relation to business was initially used to refer to the commitment to corporate social responsibility, now business is often used as evidence of social value, as demonstrated by its expansion to rural and slum areas (McGoey 2014: 84). In the case of M-Pesa, the growth of Safaricom as a Kenyan corporation (although Vodafone owns 40 per cent of it and investors 25 per cent) and its commitment to social objectives has contributed to promoting a narrative of corporations creating not only capital but also, and particularly, social value.

Collaboration with NGOs and local organisations has reinforced this narrative, promoting social values within frameworks and categories provided by international institutions such as the UN, the IMF and the World Bank. These categories are premised on the developed-developing dichotomy which, even where it considers local needs, rarely considers local inequalities as the reflection of unequal structural conditions in the global economy. Although promoted as complementary to governmental efforts, mobile money partnerships tend to favour well-established mechanisms and well-resourced players (products such as M-Kopa are examples of this) and often focus on immediate inclusive solutions, deflecting attention from the problems causing exclusion. As Banks and Hulme (2014: 192) argue, discussions of exclusion tend to focus on market products and services rather than 'the inequalities in power and voice that keep poor populations systematically, socially and politically excluded'. In this context gender equality is reduced to a simple, measurable and profitable goal that can be achieved by increasing the number of women having access to mobile money services.

The second consideration is that products, services and programmes built on the M-Pesa platform are based on a logic of opportunity rather than a politics of redistribution. This is important in defining the terms and conditions of financial inclusion and evaluating its gender implication. Narratives such as social entrepreneurship, creative and BoP capitalism, shared value and philanthrocapitalism place emphasis on increasing the productivity and growth of the poor rather than the redistribution of resources and responsibilities that is necessary for substantive gender equality and, more generally, social justice. M-Pesa has created new opportunities via mobile money products and services; however, offering opportunities to women living on a low and irregular income without providing them with the necessary resources to take advantage of such opportunities can result in restricting rather than expanding their choice and ability to challenge inequalities (Kabeer 2015: 202). Mobile money partnerships have contributed to promoting the idea of more efficient and inclusive reconfiguration of social welfare and work which, as emerged from the products and services illustrated in this chapter, has called on individuals to assume responsibility and risk in new ways that are likely to create even more inequality. Fee-based products and services delivered through M-Pesa depend on people's ability to access not only the service but also the resources needed to take advantage of them. This means that these opportunities do not challenge the precarious status of people at the lower end of the income distribution.

The idea of opportunity is also oriented towards the future and promoted in terms of possibility and promise. M-Pesa is portrayed as an example of inclusive financial innovation. However, this idea risks obfuscating the unequal power relations embedded in the mobile money system. As Harvey (2010: 26) comments, 'the relationship between representation and reality under capitalism has always been problematic'. M-Pesa, after all, was developed in a framework of reinvented entrepreneurial and philanthropy-related capitalism and built on the assumption that poverty depends on a country's internal problems and can be remedied by technology and financial inclusion. This assumption is based on a tenacious wider mainstream development problem that does not see poverty as linked to colonialism and subsequent development interventions but promotes aid and market interventions in poorer countries as the solution, rather than reversing the paradigm and considering the much greater debt that the Global North owes the Global South. As a result, the wealth generated by M-Pesa, including the philanthropic investment, is not redistributed to address collective needs such as clean water, healthcare and education via publicly accessible services and social assistance. The M-Pesa infrastructure could then be used to facilitate this process of redistribution, addressing women's disproportionate responsibility for unpaid work and producing a greater impact on unequal social and gender relations, particularly at the lower end of the income distribution.

Notes

1 Borrowing Blowfield and Dolan's (2014: 23) words, 'business' here is used as a conceptual category that embraces any organisation engaging in commerce and trade, from the start-up enterprise to the multinational corporation.

2 Included in the private sector, as also stated in the SDGs, are microenterprises, cooperatives and multinational corporations. See UN General Assembly, *Transforming Our World: The 2030 Agenda for Sustainable Development*, 2015, par. 67, www.un.org/ga/search/view_doc.asp?symbol=A/RES/70/1&Lang=E (accessed 15 July 2019).

3 See for example the gender equality projects on the Shared Value website, https://sharedvalue.org/social-issues/gender-equality (accessed 12 March 2019).

4 According to the overview of the Bill and Melinda Gates Foundation Financial Services for the Poor, '[w]omen are excluded from these beneficial financial systems more often.

Nearly one billion are still left out of the formal financial system, and there is a 9 per cent persistent gender gap in financial inclusion in developing economies', www.gatesfoundation.org/What-We-Do/Global-Development/Financial-Services-for-the-Poor (accessed 20 August 2019).

5 See for instance Oxfam, *An Economy for 1%*, Oxfam Briefing Paper, January 2016. According to this report the richest 1 per cent owns more wealth than the rest of the world combined, www.oxfam.org/en/research/economy-1 (accessed 15 August 2019).

6 Safaricom PLC, 219 Full Year Results, www.safaricom.co.ke/images/Downloads/Safaricom_Annual_Report_2019.pdf (accessed 22 August 2019).

7 M-Pesa Holding Co Limited Declaration of Trust, www.safaricom.co.ke/images/Downloads/Personal/M-PESA/deed_of_amendment_to_declaration_of_trust_-_mpesa_account_holders.pdf (accessed 3 May 2019).

8 This platform has been contested by some local groups as 'usurping Kenyans' idea' following copyright cases brought against Safaricom, www.safaricom.co.ke/zindua/ (accessed 20 August 2019).

9 See http://mpesafoundationacademy.ac.ke/ (accessed 3 May 2019).

10 Health Enablement and Learning Platform project, www.m-pesafoundation.org/projects/improving-community-health/ (accessed 2 May 2019).

11 1 KES = 0,0099 USD / 0,0076 GBP The M-Pesa fee is currently 10 KES to withdraw/cash out 50–100 KES.

12 FistulaCare project, www.fistulacare.org/pages/pdf/technical-briefs/mobile_phone_brief_updated4.5.2011.pdf (accessed 2 May 2019).

13 M-Pesa in Tanzania was launched after the development of M-Pesa in Kenya and is provided by Vodacom Tanzania, also local partner of Vodafone.

14 According to the current M-Pesa charges, M-Pesa users will pay a fee of 56 KES to transfer 2,999 KES, but the transfer of 50 KES to registered customers/institutions will be free. Initially, customers had to pay between 1 and 3 KES to transfer up to 100 KES to other M-Pesa users, including companies. See www.safaricom.co.ke/personal/m-pesa/getting-started/m-pesa-rates (accessed 2 May 2019).

15 Grundus-Lifelink project, www.grundfos.com/cases/find-case/grundfos-lifelink-projects-in-kenya.html (accessed 10 March 2019).

16 Enterprises are registered under either the Registration of Business Names Act (Laws of Kenya Cap. 499) or the Companies Act (Laws of Kenya Cap. 486).

17 Focus groups: Kawangware, Nairobi, 29 November 2012; Mathare, Nairobi, 4 December 2012; Ngando, Nairobi, 8 and 9 December 2012.

18 *Matatus* are privately owned mini-buses and a main form of public transport in Nairobi.

19 Government of the Republic of Kenya, *Kenya Vision 2030*, 2007, www.vision2030.go.ke/ (accessed 8 August 2019).

20 When customers deposit/cash in money the mobile money agent's e-money float decreases and the amount of cash increases and for this reason the agent needs to deposit/cash in one of the commercial banks where the M-Pesa funds are kept. On the contrary, if customers withdraw/cash out money the agent's sum of cash decreases and the agent must rebalance liquidity by converting the e-float into cash withdrawn from the M-Pesa bank account.

21 Interviews with 14 M-Pesa agents in Kawangware, Nairobi, 12 December 2012, and 14 M-Pesa agents in Ngando, Nairobi, 13 December 2012.

References

Armendariz, B. and Morduch, J. (2010) *The Economics of Microfinance*. London: Massachusetts Institute of Technology.

Bakker, I. (1994) *The Strategic Silence: Gender and Economic Policy*. London: Zed Books with North-South Institute.

Banerjee, S. B. (2008) Corporate Social Responsibility: The Good, the Bad and the Ugly. *Critical Sociology* 34(1), 51–79.

Banks, N. and Hulme, D. (2014) New Development Alternatives or Business as Usual with a New Face? The Transformative Potential of New Actors and Alliances in Development. *Third World Quarterly* 35(1), 181–195.

Bateman, M., Duvendack, M. and Loubere, N. (2019) Is Fin-Tech the New Panacea for Poverty Alleviation and Local Development? Contesting Suri and Jack's M-Pesa findings published in Science. *Review of African Political Economy*. DOI: 10.1080/03056244.2019.1614552

Benería, L. (2003) *Gender, Development and Globalisation: Economics as if All People Mattered*. New York: Routledge.

Benería, L. and Feldman, S. (1992) *Unequal Burden: Economic Crises, Persistent Poverty, and Women's Work*. Boulder, CO: Westview Press.

Bishop, M. and Green, M. (2008) *Philanthrocapitalism: How the Rich can Save the World*. London: Bloomsbury Press.

Blowfield, M. (2010) Business and Poverty Reduction, in P. Utting and J. C. Marques (eds) *Corporate Social Responsibility and Regulatory Governance: Towards Inclusive Development?* New York: Palgrave Macmillan.

Blowfield, M. and Dolan, C. S. (2014) Business as a Development Agent: Evidence of Possibility and Improbability. *Third World Quarterly* 35(1), 22–42.

Chant, S. and Sweetman, C. (2012) Fixing Women or Fixing the World? 'Smart Economics', Efficiency Approaches, and Gender Equality in Development. *Gender and Development* 20(3), 517–229.

Cherie Blair Foundation for Women (2010) Women and Mobile: A Global Opportunity. A Study on the Mobile Phone Gender Gap in Low and Middle-Income Countries. London: GSMA, www.cherieblairfoundation.org/wp-content/uploads/2012/07/women_and_mobile_a_global_opportunity.pdf (accessed 20 August 2019).

Cherie Blair Foundation for Women (2011) Women Entrepreneurs in Mobile Retail Channels: Empowering Women, Driving Growth. London: Cherie Blair Foundation for Women, www.cherieblairfoundation.org/wp-content/uploads/2012/07/Women-Entrepreneurs-in-Mobile-Retail-Channels.pdf (accessed 20 August 2019).

Cherie Blair Foundation for Women (2012) Mobile Value Added Services: A Business Growth Opportunity for Women Entrepreneurs. London: Cherie Blair Foundation for Women, www.cherieblairfoundation.org/wp-content/uploads/2012/07/Mobile-Value-Added-Services-digital-report.pdf (accessed 20 August 2019).

De Soto, H. (2000) *The Mystery of Capital: Why Capitalism Triumphs in the West and Fails Everywhere Else*. London: Bantam Press.

De Sousa, Santos B. (2006) Globalizations. *Theory, Culture and Society* 23(2–3), 393–399.

Dolan, C. (2012) The New Face of Development. *Anthropology Today* 28(4), 3–7.

Eisenstein, H. (2005) A Dangerous Liaison? Feminism and Corporate Globalization. *Science and Society* 69(3), 487–518.

Elkington, J. and Hartigan, P. (2008) *The Power of Unreasonable People: How Social Entrepreneurs Create Markets That Change the World*. Cambridge, MA: Harvard University Press.

Elson, D. (1989) The Impact of Structural Adjustments on Women: Concepts and Issues. in B. Onimode (ed.) *The IMF, the World Bank and the African Debt. Volume 2: The Social and Political Impact*. London: Zed Press.

Elson, D. (1991) Structural Adjustment: Its Effect on Women, in T. Wallace and C. March (eds) *Changing Perceptions: Writings on Gender and Development*. Oxford: Oxfam.

Elson, D. (1992) Male Bias in Structural Adjustment, in H. Afshar and C. Dennis (eds) *Women and Adjustment Policies in the Third World*. London: Macmillan.

Elumelu, T. (2014) The Rise of Africapitalism. *The Economist*, 14 November.

Elyachar, J. (2002) Empowerment Money: The World Bank, Non-governmental Organisations, and the Value of Culture in Egypt. *Public Culture* 14(3), 493–513.

Elyachar, J. (2005) *Markets of Dispossession: NGOs, Economic Development, and the State in Cairo*. Durham, NC: Duke University Press.

Elyachar, J. (2012) Next Practices: Knowledge, Infrastructure, and Public Good at the Bottom of the Pyramid. *Public Culture* 24(1), 109–129.

Escobar, A. (2010) *Encountering Development: The Making and Unmaking of the Third World*. Princeton, NJ: Princeton University Press.

Ferguson, J. (1994) *The Anti-Politics Machine: 'Development', Depoliticization, and Bureaucratic Power in Lesotho*. Minneapolis: University of Minnesota Press.

Ferguson J. (2007) Formalities of Poverty: Thinking about Social Assistance in Neoliberal South Africa. *African Studies Review* 50(2), 71-86.

Fisher, M. (2009) *Capitalist Realism: Is There No Alternative?* Hants: Zero Books.

Fraser, N. (2014) Can Society be Commodities all the Way Down? Post-Polanyian Reflections on Capitalist Crisis. *Economy and Society* 43(4), 541–558.

FSD Kenya and The Steadman Group Research Division (2007) *Financial Access in Kenya: Results of the 2006 National Survey*. Nairobi: FSD Kenya.

FSD Kenya, Central Bank of Kenya, National Bureau of Statistics (2019) *2019 Finaccess Household Survey*. Nairobi: FSD Kenya.

Gabor, D. and Brooks, S. (2016) The Digital Revolution in Financial Inclusion: International Development in the Fintech Era. *New Political Economy* 22(4), 423–436.

Gates, B. and Kiviat, B. (2008) Making Capitalism More Creative. *Time*, 31 July.

Goetz, A. M. (1996) Who Takes Credit? Gender, Power and Control over Loan Use in Rural Credit Programs in Bangladesh. *World Development* 24(1), 45–63.

GSMA (2017) Person-to-Government (P2G) Payment Digitisation: Lessons from Kenya. London: GSMA.

Guilhot, N. (2007) Reforming the World: George Soros, Global Capitalism and the Philanthropic Management of the Social Sciences. *Critical Sociology* 33, 447–477.

Haas, S. and Nagarajan, G. (2011) *Water Delivery Through Payment Platform: M-PESA Pushes the Rural Frontiers*. College Park Maryland: Financial Services Assessment.

Harvey, D. (2010) *The Enigma of Capital and the Crises of Capitalism*. London: Profile Books.

Helix Institute of Digital Finance (2015) Agent Network Accelerator Survey: Kenya Country Report 2014. Nairobi: HELIX, www.helix-institute.com/sites/default/files/Publications/161101%20ANA%20Kenya%20II%20Country%20Report%202014%20FINAL-REV.pdf (accessed 20 August 2019).

International Labour Organisation (2008) *Women Entrepreneurs in Kenya: A Preliminary Report & Factors Affecting Women Entrepreneurs in Micro and Small Enterprise in Kenya: A Primary Research Report*. Geneva: ILO.

K'Akumu, O. A. (2004) Privatisation and the Urban Water Supply in Kenya: Policy Options for the Poor. *Environment and Urbanization* 16(2), 213–222.

Kabeer, N. (2001) Conflicts over Credit: Re-evaluating the Empowerment Potential of Loans to Women in Rural Bangladesh. *World Development* 29(1), 63–84.

Kabeer, N. (2012) *Women's Economic Empowerment and Inclusive Growth: Labour Markets and Enterprise Development*. Supporting Inclusive Growth Working Paper 2012/1. UK.

Kabeer, N. (2015) Evolving Meanings of 'the Social' in the International Development Agenda. *Journal of International and Comparative Social Policy* 31(2), 114–131.

Kaijage, E. and Wjeeler, D. (2013) *Supporting Entrepreneurship Education in East Africa*. DFID, Plymouth University and University of Nairobi, https://assets.publishing.service.gov.uk/media/57a08a3440f0b652dd0005fc/Entrepreneurship-Education-East-Africa-2013_.pdf (accessed 20 August 2019).

Kameri-Mbote, A. P. and Cullet, P. (1997) Law, Colonialism and Environmental Management in Africa. *Review of European Community and International Environmental Law* 6(1), 23–31.

Karim, L. (2011) *Microfinance and its Discontent: Women in Debt in Bangladesh*. Minneapolis: University of Minnesota Press.

Kendall, J., Maurer, B., Machoka, P. and Veniard, C. (2012). An Emerging Platform: From Mobile Money Transfer System to Mobile Money Ecosystem. *Innovations* 6(4), 49–64.

Lairap-Fonderson, J. (2002) The Disciplinary Power of Microcredit: Examples from Kenya and Cameroon, in J. L. Parpart, S. M. Rai and K. A. Staudt (eds) *Rethinking Empowerment: Gender and Development in a Global/Local World*. London and New York: Routledge.

Mas, I. and Ng'weno, A. (2012) *Why Doesn't Every Kenyan Business Have a Mobile Money Account?* Nairobi: Financial Sector Deepening Kenya.

Maurer, B. (2012) The Disunity of Finance: Alternative Practices to Western Finance, in K. K. Cetina and A. Preda (eds) *The Oxford Handbook of the Sociology of Finance*. Oxford: Oxford University Press.

Maurer, B. (2015) *Who Would You Like to Pay? How Technology Is Changing the Future of Money*. Durham, NC: Duke University Press.

Maurer, B., Nelms, T. C. and Rea, S. C. (2013) 'Bridges to Cash': Channelling Agency in Mobile Money. *Journal of the Royal Anthropological Institute* 19(1), 54–74.

Mazzucato, M. (2013) *The Entrepreneurial State: Debunking Public vs. Private Sector Myths*. London: Anthem Press.

Mbithi, L. M. (2014) Barriers Faced by Women-Owned Businesses. *Journal of African Women Studies Centre* 1, 105–123, http://journals.uonbi.ac.ke/index.php/aws/article/viewFile/1340/1123 (accessed 20 August 2019).

McGoey, L. (2014) The Philanthropic State: Market-state Hybrids in the Philanthrocapitalist Turn. *Third World Quarterly* 35(1), 109–125.

McGoey, L. (2015) *No Such Thing as A Free Gift: The Gates Foundation and the Price of Philanthropy*. London: Verso.

Molyneux, M. (2006) Mothers at the Service of the New Policy Agenda. *Journal of Social Policy and Administration* 40(4), 425–449.

Moyo, D. (2009) *Dead Aid: Why Aid Is Not Working and How There is a Better Way for Africa*. London: Penguin Books.

Muiruri, P. (2010) *Women Street Vendors in Nairobi, Kenya: A Situational and Policy Analysis Within a Human Rights Framework*. Addis Ababa, Ethiopia: Organisation for Social Science Research in Eastern and Southern Africa.

Nicholls, A. (2006) *Social Entrepreneurship: New Models of Sustainable Social Change*. Oxford: Oxford University Press.

Pearson, R. (2007) Beyond Women Workers: Gendering Corporate Social Responsibility, *Third World Quarterly* 28(4), 731–749.

Pearson, R. and Seyfang, G. (2001) New Hope or False Dawn? Voluntary Codes of Conduct, Labour Regulation and Social Policy in a Globalising World. *Global Social Policy* 1(1), 49–78.

Porter, M. E. and Kramer, M. R. (1999), Philanthropy's New Agenda: Creating Value. *Harvard Business Review* 77(6), 121–130.

Porter, M. E. and Kramer, M. R. (2006) Strategy and Society: The Link Between Competitive Advantage and Corporate Social Responsibility. *Harvard Business Review* 84(12), 78–92.

Porter, M. E. and Kramer, M. R. (2011) Creating Shared Value. *Harvard Business Review* 89(1/2), 62–77.

Prahalad, K. (2004) *The Fortune at the Bottom of the Pyramid: Eradicating Poverty Through Profits*. State College, PA: Wharton School Publishing.

Rahman, A. (1999) *Women and Microcredit in Rural Bangladesh*. Boulder, CO: Westview Press.

Rankin, K. N. (2001) Governing Development: Neoliberalism, Microcredit and Rational Economic Woman. *Economy and Society* 30, 18–37.

Rankin, K. N. (2002) Social Capital, Microfinance, and the Politics of Development. *Feminist Economics* 8(1), 1–24.

Ribot, J. C. and Peluso, N. L, (2003) A Theory of Access. *Rural Sociology* 68(2), 153–181.

Richey, L. A. and Ponte, S. (2011) *Brand Aid: Shopping Well to Save the World*. Minneapolis: University of Minnesota Press.

Rittich K. (2006) The Future of Law and Development: Second-Generation Reforms and the Incorporation of the Social, in D. M. Trubek and A. Santos (eds) *The New Law and Economic Development: A Critical Appraisal*. Cambridge: Cambridge University Press.

Roberts, A. (2014a) Gender, Financial Deepening and the Production of Embodied Finance: Towards a Critical Feminist Analysis. *Global Society* 29(1), 107–127.

Roberts, A. (2014b) The Political Economy of 'Transnational Business Feminism'. *International Feminist Journal of Politics* 17(2), 209–231.

Roberts, A. and Soederberg, S. (2012) Gender Equality as Smart Economics? A Critique of the 2012 World Development Report. *Third World Quarterly* 33(5), 949–968.

Robinson, M. (2001) *The Microfinance Revolution: Sustainable Finance for the Poor*. Washington, DC: World Bank and New York: Open Society Institute.

Rowlingson, K. (1994) *Money Lenders and Their Customers*. London: Policy Studies Institute.

Safaricom (2019) Safaricom Annual Report and Financial Statements. Nairobi: Safaricom PLC, www.safaricom.co.ke/images/Downloads/Safaricom_Annual_Report_2019.pdf

Sandbrook R. and J. Barker (1985) *The Politics of Africa's Economic Stagnation*. Cambridge: Cambridge University Press.

Sen, A. (1999) *Development as Freedom*. Oxford University Press.

Tamanaha, B. Z. (2011) The Rule of Law and Legal Pluralism in Development. *Hague Journal on the Rule of Law* 3(1), 1–17.

The Economist (2008) Africa Calling, 5 June.

The Economist (2012) Africa Rising – A Hopeful Continent, 2 March.

UN Women (2015) Progress of the World's Women: Transforming Economies, Realising Rights. New York: UN Women.

UNDP, Commission on the Private Sector and Development (2004) *Unleashing Entrepreneurship: Making Business Work for the Poor*. New York: United Nations.

Williams, T. (2001) Requiem for Microcredit? The Decline of a Romantic Ideal. *Banking and Finance Law Review* 19(2), 145–198.

World Bank (1997) *Kenya Women Finance Trust: A Case Study of a Micro-finance Scheme*. Washington, DC: World Bank.

World Bank (2006) *Gender Equality as Smart Economics: A World Bank Group Gender Action Plan.* Washington, DC: World Bank.

World Bank (2012) *World Development Report 2012: Gender Equality and Development.* Washington, DC: World Bank.

World Bank (2015) *Women, Business and the Law 2016: Getting to Equal.* Washington, DC: World Bank.

World Economic Forum (2009) *The Next Billions: Unleashing Business Potential in Untapped Markets* Geneva: WEF.

Yenkey, C., Doering, L. and Aceves, P. (2015) *The Financialisation of Everyday Life: Mobile Money and (In)formal Activity in a Developing Context.* Toronto: Rotman School of Management Working Paper.

Yunus, M. and Weber, K. (2010) *Building Social Business: The New Kind of Capitalism that Serves Humanity's Most Pressing Needs.* New York: Public Affairs.

5 The gendered governance of mobile money

From local to global and back

Gender, law and postcolonial governance

Social inequality, access to finance and the norms and institutions governing political economic relations are interdependent. The financial exclusion of women is linked to their gendered socio-economic disadvantage which can be created, exacerbated, ignored or mended by the law. As discussed in Chapter 1, under colonialism the law was used to control local matters and protect Western economic interests. The commodification of land, the introduction of property rights and the wage economy contributed to institutionalising the role of the male household head and breadwinner. Customary norms filtered via the repugnancy clause reinforced the subordination of women, particularly in areas of domestic and family law such as marriage, divorce, inheritance and land and burial rights. After the former colonies gained their independence the law acquired a different role in response to the changing interests and goals driving the development project (Kennedy 2006; Tamanaha 2011).

In the postcolonial and post-Cold War period multilateral and bilateral development institutions began to pay increasing attention to the law and legal reform as an important political arena. They saw the law as necessary for the establishment of a global market economy generally associated with the norms and institutions attached to global capitalism and liberal democracy, two pillars of the neoliberal project (Harvey 2005). As the Kenyan scholar Nyamu-Musembi (2005: iv) explains, in Sub-Saharan Africa structural adjustment programmes (SAPs) and subsequent interventions included legal and institutional reforms focusing on creating the legal and institutional market environment seen as a necessary and sufficient condition for growth and thus development. Although some attention was paid to democratic rule, particularly through electoral and constitutional reforms, more incisive changes were made to the role of the judiciary to protect business against government interference, and to local legislation to facilitate Kenya's integration into the world economy (Nyamu-Musembi 2005). These reforms included subsidy cuts, price control, the privatisation of services, the removal of import tariffs and monetary policy targeting low inflation (Chang 2008). No particular attention was paid to social justice or redistribution as specific elements of substantive gender equality, or to the law more generally as an instrument for protecting the vulnerable and the disadvantaged.

Grassroots women's groups, however, also under the influence of the UN Conference for Women in Nairobi in 1985, became more and more aware of how the law could affect their recognition and status (Nzomo 1997). A publication from the Women, Law and Development seminar in Kenya in 1987 following the UN Conference (Mbeo and Ooko-Ombaka 1989) recognises the law as an instrument of both domination and emancipation.[1] Okeyo (1989) was already advocating strategies looking beyond the issue of equality per se, namely formal equality, to question the fairness of the socio-economic structure within which women act, namely substantive equality. According to Mbeo and Ooko-Ombaka (1989: 3 and 31), substantive equality could be achieved if women acted together as a social movement seeking political, legal and judicial articulation for women's issues.

The adoption of the UN Millennium Development Goals (MDGs) that followed the criticism of SAPs highlighted the need for greater attention to the social dimensions of development, including gender equality as well as factors such as democracy, human rights and the rule of law (Rittich 2006). The Sustainable Development Goals (SDGs) that have replaced the MDGs continue to promote social goals and democratic institutions, but also embrace new forms of governance including collaboration with the private sector, philanthropic foundations and non-state actors such as NGOs, and country-led grassroots approaches with a particular emphasis on the people's autonomy and self-reliance. The law, in the form of legislation, regulation, policy and soft law, is increasingly seen as important to achieving these aims. This approach to development, rejecting the strong neoliberal presumption against regulatory law, has accepted the need for regulation to create efficiency, reduce transaction costs and compensate for market failures (Kennedy 2006: 152). The aims of economic growth and financial development have maintained a centrality over social provisioning; for instance the World Bank report *Women, Business and the Law 2016: Getting to Equal* (2015) points out that law, regulation and policy should facilitate women's access to credit and economic opportunities as a key factor for gender equality (ibid.: 17).

In light of this overview, this chapter shows how M-Pesa has been regulated with the aim of removing the main legal constraints to accessing financial services. However, similarly to previous financial inclusion projects such as microcredit, these measures have not been coordinated with reforms to realise socio-economic rights such as employment, housing, healthcare, education and so on. In other words, the regulation of mobile money has focused on creating an enabling environment for financial inclusion, but it has not focused in the same way on providing people, and particularly women in poverty or on a low and irregular income, with the resources they need to really take advantage of financial services.

To illustrate this argument, the second section makes a distinction between social objectives and socio-economic rights. I argue that financial inclusion policies frame gender equality as an objective achievable via financial products and services rather than focusing on realising the socio-economic rights necessary to address the unequal gender relations that cause financial exclusion. The section illustrates this distinction in the Kenyan context by examining two key legal frameworks for financial inclusion and gender equality: Kenya Vision 2030, which focuses on economic growth and financial development, and the 2010 Kenyan Constitution, which is seen as the result of a long struggle for the recognition of gender equality and socio-economic rights. The third section analyses the regulation of M-Pesa and highlights its gender implications. It explains how the National Payment Systems Regulations 2014 formalised the regulatory practices developed by the Central Bank of Kenya (CBK) since M-Pesa's launch in 2007. This 'test and learn' approach to the regulation of mobile money favours financial development according to the principles contained in the Kenya Vision over the more redistributive measures necessary to realise the rights stated in the Constitution. The fourth section extends the analysis to the global context, illustrating the trajectory of the regulation of mobile money and the institutions that shape the digital financial inclusion agenda: Financial Sector Deepening (FSD), the Groupe Spéciale Mobile Association (GSMA), the Consultative Group to Assist the Poor (CGAP), the Alliance For Financial Inclusion (AFI), the Better than Cash Alliance and the Bill and Melinda Gates Foundation. I argue that these institutions have endorsed the regulatory approach to mobile money adopted in Kenya and consider gender equality a measurable and profitable goal for social legitimacy rather than as an essential part of social justice.

Social objectives v. socio-economic rights

Gender equality is often presented as one of M-Pesa's key social gains (Suri and Jack 2016). The gender aspects of mobile money governance can be examined by looking at how the social benefits of digital financial inclusion are framed in legal and policy documents. Financial inclusion policies tend to consider gender equality as a social objective achievable by facilitating access to financial products and services. The language of rights, particularly socio-economic rights, and of accountability are largely absent in these documents. As seen in Chapter 2, socio-economic rights require positive action, generally by the state, which should also be accountable for their realisation. Social objectives, on the other hand, are declarative aims that are often supported by various development actors such as international organisations, philanthropic foundations, NGOs or even corporations. However, there is little to hold these actors accountable when they deliver social objectives in ways that do not challenge inequalities, or even use them as instruments of social legitimacy while making profits (Kabeer 2015a).

In the Kenyan context the distinction between social objectives and socio-economic rights can be found in two key documents: Kenya Vision 2030 and the 2010 Kenyan Constitution. These documents have been influenced by the international development discourse and can be considered Kenya's main legal financial inclusion and gender equality frameworks. Both embrace the global commitment to poverty reduction, gender equality, the rule of law and good governance. Kenya Vision frames poverty reduction and gender equality as social objectives, while the Constitution focuses on rights, including socio-economic rights. These documents are seen as marking a period of social transformation in Kenya and reaffirming the country's role in the global economy, particularly following the post-election crisis of 2007–2008 (Adam, Collier and Ndung'u 2010; Kanyinga and Long 2012). The violence that followed the contested presidential election of 2007 affected tourism, commerce, agriculture and livelihood more generally (Adam, Collier and Ndung'u 2010). Research shows how M-Pesa, as a money transfer system launched few months before the crisis, was used by NGOs such as Oxfam and international organisations to implement cash transfer programmes, and by the population to transfer money to family and friends, bypassing the street blockages and the closure of financial institutions caused by the revolt (Morawcznski 2009).

In response to the crisis the African Union, with the support of international organisations, constituted a panel of African leaders headed by Kofi Annan as UN Secretary General (Lindenmayer and Kaye 2009). The panel established the Kenya National Dialogue and Reconciliation (KNDR), proclaiming its aims of addressing long-term political, economic and social challenges such as 'poverty, the inequitable distribution of resources and perceptions of historical injustices and exclusion on the part of segments of Kenyan society'.[2]

Kenya Vision 2030 can be seen as a political statement addressing some of these reforms, but also, as Manji (2015: 2) argues, as a 'document of neoliberal master planning'. It was completed in 2007 but, due to the crisis, launched in 2008 by President Kibaki and embraced by President Kenyatta on his election in 2013. It represents a development programme for the transformation of Kenya into a middle-income country by the year 2030 (Otieno and Ndung'u 2010: 40). The Vision has three pillars – economic, social and political – underpinned by institutional and regulatory interventions aiming for macroeconomic stability, opportunities for people living in poverty, infrastructure, science, technology and innovation, land reform, security and public sector reforms (Government of Kenya 2007: 6).

As mentioned in Chapter 3, Kenya Vision 2030 places particular emphasis on economic growth and considers financial sector development both a major objective of the economic pillar and relevant to the social and political pillars. In particular it recognises the necessity of financial services for the creation of jobs and facilitation of savings, which are considered essential to finance Kenya's overall investment needs (ibid.: 15). The Vision offers two main steps towards financial sector development: extend access to finance to excluded segments of the population and micro- and small-scale enterprises, and promote institutional and legal reforms to increase transparency and trust. It sees these two steps as linked, and addressing the problem of financial exclusion as requiring the formalisation of rotating credit and savings associations (ROSCAs) and an effective regulatory framework for microfinance institutions to increase public trust and allow banks and other deposit-taking institutions to securely handle the public's savings. Importantly, M-Pesa has contributed to formalising informal financial practices, and facilitated access to banks via products such as M-Shwari that link M-Pesa accounts to savings accounts (Cook and McKay 2015).

The focus on financial services as a means of increasing savings and investment is expressed in the deflationary monetary policy adopted by the Vision, which also confirms its neoliberal tenor. Kenya Vision 2030 sees anti-inflationary or deflationary policy as able to promote entrepreneurship, savings, lending and investment, an approach adopted by the CBK since the introduction of SAPs.[3] Anti-inflationary policy is a key feature of the neoliberal approach to monetary development policy and is considered necessary to attract foreign capital. The obligation to maintain low inflation is based on the assumption that monetary policy makes its best contribution to long-term development by maintaining relatively low inflation and a strong financial system. In this way market participants, and in particular investors, know that when conflict arises between price stability and competing socio-economic needs such as employment or social services, central banks prioritise price stability (Adam *et al.* 2010: 142). However, anti-inflationary policy risks undermining living standards (Chang and Grabel 2004: 185) and can reinforce gender inequality. As discussed in Chapter 2, this policy is one of the biases that increase women's disproportionate responsibility for social reproduction work with negative impacts on their employment and access to social services (Elson and Cagatay 2000). Anti-inflationary policy often results in the promotion of informal micro-entrepreneurship to compensate for the lack of waged employment which negatively affects the status of women on a low income (Braunstein and Heintz 2008, 2011).

Kenya Vision 2030's social pillar focuses on six social objectives: education, healthcare, water and sanitation, environmental protection, adequate housing and the commitment to increase opportunities for women, youth and 'all disadvantaged people' (Government of Kenya 2007: 21). Gender equality is one of the Vision's objectives: the document mainly uses the language of opportunity, empowerment and capabilities and aims to provide women with access to capital, education and training which would allow them to contribute to Kenya's economic development, in line with the World Bank's framework of 'gender equality as smart economics'. According to Kenya Vision, these social objectives are to be achieved by implementing the policies prescribed under the economic pillar and within the framework of the political pillar. The political pillar concerns the national governance system and places particular emphasis on democracy, non-discrimination and the rule of law. The Vision sees the rule of law as adherence to a 'system based on a market economy in a human-rights respecting state' (Government of Kenya 2007: 21), reflecting the tendency of Western liberal democracy to conflate a free market, fundamental rights and good governance.

The Kenyan Constitution, adopted in 2010, was also part of the post-election-violence reform to achieve the aims defined by the Kenya National Dialogue and Reconciliation panel. However, its history and intention are different to those of

Kenya Vision 2030. The Constitution replaced the 1963 Independence Constitution and was officially adopted following a national referendum. Previous attempts to obtain a public majority to adopt a new Constitution had failed, showing the difficulty of adopting a national constitutional document in a country characterised by plural legal realities. The 2010 Constitution recognises the key provision of international law (article 2.5),[4] but also recognises Kenya's different ethnic and religious communities, for instance the Kadhi courts, which govern Muslims' personal issues such as marriage, divorce and inheritance (Kramon and Posner 2011). The Constitution received strong support from both international institutions and civil society amid high expectations that it would make a considerable difference to citizen welfare (Kanyinga and Long 2012: 47).

Particularly relevant in this light is the Constitution's introduction of provisions on gender equality and socio-economic rights. Article 21(3) makes the state responsible for addressing the needs of vulnerable groups, including women. Article 27 prohibits discrimination on various grounds including gender. Article 27(8) obliges the state to implement the principle that no more than two-thirds of elective or appointive bodies are of the same gender. Article 45(3) provides that parties to a marriage are entitled to equal rights before, during and after marriage. Article 53(1) states that parental responsibility must be shared between parents, and article 68(c) requires parliament to enact legislation on the recognition and protection of matrimonial property during and at the termination of a marriage. Article 59 establishes the Kenya National Human Rights and Equality Commission, whose main task is to promote respect for human rights, including gender equality and equity. As provided by article 59(4), in 2011 an Act of Parliament established the National Gender and Equality Commission to ensure that 'the concerns of women and men form an integral dimension of the design of all policies, laws and administrative procedures in all political, economic and social spheres' (Act No. 15 2011). Article 60 provides for the elimination of gender discrimination in laws, customs and practices related to land.[5] Article 2(4) recognises customary law unless it leads to discrimination against women, in which case should not be legally applicable (FIDA 2013). According to Kabira (2011), these provisions are the result of the involvement of civil society groups, particularly women's rights groups, in the drafting of the Constitution. Mutua (2006) contends that this involvement demonstrates how women across different socio-economic, ethnic and religious backgrounds see the potential in the law for social change.

Article 43 is an important provision that specifically addresses economic and social rights. As discussed in Chapter 2, socio-economic rights are important in addressing gender inequality because of women's disproportionate responsibility for social reproduction work. This is particularly the case for women living in poverty or on a low income, as their conditions depend on the provisioning of basic resources and physical and social infrastructure. The importance of socio-economic rights also reflects the development concerns that for years have been claimed by African women, such as the availability of clean water and food (Oyèwùmí 1997; Cornwall and Nyamu-Musembi 2005).

Under article 43, socio-economic rights include healthcare, housing and sanitation, adequate food, clean and safe water, social security and education. In addition, according to article 56 women, and other marginalised group, should benefit from the state's obligation to put affirmative action programmes into place that encourage female participation in governance, provide special opportunities in education, the economy and employment, and give them reasonable access to water and health services. Article 21 of the Constitution recognises that the state's primary obligation is to adopt legislative, policy and other measures to achieve the 'progressive realisation' of socio-economic rights.[6]

According to the literature on the implementation of the International Covenant on Economic, Social and Cultural Rights, 'progressive realisation' means that states are obliged to take steps to implement these rights according to their resources (Robertson 1994; Odinkalu 2001; Baderin and McCorquodale 2007).[7] To achieve this they can use public resources, private sector funding and/or rely on international assistance. The allocation and distribution of resources is a key factor in the realisation of socio-economic rights. Private companies have become increasingly involved in providing social services, generally in partnership with governments, financial institutions and philanthropic foundations. However as discussed in Chapter 4, these services are often premised on a narrative of social entrepreneurship, namely making profits while contributing to social development, raising the question of who is accountable for the realisation of social objectives.

Facilitating access to privately provided social services does not necessarily benefit people at the lower end of the income distribution and can even increase gendered responsibilities for social reproduction work. For instance, providing access to basic resources and services via financial services such as microcredit programmes can result in a debt trap that can absorb resources otherwise destined for food, health and education. Or it can result in over-reliance on micro-entrepreneurship, which often fails to fulfil the expectation that it will improve poor people's welfare, or in a new market that produces profit that is not redistributed among the people, as in the case of mobile money-enabled products. Financial inclusion cannot be a substitute for long-term reform and social programmes. This point is crucial in thinking about how funds from the private sector and the international aid and philanthropy community are or should be channelled to realise socio-economic rights without creating further inequality such as that deriving from the financialisation of basic resources.

Provisions removing the legal barriers to women's equal access to property, land ownership and financial services can certainly contribute to their autonomy, but need to be accompanied by programmes addressing their socio-economic disadvantages. As Kabeer (2015) mentions in relation to the UN High Level Panel report (2014) that fed into the post-MDGs agenda and SDGs negotiations, the only rights explicitly mentioned under the gender equality goal are the rights to inherit property, sign a contract, register a business and open a bank account: all rights related to the aim of economic and financial inclusion. Kabeer (2015: 391) argues that these are 'unlikely to be relevant to the large number of poor women who are struggling to feed themselves and their families through casual, poorly paid and exploitative work on the margins of the informal economy'.

This section has showed how Kenya Vision 2030, adopted at about the time of M-Pesa's launch, has served as a policy framework for financial development and financial inclusion. The Constitution, adopted a few years later, provides the legal framework for gender equality and socio-economic rights. While Kenya Vision 2030 more specifically addresses issues of financial inclusion, the provisions and reforms mandated by the Constitution are crucial to analysing the relationship between financial inclusion and gender equality, the interaction between the pursuit of financial development and socio-economic rights and the potential of the law to put finance at the service of social reproduction.

The analysis has demonstrated how the gendered legal structures of exclusion that have shaped access to finance and the organisation of socio-economic rights in Kenya since the colonial era are being reshaped both internationally and nationally by new ideas of inclusion. Some international legal concepts and ideas have been re-embedded in Kenya to support local struggles such as for gender equality. Other legal concepts and ideas have supported economic and financial development with the aim of affirming Kenya as a rapidly developing country, and M-Pesa and mobile money have become key in supporting this view.

Regulating mobile money: from Kenya to global and back

In line with mainstream development discourse, Kenya Vision 2030 assumes a causal link between financial inclusion, economic growth and the achievement of social goals such as poverty reduction and gender equality, and supports legal and institutional reforms as necessary steps to achieving these goals. The relationship between the development of the financial sector and economic growth has strong roots in Western economic research. It acquired importance in development economics in the 1970s, with the McKinnon (1973) and Shaw's (1973) argument for the growth-inducing effects of financial liberalisation, influencing the neoliberal policies that constituted the SAPs. This view suggests that the expansion and deepening of financial services and markets can assist the accumulation and mobilisation of savings, provide financial services that facilitate the purchase and exchange of goods, produce and process information to enable efficient allocation of funds and help to manage risk, and that the law should facilitate these activities.

These studies have motivated, influenced and legitimised international organisations and governments in their adoption of policies supporting financial inclusion, reinforcing the uncontested assumption that bringing people into the formal financial sector is a key aspect of economic and social development. The regulation of M-Pesa has been guided by these ideas but has also developed an unprecedented approach to the regulation of mobile money, influencing the governance of global financial inclusion. This section examines the regulation of M-Pesa and reflects on its gender implications. It argues that while the approach to the regulation of mobile money in Kenya has been driven by a 'test and learn' approach aimed at developing an environment that enables the service to grow, it has not considered redistributing part of M-Pesa's revenue to adopt measures to address the socio-economic inequalities that cause and reproduce financial exclusion.

M-Pesa was created at the intersection between finance and telecommunications, and at the time of its pilot in 2005 there was no regulation in place for MNO- rather than bank-based mobile money payment services on which to draw. An MNO-based service is different from the mobile banking used in Western countries, in which the MNO is not involved in the financial transactions that pass through the client's bank account and the bank assumes responsibility for the transaction (AFI 2010; Klein and Mayer 2011). When M-Pesa was developed, an MNO-led service was considered necessary to achieve financial inclusion for those without access to conventional banking. However, this generated concern about the legitimacy and possible risks of a financial service provided by an MNO and the extent to which this service could be justified on grounds of financial inclusion. As discussed in Chapter 3, just before the launch of M-Pesa FSD Kenya published a FinAccess survey (FSD 2007) which showed that almost 40 per cent of the adult population was financially excluded. The CBK, the regulatory body for banking and payment services, adopted a 'test and learn' approach to regulation to balance security and regulatory requirements with the purpose of financial inclusion. This approach means that the CBK has supervised the service in partnership with the MNO, ensuring legal and risk assessments and compliance with rules such as anti-money laundering (AML) and counter-terrorist financing (CTF), while remaining open to new financial services and providers entering the mobile money market.

The supervisory role of the CBK and the regulatory practices developed since the launch of M-Pesa in 2007 were formalised in the National Payments System (NPS) Regulations 2014, which followed the adoption of the NPS Act 2011. Before analysing the key aspects of the NPS Regulations and their gender implications it is important to provide an overview of the regulatory framework for financial services in Kenya. CBK is responsible for the regulation and supervision of banks under the Central Bank of Kenya Act 1966 (as amended to 1 January 2014) and The Banking Act 1995 (as amended to 15 September 2015). Over the years there have been numerous revisions of these documents and the adoption of prudential guidelines aimed at reinforcing the CBK's supervisory role (Beck *et al.* 2010: 332).

In 2000 the CBK adopted the Basel I standards, a reform reflecting the global trend requiring financial institutions to maintain capital commensurate with the credit risk inherent in their activities, and included some features of Basel II and Basel III in the CBK guidelines that came into force in January 2013 (Mwega 2014). Following the IMF and World Bank Financial Sector Assessment Program in 2003, Kenya undertook a series of legal and regulatory reforms which included significant changes to the Banking Act and to prudential guidelines in relation to banking licensing, corporate governance, capital adequacy, risk classification of assets and overall risk management. In 2003 the Central

Bank of Kenya Act was amended to give the CBK a broad mandate to oversee payment systems, which was further expanded following the launch of M-Pesa. Under section 4 A (i)d of the Act, the CBK must formulate and implement policies that promote the establishment, regulation and supervision of payments, providing a strong basis upon which the Bank can promote innovations in retail payment.

At around the time of the M-Pesa pilot, the Kenyan Parliament adopted the Microfinance Act 2006, and the Deposit-Taking Microfinance Regulations were finalised in 2008. Microfinance institutions in Kenya operate under diverse forms of legislation ranging from informal *chamas* that can be registered as self-help groups with the Ministry of Gender, Children and Social Development to NGOs and deposit-taking and non-microfinance institutions and banks licensed under the Banking Act. With the Microfinance Act the CBK wanted to increase the efficiency, outreach and sustainability of microfinance institutions by developing a regulatory framework for the establishment, licensing and supervision of deposit-taking microfinance institutions. The Act aimed to provide an opportunity for the sector to grow while increasing access to financial services. According to Atieno, Barako and Bokea (2010: 391), with the adoption of the Act there was an expectation by the CBK, later fulfilled by M-Pesa, that microfinance institutions would achieve a reduction in the high fixed costs associated with running branches, especially in rural areas, allowing microfinance institutions to expand their outreach.

However, according to an FSD (2012) study commissioned by the CBK after the adoption of the Act, setting up branches was still considered expensive and the regulations for deposit-taking microfinance institutions, including the installation of security systems, establishing high-quality technology infrastructure and recruiting staff with prior banking experience, were costly to implement. The FSD study in particular analyses the transformation of Faulu Kenya and the Kenya Women Finance Trust (now called Kenya Women Microfinance Bank), the first two institutions to be granted a deposit-taking licence, and shows that despite their functioning well as microfinance institutions in Kenya, the transformation of both required more resources and took longer than expected, and did not facilitate access, particularly for people living on a low income.

If the Act failed to benefit microfinance institutions, it did result in some commercial banks choosing to provide services and products for the low-income market; for instance, Barclays Bank of Kenya registered Barclays Deposit-Taking Microfinance Ltd (Atieno, Barako and Bokea 2010: 391). Some deposit-taking microfinance institutions such as Jami Bora bought existing small local banks to broaden their delivery of financial services. According to the FSD surveys (FSD 2007, 2009, 2013, 2016, 2019), however, the expansion of deposit-taking microfinance institutions envisaged by the Act has not resulted in more convenient microfinance services or facilitated access to microfinance services for people living on a low income. This demonstrates where M-Pesa fits in the regulatory debate on facilitating financial inclusion in Kenya. As discussed in Chapter 3, while the Vodafone team initially saw M-Pesa as a system to facilitate microfinance transactions and reduce the costs of microfinance institutions, the pilot demonstrated that it was more useful as a platform for micropayments than as one for improving the efficiency of microfinance institutions.

To authorise the launch of M-Pesa in February 2007 the CBK issued Safaricom with a letter of no objection after conducting various legal and risk assessments and authorised two external audits. The letter, which represented the M-Pesa's regulatory framework until the adoption of the NPS Act 2011 and the related Regulations in 2014, specified obligations and prudential and market conduct rules identified during the pilot and subsequent investigations. The CBK allowed Safaricom to operate under a special Communications Commission of Kenya licence without a banking licence, and the Communications Act 1998 (part VI A) was amended in 2009 to recognise electronic transactions. This approach allowed M-Pesa to function under the oversight of the CBK pending a complete regulatory framework for payment systems, later provided by the NPS Regulations drawing on the M-Pesa experience to develop a regulatory framework for mobile money more generally. Two aspects of the NPS Regulations are relevant to this analysis of the gender implications of mobile money: the regulation of mobile money as a payment system, and how the 'test and learn' approach contributed to the proliferation of mobile money providers and products.

The CBK classified M-Pesa as a payment service and decided that the Kenya Banking Act did not provide a legal basis for either M-Pesa or the regulation of mobile money products offered by MNOs. Mobile money providers are not considered financial intermediaries and mobile money services are not classified as banking businesses. According to the Kenyan Banking Act, a banking business involves not only accepting money from the public but also 'the employing of money held on deposit on current accounts, or any part of the money, by lending, investment or in any manner for the account and at the risk of the person so employing the money' (Part I section 2C). The M-Pesa system is rather designed to provide a money transfer service converting cash into e-money and e-money into cash through mobile money agents acting as cash merchants. These transactions are managed via the mobile phone and are reflected in the customer's e-wallet. Customers cashing in/depositing money on their M-Pesa account purchase electronic units for cash that can be transferred or cashed out/withdrawn for a fee set by the MNO. As discussed in Chapter 3, the fee has an important regulatory role itself in defining access to the service and the profit for the MNO.

In the M-Pesa system the customer remains in control of the electronic money in their e-wallet at all times. There is no financial intermediation in banking terms between M-Pesa customers and mobile money agents. The agents do not perform bank credit assessments or risk management, nor do they lend or invest the money as deposit-taking banking institutions do: they only exchange cash for electronic money and vice versa. While customers may view money stored on their M-Pesa account as savings, it is not the case from a regulatory perspective and the CBK has been very careful to make this clear from the beginning. Even though mainstream banking terms such as 'withdrawal' and 'deposit' are used in M-Pesa transactions, in practice customers are just exchanging cash for e-money and transferring e-money for a fee.

While the MNO receives a secure source of profit via the fees, customers are paid no interest on the money they keep in their M-Pesa account, which is physically kept in pooled trust accounts under the custody of a trustee, the non-profit M-Pesa Holding Company.[8] The NPS Regulations (2014: section 25.3 b, f) confirm that mobile money is to be held in trust funds, sufficiently diversified and placed in commercial banks licensed under the Banking Act. Trusts should be established by the payment service provider, who should also ensure that at no time does the fund amount to less than customers are keeping in their e-wallets (section 25.3 a, c). Other precautionary measures are aimed at keeping mobile money funds isolated from service providers' funds and protected from their creditors, and at prohibiting providers transferring any funds to themselves or mixing trust funds with other funds (section 25.3 d, e). The document states that 'e-money shall not earn interest or any other financial return to e-money holder or customer', and that lending and investment activities are not permitted (sections 44.2 and 45). According to the Regulations 'any income generated from placement of these trust funds shall be used in accordance with Trust legislation and in consultation with the Bank [or] donated to public charitable organisations for use for public charitable purposes' (section 25.5). As discussed in Chapter 4, the M-Pesa trust agreement claims that the M-Pesa Foundation, created for this purpose in 2010 as an independent charitable trust, uses the interest on customers' deposits held by the M-Pesa Holding Company to benefit Kenyans.

While these precautions are presented as necessary to protect customers' funds, the obligation to use the interest generated from trust accounts for 'public charitable purposes' has reinforced the link between philanthropy, in the form of philanthrocapitalism, financial technology and development (Gabor and Brooks 2017: 2). According to the NPS Regulations (section 25.3), mobile payment providers must set up a trust and specify the use of the income generated by the trust fund, although the nature of 'charitable purposes' is not specified. This focus on charitable activities is relevant not only because they are based on a logic of opportunity rather than a politics of redistribution, as discussed in Chapter 4, but also because the trustees take the decision on how to employ the funds away from the people without recognising them as the rightful owners of this money.

It is interesting that since its launch, M-Pesa has been used but also promoted by mobile money agents as a service that stores money safely, particularly for people with limited resources, integrating or replacing home banking and individuals working as savings-keepers.[9] This is also facilitated by M-Pesa's fee structure, as 'deposits' incur no fee. However, the amounts of money stored on the accounts are very small – about 300 KES per person in 2012 (Johnson, Brown and Fouillet 2012) – allowing the CBK to make sure that this money is not treated as savings, contravening the Banking Act. For this reason, Safaricom has partnered with banks and deposit-taking microfinance institutions to encourage M-Pesa customers to open interest-earning savings accounts such as M-Shwari (Cook and McKay 2015). These products, however, not only offer instant automated fee-based loans that create profit for the MNO and financial institution involved and increase the risk of debt (Gordon and Lyon 2017), they also fail to consider the difficulties that people living in poverty and on a low income experience in saving money.

Although saving is often presented as the ability to manage money effectively, these difficulties generally derive from complex issues such as lack of resources and a stable source of income. For instance, according to FSD survey 2016 between 2006 and 2016 the number of savings instruments increased from 12.4 to 24 per cent, of which 10.4 were bank accounts and 16.8 per cent were mobile-enabled accounts. However, the survey shows that 22.3 per cent of the bank accounts were dormant or closed, the main reason being loss of income. This clearly demonstrates that facilitating access to bank accounts and their savings products without creating the necessary conditions for people to access sufficient resources to save does not challenge unequal social relations. Savings accounts are often seen as useful for women to navigate their social reproduction roles (Dupas and Robinson 2013), but providing them without addressing issues such as access to employment, basic resources and public services risks reproducing gender inequality. The fees for using the mobile money service and the loss of the interest gained on customers' funds can also have an impact on gender inequality, considering that small amounts of money represent a large part of people's already limited household resources.

The question of interest paid on mobile money accounts is being debated among other African countries, and some have suggested a different approach. Tanzania has proposed the distribution of profits earned from a pooled trust account to its customers, and the Bank of Ghana recently issued draft Guidelines for E-Money Issuers which expressly allow interest to be passed directly to the customers.[10] The underlying question is not only about the allocation of interest gained on the trust accounts but more generally whether and how unbanked poor customers should benefit from the value created by mobile money. As discussed, M-Pesa's fees are defined by the MNO and represent a secure source of private profit. The fees have changed and increased over time without contributing to the redistribution of income. For instance, in 2013 the Kenya National Treasury introduced a 10 per cent excise duty on transaction fees for money transfers, including mobile money services.[11] This consumption tax was passed on to mobile money consumers through higher transaction charges, affecting people who had integrated M-Pesa into their everyday financial practices. The way in which this consumption tax affects people at the lower end of the income distribution needs to be compared to the share of taxes paid by local and foreign MNOs such as Safaricom and Vodafone,[12] and reflect on whether and how this income could be used to realise socio-economic rights, perhaps through public services and social assistance. In 2018 the government proposed a 2 per cent tax on mobile money transactions to fund a universal healthcare programme, a plan opposed by Safaricom and Vodafone on the grounds that the tax would make the service more expensive and arrest financial inclusion (Kazeem 2018).

The second aspect of the NPS Regulations relevant to this chapter's analysis is how they have contributed to the expansion of mobile money. As Muthiora

(2015: 20) explains, with the NPS Regulations the CBK wanted to ensure the system's integrity and security, but also to give greater legitimacy to evolving mobile money business models developed around the idea of social entrepreneurship. The Regulations allow both banks and non-banks to provide mobile money services.[13] In this way the NPS Regulations allow mobile money agents to offer products from other providers besides Safaricom, and favour interoperability among different mobile money services.

As discussed, the presence of M-Pesa agencies in the form of airtime resellers, kiosks and shops in urban and rural areas has removed most of the barriers to facilitating financial inclusion. Since its launch in 2007 Safaricom has been allowed to conclude exclusive agreements with cash in, cash out agents, who are seen as cash merchants rather than banking intermediaries, who perform credit assessments and banks' management role. Banks, on the other hand, were not permitted to use agents to take deposits on their behalf until the 2009 Finance Bill amended the Banking Act, and the CBK's adoption of the Guidelines on Agent Banking in 2010.[14] The NPS Regulations have legitimised and expanded the role of mobile money agents. According to the Regulations (section 14) a payment service provider can conclude an agreement with an agent to undertake certain services on its behalf, such as sending, receiving, storing and processing payments and providing cash services. The Regulations specify that the payment service provider can appoint an agent or cash merchant to perform cash services, defined as the exchange of cash for e-money and e-money for cash (section 15).[15] The provider is also responsible for the operations of the agent within the scope of the agency agreement (section 14.4) and should provide adequate training and maintain effective oversight of its operation (section 19). There are no clear indications concerning the scope of the agency agreement, but it is the agent's responsibility to comply with security measures including anti-money-laundering legislation (section 16.2).

The NPS Regulations allow agents to work with multiple providers and rule out the possibility of an exclusive contract for the provision of retail cash services (section 15.2). Safaricom opened up its network of M-Pesa agents in July 2014, just before the Competition Authority of Kenya issued a letter ordering it to remove M-Pesa agents' exclusivity (Ochieng 2019). This was motivated by the aim of promoting competition among providers and entrepreneurship among agents, enabling the latter to potentially make more profit by offering a variety of providers' mobile money services. While the regulation states that providers must notify the CBK of their procedure for recruiting agents and cash merchants (section 16.2a), there is no indication of or reference to the content of the contractual relationship between provider and retail agent. As discussed in Chapter 4 this can have important gender implications, as mobile money agencies, promoted as an entrepreneurial opportunity, especially for women, often do not result in a stable source of income for women because of the large number of agents and the risks that the business entails. No agreements have been concluded to address these factors.

The NPS Regulations also address the issue of interoperability (sections 21 and 22), defined in the preliminary section as 'commercial interconnectivity between providers of different payment systems or payment instruments including the capability of electronic systems to exchange messages and "interoperable" shall be construed accordingly' (sections 21 and 22). As mentioned, one of the main aspects of M-Pesa's rapid development in Kenya has been the dominant market presence of Safaricom and the favourable regulatory approach that it has enjoyed as part of the M-Pesa financial inclusion project. Since 2007 the mobile money market has been very much controlled by Safaricom (Donovan 2012). This monopolisation has been attributed not only to the exclusive agreement between Safaricom and its agent network, but also to a lack of interoperability among providers.[16] The NPS Regulations provide a framework for market-led interoperability in line with which the Communications Commission of Kenya granted mobile virtual network operator licences to mobile money companies, MNOs and banks in May 2014.[17]

The rationale behind promoting interoperability is that it will expand the mobile money market, creating new opportunities for providers and agents and lower transaction costs for consumers (World Bank 2012a; Muthiora 2015: 26). However, as Maurer argues, competition among payment systems does not necessarily bring prices down, as would be expected of a market mechanism, as the provider and not the market sets the consumer fees (Maurer 2012a: 25). Interoperability and competition can facilitate access and the development of new products for the low-income or, in Prahalad's words (2004), bottom-of-the pyramid (BoP) market and contribute to financial inclusion.

The NPS Regulations balance this opening up of the mobile money market with consumer protection provisions in accordance with international rules, the Kenyan Constitution, which contains an article on consumer rights (Article 46), and consumer education programmes development by institutions such as FSD Kenya. In particular, the Regulations contain provisions on the transparent communication of terms, conditions and charges (section 35), complaint-handling mechanisms (section 38), privacy and the confidentiality of customer data (section 42). These measures are considered necessary in the growing mobile money network and market to facilitate the CBK's supervisory role ensuring that the system functions well and with integrity and conform to international financial rules.

This section argues that M-Pesa has been regulated more in line with the objective of financial development, as laid out in Kenya Vision 2030, than with the idea of rights, and in particular socio-economic rights, on which the Kenyan Constitution focuses. The examination shows how the NPS Regulations have formalised the mobile money regulatory practices developed since M-Pesa's launch in 2007. These practices have favoured the rapid expansion of the M-Pesa payment infrastructure and the proliferation of the mobile money business while complying with international requirements.

The regulatory framework has facilitated women's access to the service by removing regulatory barriers to access. However, mobile money products and services support gender equality only to the extent of providing women with money management tools and entrepreneurial opportunities to make their paid and unpaid work more efficient. As discussed throughout this book, this can result in increased responsibility and inequality for women unless accompanied by measures to provide them with the resources, social support and employment protection necessary for them to take full advantage of financial inclusion. The analysis in this section raises questions about the fairness of customers not earning interest on the money kept on their M-Pesa accounts, the limits of a philanthrocapitalist approach to the management of these funds and the possible use of taxation in order to redistribute part of the profit from mobile money to realise socio-economic rights via publicly provided social services.

If we consider that regulation can help us to understand where the forces of legitimacy, authority and power are located in a society (Black 2002: 27) we can say that with mobile money the Central Bank and the MNO have assumed their position at the top of the pyramid, privileging the aims of financial deepening and the mobile money business. This generates questions about how central banks and MNOs could or should act to challenge gender inequality. First, both the financial and the telecommunication sectors are characterised by ideas of inclusion, innovation and opportunity, but are often criticised for unfair commercial practices. The convergence of the two sectors in mobile money can result in the unfair distribution of risk, responsibility and profits, and in more inequality, particularly if there is no collaboration with other sectors to guarantee people's welfare.

Second, the CBK's key role in mobile money reflects what Holmes (2014: 6) has called the 'performative art' of central banks which 'cultivate networks of interlocutors that generate knowledge about the social and cultural character of the economy animated by precisely the contextual and situational information that is typically stripped out from conventional macroeconomic and financial analysis'. A question that is outside the scope of this research but which might require more investigation is how central banks could use their role in the context of mobile money to adopt more gender-equitable policies and interventions. This could be an innovative and also potentially performative approach, considering that Kenya has been used as an example of mobile money regulation for other countries in the Global South, as I discuss in the next section.

Gender in mobile money governance

The regulation of mobile money is not just the result of national discussions on financial development in Kenya: it also has been influenced by international economic relations and development policies and has defined the global discourse on digital financial inclusion. While this discourse has a strong focus on the Global South's ability to inspire new financial practices (Collins *et al.* 2009), its agenda has been driven by Western countries, multilateral and international institutions, governments, corporations and philanthropic foundations. The digital financial inclusion agenda is based on the underlying assumption that access to finance contributes to economic and social development. This idea guides the financial inclusion agenda built around the World Bank policy research report *Finance For All?*, adopted in 2008, and its universal financial access (UFA) 2020 initiative; the G20 Principles for Innovative Financial Inclusion 2010; the IMF financial access survey monitoring financial inclusion; and the financial inclusion initiatives of the UN Secretary General's Special Advocate for Inclusive Finance for Development and UN Capital Development Fund (UNCDF), which highlight financial inclusion as a key tool for the implementation of the SDGs, including gender equality (UNCDF 2018). All of these documents, institutions and programmes see M-Pesa as a model of digital financial inclusion in the Global South, and gender equality as an important policy element and social objective of the universal financial inclusion agenda. This section explores some of the global and local institutions that have shaped the governance of mobile money, and illustrates the role of gender equality in this framework. While M-Pesa has contributed to globalising the debate on the role of mobile money in the digital financial inclusion agenda, the evolution of this debate is now shaping the further development of M-Pesa.

There are two important aspects to consider to understand the role of M-Pesa in defining the trajectory of mobile money governance. The first is that the rise of M-Pesa coincided with the general distrust of finance that followed the global financial crisis (Maurer 2012a: 18). In particular, the consequences of the financial crisis for more vulnerable groups across the gender, racial and class spectrums (Montgomerie and Young 2011; Young, Bakker and Elson 2011; Roberts 2012) created distrust in the causal link between financial inclusion and the realisation of social goals and rights. In these conditions the rapid growth of M-Pesa has been used to support the idea that digital financial services such as mobile money can raise household welfare and increase growth, stability, poverty reduction and gender equality as maintained in influential studies such as those of Jack and Suri (2011, 2014). Suri and Jack's study of 2016 is mentioned on the Bill and Melinda Gates Foundation website as evidence that financial inclusion via mobile money contributes to gender equality.[18] Recent scholarship (Bateman, Duvendack and Loubere 2019) has questioned these claims, highlighting their methodological flaws and omissions regarding the risk of reproducing negative patterns of micro-credit such as over-indebtedness and local exploitation in favour of profit for corporations and foreign investors. However, Jack and Suri's studies have strongly influenced the digital financial inclusion agenda and the link between mobile money and economic and social development.

The second point is M-Pesa's legitimisation of a novel approach to the regulation of financial services, namely by creating an environment that enables financial inclusion by removing regulatory obstacles to accessing financial services under the supervision of a country's central bank with the support of the government as well as the private sector. Maurer (2012b: 303) considers regulation in the field of mobile money a 'retrospective ethnography of potential' rather than 'proscriptive or restrictive of human action', meaning that mobile money regulation offers an account of the past by considering the obstacles to accessing finance, is responsive to the present by adopting a 'test and learn' approach, and keeps an eye on the future according to the aims of financial inclusion.

This regulatory approach is supported by DFID, the UN, the IMF, the World Bank and the G20, among others, and was developed by five institutions in particular: FSD, GSMA, CGAP, the AFI and the Better than Cash Alliance, to which we can add the Bill and Melinda Gates Foundation as the philanthropic arm of the mobile money industry (Donovan 2015). These institutions lead debates on mobile money, undertake research and develop indicators and policy documents. As mentioned in Chapter 1, research on mobile money is mainly conducted by an interlinked network of mobile money professionals located in these core institutions and defined by Maurer (2012b: 301) as 'mobile money intellectuals'. The Bill and Melinda Gates Foundation funds most projects and research on mobile money and has funded the Institute for Money, Technology and Financial Inclusion (IMTFI), established in 2008 with the aim of supporting mainly ethnographic research on the everyday financial practices of the poor and people on low incomes (Schwittay 2014; Maurer, Musaraj and Small 2018). It also plays an indirect although key role in shaping regulatory and policy debates on digital financial inclusion by funding the key institutions that lead these debates such as AFI and GSMA.

Gender has become an important aspect of mobile money programmes, research and policies. The Bill and Melinda Gates Foundation aims to close the gender gap in access to finance by supporting public- and private sector development of 'accessible, affordable and profitable' financial services, particularly in the form of digital payments such as mobile money.[19] Gender equality is presented as the inclusion of women in the financial system but also as a driver of economic growth due to women's contribution to the wellbeing of their communities and countries. This approach clearly reflects the international narrative of 'gender equality as smart economics' (World Bank 2006, 2012b). The Foundation considers the digitisation of payments for social protection programmes part of its gender equality strategy, but focuses on supporting the payment infrastructure rather than the social programmes themselves. While social programmes can contribute to addressing women's socio-economic disadvantages and support their responsibility for social reproduction work, facilitating payments alone has little impact on substantive equality. Research by IMTFI, as mentioned also funded by the Foundation, has shed light on local gender dynamics and given voice to researchers from the Global South (Kusimba, Krunyu and Gross 2018). However, it upholds the underlying assumption that financial inclusion is good for gender equality and gender equality is good for development. FSD, CGAP, GSMA and AFI also share the view that financial inclusion is positive and even necessary for gender equality, and that removing barriers to women's access to financial services is a main condition for realising their financial inclusion and improving their status.

FSD Kenya, introduced in Chapter 3, was established by DFID in 2005 as an independent trust with the aim of developing financial markets in Kenya, and has received funding from various partners over the years including the International Finance Corporation, the Swedish government and the Bill and Melinda Gates Foundation. FSD trusts have also been established in other African countries such as Mozambique, Nigeria, Rwanda, Tanzania, Uganda and Zambia. In 2012 DFID invested over 35 million GBP in FSD Africa, a regional financial sector development programme based in Nairobi.[20] FSD Kenya has played a key role in the development of M-Pesa by coordinating the FinAccess surveys (FSD 2007, 2009, 2013, 2016, 2019) that justified M-Pesa's adoption and regulatory framework, and conducting a variety of studies on digital financial inclusion in Kenya. It coordinates research and policy analysis, provides technical advice to the government, regulators and the private sector, and supports a variety of financial inclusion projects. Gender equality has a relevant focus in FSD's studies, providing important insights (Johnson 2015; Mintz-Roth 2018). However, the partnerships developed by FSD have focused more on expanding the reach of financial services and markets than on addressing women's socio-economic inequalities. For instance, in November 2013 FSD Africa concluded a partnership with the global NGO Women's World Banking with the aim of developing policy 'to raise awareness of the role of women as drivers of economic change and managers of household security, as well as market opportunities to serve women clients'.[21]

CGAP is a donor forum based at the World Bank whose main goal is to advance financial inclusion. For years it has worked to build a global microfinance industry and expand financial markets (Roy 2010: 26). Following the rapid growth of M-Pesa in Kenya CGAP also focused on mobile money and digital financial inclusion, contributing to defining the regulation of branchless banking, interoperability and consumer protection. Research and policy work conducted at CGAP is premised on the idea that financial services at the macro level can favour economic growth and at the micro level can improve household welfare. In line with the social entrepreneurship and Prahalad's BoP (2004) models discussed in Chapter 4, CGAP has increasingly supported the idea of innovation as a digital business model that gives poor consumers access to finance while creating profit for its providers. Accordingly, CGAP advocates a regulatory framework that favours the expansion of financial markets while suggesting measures for the protection of consumers.

In terms of gender equality, besides reiterating the need to remove barriers to women's access to financial services, CGAP recognises the link between gender inequality and social support. In a project conducted with the support of the Ford Foundation it also considers women's disproportionate responsibility for social reproduction work (de Montesquiou and Sheldon 2014: 72). However, instead of envisaging measures to put finance at the service of people and of social reproduction, the project aims to 'lower barriers to entering the market economy' and encourages financial service providers 'to design more appropriate products and delivery channels and pay increased attention to efficiency, incentives and marketing' (Montesquiou and Sheldon 2014: 22).

GSMA is the association of mobile money operators and became particularly involved in financial inclusion following the rapid growth of M-Pesa in Kenya and the development of mobile money projects. While CGAP is mainly a donor network, GSMA represents the private sector in mobile money and has established a Mobile Money Programme funded by the Bill and Melinda Gates Foundation, the Mastercard Foundation and the Omidyar Network, a philanthropic investment organisation created by Pierre and Pam Omidyar. Pierre Omidyar is the entrepreneur who founded eBay. GSMA plays a key role in the regulation of mobile money by coordinating research studies, policy analysis, handbooks and training for mobile money providers. The GSMA Mobile Money Programme has a particular focus on policy and regulation aimed at creating an enabling global environment for the growth of mobile money.[22] GSMA also runs a Connected Women Programme that aims to reduce the gender gap in mobile money services and create socio-economic opportunities for women. In line with the gender equality as smart economics narrative the programme encourages MNOs and companies to develop gender equality projects not only to advance women's digital and financial inclusion, but also to 'unlock significant growth potential for the mobile money industry'.[23] According to GSMA, including more women in the mobile money market could increase MNO revenues by 140 billion USD. However, in the GSMA programmes there is no discussion of how this income could be redistributed to address gender inequality.

The AFI constitutes a network of policymakers, central banks and financial regulatory authorities from 90 countries in the Global South and was established in 2008 with funding from the Bill and Melinda Gates Foundation and the Omidyar Network. It became an independent organisation in 2016. According to the Maya Declaration, a set of flexible principles and purposes adopted in 2011, the AFI is committed to defining clear targets for the realisation of financial inclusion, in this way contributing to the SDGs. While it assumes a causal nexus between financial inclusion and development, it also commits to the SDGs by developing partnerships with the private sector and facilitating the adoption of regulatory frameworks that balance access to finance, inclusive growth, stability, integrity, interoperability, competition and consumer protection. M-Pesa's regulation is seen as a successful example of this balance (AFI 2010), and interestingly Njuguna Ndung'u, the governor of the CBK from 2007 to 2015 who coined the 'test and learn' approach to the regulation of mobile money, was also the first chair of the AFI.

Like the other institutions involved in mobile money governance, the AFI considers gender equality an instrument and objective of financial inclusion. In 2016 it adopted the Denarau Action Plan seeking to bridge the gender gap in access to financial services by 2021, and it has concluded a partnership with the Swedish International Development Agency to achieve this goal.[24] The Plan regards gender equality and poverty reduction as commensurate goals, maintaining that increasing gender equality automatically contributes to poverty reduction. Gender equality, however, is mainly considered as the number of women with access to financial services, and the AFI suggests combining policies on women's financial inclusion with national inclusion strategies, with no mention of social programmes or socio-economic rights.

The Better Than Cash Alliance is a consortium of donors, governments and corporations housed at the UN and also funded by the Bill and Melinda Gates

Foundation and the Omidyar network. It is one of the implementing partners in the G20 Partnership for Financial Inclusion together with CGAP, AFI, the Organisation for Economic Cooperation and Development (OECD), the International Finance Corporation, the International Fund for Agricultural Development, the Small and Medium Enterprise (SME) Forum and the World Bank. The Better Than Cash Alliance promotes the idea that the digitisation of transactions and the elimination of cash would contribute to the SDGs, including gender equality. A report prepared by the Better Than Cash Alliance, the Bill and Melinda Gates Foundation, Women's World Banking and the World Bank (2015) for the G20 Partnership for Financial Inclusion argues that digital financial services increase women's financial autonomy, their participation in the economy and the performance of their businesses. Drawing on the experience of M-Pesa, it suggests that governments should adopt a regulatory framework that facilitates access to digital financial services for women, promote formal savings, and set up digital payment systems for school fees, utilities, employment and social benefits. However, while it makes the point that digital payments are affordable, secure, transparent and convenient ways of moving money, it assumes that citizens have work and social benefits, which is often not the case. In other words, it assumes that the problem with gender equality is a lack of financial services and rapid and secure transactions rather than the structural inequalities that reproduce women's socio-economic disadvantages. Moreover, while cash is a public good with an infrastructure not restricted or controlled by private companies or usage fees (Maurer 2012c), this is not the case with digital payments, which are privately owned and allow mining of the poor's digital financial transactions (Bateman *et al.* 2019: 8).

This overview of the key institutions that form part of the governance of mobile money demonstrates how financial inclusion is promoted as a one-size-fits-all solution to gender inequality. Consistent with the narrative of 'gender equality as smart economics', gender equality is considered a valuable instrument for poverty reduction, financial development and economic growth. The institutions involved in the mobile money governance have contributed to shaping the regulatory and policy framework for digital financial inclusion, focusing on eliminating barriers to women's access to financial services without addressing issues of structural inequality, access to resources and social infrastructure. For example, while some of these institutions recognise the importance of social welfare, they tend to see the solution to inequality in the digitisation of cash transactions. There is no discussion of how the revenue produced by a privately owned payment infrastructure could contribute to addressing women's socio-economic disadvantage. The research and studies conducted by these institutions could be used to define ways of redistributing this wealth and supporting women's local struggles.

Conclusion

This chapter has explored the governance of mobile money and reflected on its gender aspects by analysing the role of the law and regulations in defining the trajectory of digital financial inclusion, both in Kenya and globally. 'Gender, law and postcolonial governance' has explained how norms and institutions introduced since the colonial era have prioritised the aims of economic and financial integration over socio-economic rights, and how the rule of law and good governance have increasingly become instruments for financial development and gender equality. 'Social objectives v.socio-economic rights' has examined two key legal frameworks for financial inclusion and gender equality in Kenya: Kenya Vision 2030 and the 2010 Constitution. These two documents, both premised on the idea of Africa Rising, encapsulate two different approaches to financial inclusion and gender equality. While the first is based on the idea of economic growth and financial development, the second is seen as the result of a long struggle for the recognition of rights including gender equality and socio-economic rights at the national level. 'Regulating mobile money: from Kenya to global and back' has analysed the regulation of M-Pesa and highlighted its gender implications, focusing on the key aspects of the National Payment Systems Regulations 2014 which formalised the regulatory practices developed since the launch of M-Pesa in 2007. It has shown how the regulatory framework for mobile money has facilitated the expansion of the service, increasing the number of women able to access the service but failing to adopt measures to address the gendered socio-economic disadvantage that causes financial exclusion. 'Gender in mobile money governance' has extended the analysis to the global level to demonstrate how the regulatory approach to M-Pesa influenced the global institutions that shape the digital financial inclusion agenda. This agenda considers gender equality an important aspect of the global commitment to financial inclusion. However, it regards the digitisation of payments and elimination of regulatory barriers to accessing financial services a solution to inequality without engaging in more complex discussion of global and local structural inequalities.

The analysis of the mobile money governance conducted in this chapter shows how international legal concepts have been re-embedded locally in different ways to support local struggles and/or contrasting local interests. Neoliberal ideas, for instance, have been recontextualised locally and have taken on a shape of their own, sometimes resulting in new regulatory trends. As Gathii (2011) argues in relation to development policies, while at the time of the SAPs neoliberal measures were almost exclusively an exogenous coercive imposition through conditionality, today former colonial countries are consciously 'redefining their identities in terms of understandings and commitments consistent with neoliberalism' (Gathii 2011: 421). The idea of Africa Rising, consistent with narratives of social entrepreneurship and inclusive capitalism, expresses this dynamic. In Kenya the recontextualisation of global norms has also affected financial inclusion and gender equality and the relationship between them, as illustrated in the legal and policy frameworks provided by Kenya's Constitution 2010 and Kenya Vision 2030.

M-Pesa and mobile money services have been regulated in line with the principles of financial development contained in Kenya Vision 2030. The CBK has adopted a 'test and learn' approach to the regulation of mobile money and has collaborated with the MNO and other policy institutions to create an enabling environment for financial inclusion. Gender equality within this framework is promoted as a social objective achievable by facilitating women's access to financial services. No attention is paid to the global and local structural inequalities that have caused and continue to reproduce gender inequality and financial exclusion. After all, financial exclusion is itself the product of inequalities. While creating an enabling environment for financial development, the regulators have not aimed to create the necessary conditions to allow women at the lower end of the income distribution to benefit from financial services. The light-touch regulation has not been accompanied by redistributive measures to contribute to the socio-economic rights enshrined in the Kenya Constitution. The responsibility for the realisation of these rights, more often framed instead as objectives, is shifted to individuals who need to take advantage of the entrepreneurial opportunities offered by mobile money. In this way access to finance can exacerbate gender inequality, even though one of the premises of financial inclusion for women is that it is for coping with the unpredictable needs that life presents.

The regulation of mobile money in Kenya has become an example of good regulatory practice at the global level and is considered successful according to the values of the international development project. Law and regulation, however, should have a role beyond facilitating access to financial services and complying with international rules. This role should favour a politics of redistribution that addresses gender inequalities and contributes to social justice. This confirms, as Uma Kothari (2006) argues, that better regulation is not enough to substantially transform unequal relations; such a transformation also requires 'more and better politics'. Better politics, for instance, means entitling all people to a decent livelihood, taking into consideration gendered responsibilities and disadvantages, and not simply entitling them to access to financial and entrepreneurial opportunities. As Rankin (2013: 207) argues, this entails going beyond the 'prudent regulation' of existing practices to consider the financial system as an instrument for a more fundamental transformation oriented towards universal provisioning. This argument resonates with Elson's claim (2014: 207), analysed in Chapter 2, that the transformation of unequal gender relations requires the sphere of finance to serve the needs of social reproduction. Regulated towards this aim, M-Pesa could become a transformative financial inclusion project addressing gender justice.

Notes

1 Ooko-Ombaka argues for the need to recognise the historical imposition of the British colonial legal system which, via the repugnancy clause, destroyed some organic legal institutions while preserving others. This resulted in not only the coexistence of two different legal and value systems – Western-type law and what has been called customary law – but also discrimination against women: 'Depending on the mood, whim or politics of the situation, African culture might be invoked to oppress women, or modern society cited in efforts to eliminate the very cultural practices which safeguard the rights of women' (Adhiambo Mbeo and Ooko-Ombaka 1989: 3).

2 Kenya National Dialogue and Reconciliation, 'Statement of Principles on Long-term Issues and Solutions', 23 May 2008, http://peacemaker.un.org/kenya-statement-longtermissues2008 (accessed 10 August 2019).

3 According to article 4(1) of the Banking Act 'The principal object of the Bank shall be to formulate and implement monetary policy directed to achieving and maintaining stability in the general level of prices.' According to the CBK's Monetary Policy Statement of June 2015

> The achievement and maintenance of a low and stable inflation rate together with ensuring adequate liquidity in the market facilitates higher levels of domestic savings and private investment, leading to improved economic growth, higher real incomes and increased employment opportunities.

4 According to article 2(5) of the Constitution the general rules of international law and any Treaty or Convention ratified by Kenya constitute part of the law of Kenya. These include the Universal Declaration of Human Rights, the International Covenant on Economic, Social and Cultural Rights, the Convention on the Elimination of All Forms of Discrimination against Women, the Convention on the Rights of the Child, the Convention on the Rights of Persons with Disabilities, the International Labour Law Organisation Conventions, international and regional instruments, such as the African Charter on Human and Peoples' Rights and its protocol on the rights of women in Africa (Maputo Protocol) and the African Charter on the Rights and Welfare of the Child.

5 The land reform in Kenya acquired an important political purpose. Article 60 of the Constitution provides that

> land in Kenya shall be held, used and managed in a manner that is equitable, productive and sustainable, in accordance with stated principles, including the elimination of gender discrimination in law, customs and practices related to land and property in land.

However, as Manji (2014) explains, the new laws have not challenged the structure of landholding, as is necessary to achieve a redistributive land reform, but have rather contributed to perpetuating the country's long-running corruption, conflict, injustice and inequalities.

6 In this regard the Kenyan government adopted the Preservation of Human Dignity Bill 2018.

7 'Progressive realisation' was first entrenched in article 2 of The International Covenant on Economic, Social and Cultural Rights 1966:

> Each State Party to the present Covenant undertakes to take steps, individually and through international assistance and co-operation, especially economic and technical, to the maximum of its available resources, with a view to achieving progressively the full realisation of the rights recognised in the present Covenant by all appropriate means, including particularly the adoption of legislative measures.

8 Declaration of Trust, M-Pesa Holding Co Limited, Nairobi: 23 February 2007. According to the Declaration of Trust

> Any interest or income received in respect of any investment of the Trust Fund shall be retained by the Trustee for its own account and shall not form part or be credited to the Trust Fund and the Trustee shall have no obligation to account to any System Participant for any such interest or income. Any such interest or income shall generally be applied first to defray the Trustee's own costs of its role in the Service but may be applied for such other purposes (whether charitable or not) as the Trustee, may in its sole discretion determine.

9 Interviews with M-Pesa agents, Kawangware, Nairobi 12 December 2012; Ngando, Nairobi, 13 December 2012.

10 In the case of Ghana, Section 10 (5) of the Guidelines provides that

> E-money issuers shall pass through not less than 80 per cent of the interest accrued on the e-money float net of any fees or charges related to the administration of the pooled float accounts to e-money holders. Such fees and charges must be the standard applicable to the account type in question. Any use of frivolous fees and charges or the invention of a new account type to hold e-money float for the purposes of limiting interest below that of other account types will be seen as an attempt to defraud the e-money holders and grounds for severe sanction of the bank and any colluding partner. Such fees and charges may also not exceed the interest income generated on the account such that the balance in the account falls below the total value of the part of the e-money float held in the account in question.

11 The Financial Act 2012, supplement 221, act 57, 9 January 2013. Before this, money transfer services conducted by banks, non-bank financial institutions and mobile network operators were exempt from VAT.

12 In September 2010 Vodafone was criticised for tax avoidance schemes that enabled it to save six billion GBP, although it has a market capitalisation of 89.4 billion GBP.

13 The National Payment System Act defines a payment service provider as (i) a person, company or organisation acting as provider in relation to sending, receiving, storing or processing of payments or the provision of other services in relation to payment services through any electronic system; (ii) a person, company or organisation that owns, possesses, operates, manages or controls a public switched network for the provision of payment services; (iii) or any other person, company or organisation that processes or stores data on behalf of such payment service providers or users of such payment services. An e-money issuer is a payment service provider authorised to issue e-money (Laws of Kenya 2011: 6).

14 Central Bank of Kenya Guidelines on Agent Banking, www.centralbank.go.ke/images/docs/legislation/GUIDELINE%20ON%20AGENT%20BANKING-CBK%20PG%2015.pdf (accessed 26 August 2019).

15 The NPS Regulations define 'agent' as a person who, for a fee, provides limited payment services on behalf of a payment service provider; and 'cash merchant' as a person who, for a fee, provides cash services on behalf of a payment service provider.

16 CGAP distinguishes three types of interoperability: platform-level, where a customer of one service can send money to a customer of another; agent-level, as seen in M-Pesa, where customers of one service can serve customers of another; and customer-level, which permits customers to access their account through any SIM card (CGAP 2011).

17 In May 2014 the Communications Commission of Kenya granted Mobile Virtual Network Operator (MVNO) licences to mobile money companies ZionCell/Mobile Decisioning, Mobile Pay, and Finserve trading as Equitel on behalf of Equity Bank. An MVNO licence allows a company without a network infrastructure licence or network infrastructure of its own to resell the mobile network services of its host network under its own brand name so that it can provide mobile money services relying on the mobile network infrastructure built since the introduction of M-Pesa. MVNOs have full control over their SIM card, branding, marketing, billing and customer care operations, purchasing minutes in bulk from their host network at a discounted rate to offer voice and data services.

18 Bill and Melinda Gates Foundation, Gender Equality strategy overview, www.gatesfoundation.org/What-We-Do/Global-Growth-and-Opportunity/Gender-Equality (accessed 10 August 2019).

19 Bill and Melinda Gates Foundation, Financial Services for the Poor: Strategy Overview, www.gatesfoundation.org/what-we-do/global-growth-and-opportunity/financial-services-for-the-poor (accessed 20 August 2019).

20 DFID, 'Skills and Innovation for Micro Banking in Africa (SIMBA)', http://devtracker.dfid.gov.uk/projects/GB-1–201394/ (accessed 8 August 2019).
21 Partnership between Financial Sector Deepening and Women's World Banking, www.womensworldbanking.org/news/fsd-africa-womens-world-banking-announce-multi-year-partnership-promote-womens-financial-inclusion-africa/ (accessed 28 August 2019).
22 GSMA Mobile Money Programme, www.gsma.com/mobilefordevelopment/mobile-money/ (accessed 29 August 2019).
23 GSMA, Connected Women Programme, www.gsma.com/mobilefordevelopment/programmes/connected-women/ (accessed 29 August 2019).
24 AFI Gender Inclusive Finance, www.afi-global.org/gender-women-financial-inclusion (accessed 20 August 2019).

References

Adam C. S., Collier, P. and Ndung'u, N. S. (eds) (2010) *Kenya Policies for Prosperity*. Oxford: Oxford University Press.

Adam C. S., Maturu, B. O., Ndung'u, N. S. and O'Connell, S. O. (2010) Building a Kenyan Monetary Regime for the Twenty-First Century, in C. S. Adam, P. Collier and N. S. Ndung'u (eds) *Kenya Policies for Prosperity*. Oxford: Oxford University Press.

Alliance for Financial Inclusion (AFI) (2010) *Mobile Financial Services: Regulatory Approaches to Enable Access. Policy Note*. Kuala Lumpur: AFI.

Atieno, R., Barako, D. and Bokea, C. (2010) Policies for Prosperity, Innovation, and Financial Access: The Role of M-Pesa in Kenya, in C. S. Adam, P. Collier and N. S. Ndung'u (eds) *Kenya Policies for Prosperity*. Oxford: Oxford University Press.

Baderin, M. A. and McCorquodale, R. (2007) The International Covenant on Economic, Social and Cultural Rights: Forty years of Development, in M. A. Baderin and R. McCorquodale (eds) *Economic, Social and Cultural Rights in Action*. Oxford: Oxford University Press, 2007.

Bateman, M., Duvendack, M. and Loubere, N. (2019) Is Fin-tech the New Panacea for Poverty Alleviation and Local Development? Contesting Suri and Jack's M-Pesa findings published in *Science*. *Review of African Political Economy*. DOI: 10.1080/03056244.2019.1614552

Beck, T., Cull, R., Fuchs, M., Getenga, J., Gatere, P., Randa, J. and Trandafir M. (2010) Banking Sector Stability, Efficiency, and Outreach in Kenya in C. S. Adam, P. Collier and N. S. Ndung'u (eds) *Kenya Policies for Prosperity*. Oxford: Oxford University Press.

Better Than Cash Alliance (2015) Digital Financial Solutions to Advance Women's Economic Participation, www.gpfi.org/sites/gpfi/files/documents/03-Digital%20Financial%20Solution%20to%20Advance%20Women....pdf

Black, J. (2002) *Critical Reflections on Regulation*, CARR Discussion Papers, DP 4, Centre for Analysis of Risk and Regulation, London: London School of Economics and Political Science.

Braunstein, E. and Heintz, J. (2008) Gender Bias and Central Bank Policy: Employment and Inflation Reduction. *International Review of Applied Economics* 22(2), 173–186.

Braunstein E. and J. Heintz (2011) Central Banks, Development and Employment in Development Countries, in B. Young, I. Bakker, andD. Elson (eds),*Questioning Financial Governance From a Feminist Perspective*. London: Routledge.

CGAP (2011) *Interoperability and Related Issues in Branchless Banking*. Washington, DC: CGAP.
Chang, H.-J. (2008) *Bad Samaritans: The Myth of Free Trade*. London: Bloomsbury Press.
Chang, H.-J. and Grabel, I. (2004) *Reclaiming Development: An Alternative Economic Policy Manual*. London: Zed Books.
Collins, D., Morduch, J., Rutherford, S. and Ruthven, O. (2009) *Portfolios of the Poor*. Princeton, NJ: Princeton University Press.
Cook, T. and McKay, C. (2015) *How M-Shwari Works: The Story so Far*. Washington, DC: CGAP and FSD Kenya.
Cornwall, A. and Nyamu-Musembi, C. (2005) Why Rights, Why Not? *IDS Bulletin* 36(1), 9–18.
De Montesquiou, A. and Sheldon, T. (2014) From Extreme Poverty to Sustainable Livelihoods. CGAP, Ford Foundation, www.cgap.org/sites/default/files/graduation_guide_final.pdf
Donovan, K. P. (2012) Mobile Money, More Freedom? The Impact of M-Pesa's Network Power on Development as Freedom. *International Journal of Communication* 6, 2647–2669.
Donovan, K. P. (2015) Mobile Money, in R. Mansell and P. Hwa Ang (eds) *The International Encyclopedia of Digital Communication and Society*. Hoboken, NJ: Wiley-Blackwell.
Dupas, P. and Robinson, J. (2013) Why Don't the Poor Save More? Evidence from Health Savings Experiments. *American Economic Review* 103(4), 1138–1171.
Elson, D. (2014) Economic Crises from the 1980s to the 2010s: A Gender Analysis, in S. M. Rai and G. Waylen (eds) *New Frontiers in Feminist Political Economy*. Oxford: Routledge.
Elson, D. and Cagatay, N. (2000) The Social Content of Macroeconomic Policies. *World Development* 28(7), 1347–1364.
Federation of Women Lawyers (FIDA) Kenya (2013) *Advancing Women's Rights in Kenya*. Nairobi: FIDA Kenya.
FSD Kenya and The Steadman Group Research Division (2007) *Financial Access in Kenya: Results of the 2006 National Survey*. Nairobi: FSD Kenya.
FSD Kenya and Central Bank of Kenya (2009) FinAccess National Survey 2009: Dynamics of Kenya's Changing Financial Landscape. Nairobi: FSD Kenya.
Financial Sector Deepening (2012) *Microfinance in Kenya: The Experience of FAULU Kenya and Kenya Women Finance Trust*. Nairobi: FSD Kenya.
FSD Kenya and Central Bank of Kenya (2013) *FinAccess National Survey 2013: Profiling Developments in Financial Access and Usage in Kenya*. Nairobi: FSD Kenya.
FSD Kenya and Central Bank of Kenya, Kenya National Bureau of Statistics (2016) *The 2016 FinAccess Household Survey on Financial Inclusion*. Nairobi: FSD Kenya.
FSD Kenya, Central Bank of Kenya, National Bureau of Statistics (2019) *2019 Finaccess Household Survey*. Nairobi: FSD Kenya.
Gabor, D. and Brooks, S. (2017) The Digital Revolution in Financial Inclusion: International Development in the Fintech Era. *New Political Economy* 22(4), 423–436.
Gathii, J. (2011) The Neoliberal Turn in Regional Trade Agreements, *Washington Law Review* 86, 421.
Gordon, B. and Lyon, B. (2017) 4 Trends Driving a Looming Credit Crisis in East Africa. *Medium*, 14 August, https://medium.com/dfs-lab/4-trends-driving-a-looming-credit-crisis-in-east-africa-844b217369fd (accessed 26 November 2019).

Harvey, D. (2005) *A Brief History of Neoliberalism*. Oxford: Oxford University Press.

Holmes, D. R. (2014) *Economy of Words: Communicative Imperatives in Central Banks*. Chicago, IL: University of Chicago Press.

Jack, W. and Suri, T. (2011) *Mobile Money: The Economics of M-Pesa*. Cambridge, MA: MIT Sloan.

Jack, W. and Suri, T. (2014) Risk Sharing and Transactions Costs: Evidence from Kenya's Mobile Money Revolution. *American Economic Review* 104(1), 183–223.

Johnson, S. (2015) *Capacities to Aspire and Capacities to Save: A Gendered Analysis of Motivations for Liquidity Management*. Nairobi: FSD Kenya.

Johnson, S., Brown, G. K. and Fouillet, C. (2012) *The Search for Inclusion in Kenya's Financial Landscape: The Rift Revealed. Summary Report*. Nairobi: FSD Kenya.

Kabeer, N. (2015) Tracking the Gender Politics of the Millennium Development Goals: Struggles for Interpretative Power in the International Development Agenda. *Third World Quarterly* 36(2), 377–395.

Kabeer, N. (2015a) Evolving Meanings of 'the Social' in the International Development Agenda. *Journal of International and Comparative Social Policy* 31(2), 114–131.

Kabira W. (2011) *Time for Harvest: Women and Constitution Making in Kenya*. Nairobi: Nairobi University Press.

Kanyinga, K. and Long, J. D. (2012) The Political Economy of Reforms in Kenya: The Post-2007 Election Violence and a New Constitution. *African Studies Review* 55(1), 31–51.

Kazeem, Y. (2018) M-Pesa is Pushing Against a Tax Hike on Mobile Money services in Kenya. *Quartz*, 19 June, https://qz.com/africa/1309097/m-pesa-opposing-kenya-mobile-money-tax-increase/ (accessed 27 November 2019).

Kennedy, D. (2006) The 'Rule of Law', Political Choices, and Development Common Sense, in D. M. Trubek and A. Santos (eds) *The New Law and Economic Development: A Critical Appraisal*. Cambridge: Cambridge University Press.

Klein, M. and Mayer, C. (2011) Mobile Baking and Financial Inclusion: The Regulatory Lesson. *Policy Research Working Paper 5664*. Washington, DC: World Bank.

Kramon, E. and Posner, D. N. (2011) Kenya's New Constitution. *Journal of Democracy* 22(2), 89–103.

Kusimba, S., Krunyu, G. and Gross, E. (2018) Social Networks of Mobile Money in Kenya, in B. Maurer, S. Musaraj and I. V. Small (eds) *Money at the Margins: Global Perspectives on Technology, Financial Inclusion and Design*. Oxford: Berghahn.

Lindenmayer, E. and Kaye, J. L. (2009) *A Choice for Peace? The Story of Forty-one Days of Mediation in Kenya*. New York: International Peace Institute.

Manji, A. (2014) The Politics of Land Reform in Kenya 2012. *African Studies Review* 57(1), 115–130.

Manji, A. (2015) Bulldozers, Homes and Highways: Nairobi and the Right to the City. *Review of African Political Economy* 42, 206–224.

Maurer, B. (2012a) Payment: Forms and Functions of Value Transfer in Contemporary Society. *Cambridge Anthropology* 30(2), 15–35.

Maurer, B. (2012b) Regulation as Retrospective Ethnography: Mobile Money and the Arts of Cash. *Banking and Finance Law Review* 27, 299–313.

Maurer, B. (2012c) Credit Slips But Should Not Fall. *Distinktion: Scandinavian Journal of Social Theory* 13(3), 283–294.

Maurer, B., Musaraj S. and Small I. V. (2018) *Money at the Margins: Global Perspectives on Technology Financial Inclusion and Design*. Oxford: Berghahn.

Mbeo, A. M. and Ooko-Ombaka, O. (1989) *Women and Law in Kenya: Perspectives and Emerging Issues*. Nairobi: Nairobi Public Law Institute.

McKinnon, R. (1973) *Money and Capital in Economic Development*. Washington, DC: The Brookings Institute.

Mintz-Roth, M. (2018) *The Gender and Age Dimensions of Mobile Money Adoption in Kenya, FSD Research Brief 3, March*. Nairobi: FSD Kenya.

Montgomerie, J. and Young, B. (2011) Home is Where the Hardship is: Gender and Wealth (Dis)Accumulation in the Subprime Boom. *CRESC Working Paper Series* 79.

Morawcznski, O. (2009) Exploring the Usage and Impact of 'Transformational' Mobile Financial Services: The Case of M-Pesa in Kenya. *Journal of Eastern African Studies* 3(3), 509–525.

Muthiora, B. (2015) *Enabling Mobile Money Policies in Kenya: Fostering a Digital Financial Revolution*. London: GSMA.

Mutua A. D. (2006) Gender Equality and Women's Solidarity Across Religious, Ethnic, and Class Differences in the Kenyan Constitutional Review Process. *William and Mary Journal of Women and the Law* 13(1), 1–128.

Mwega, F. M. (2014) *Financial Regulation in Kenya: Balancing Inclusive Growth with Financial Stability. Overseas Development Institute, Working Paper 407*. London: Overseas Development Institute.

Nyamu-Musembi, C. (2005) *For or Against Gender Equality? Evaluating the Post-Cold War 'Rule of Law' Reforms in Sub-Saharan Africa*. Geneva: UNRISD.

Nzomo, M. (1995) Kenyan Woman in Politics and Public Decision Making, in G. Mikell (ed.) *African Feminism: The Politics of Survival in Sub-Saharan Africa*. Philadelphia: University of Pennsylvania Press.

Odinkalu, C. A. (2001) Analysis of Paralysis or Paralysis by Analysis? Implementing Economic, Social and Cultural Rights under the African Charter on Human and Peoples' Rights. *Human Rights Quarterly* 23(2), 327–369.

Okeyo, A. P. (1989) On Theory and Method: Issues in the Study of Women in Africa, in A. M. Mbeo and O. Ooko-Ombaka (eds) *Women and Law in Kenya: Perspectives and Emerging Issues*. Nairobi: Nairobi Public Law Institute.

Otieno, R. O. and Ndung'u, N. S. (2010) Unlocking the Future Potential of Kenya: Vision 2030, in C. S. Adam, P. Collier and N. S. Ndung'u (eds) *Kenya Policies for Prosperity*. Oxford: Oxford University Press.

Oyèwùmí, O. (1997) *The Invention of Women: Making an African Sense of Western Gender Discourses*. Minneapolis: University of Minnesota Press.

Prahalad, K. (2004) *The Fortune at the Bottom of the Pyramid: Eradicating Poverty through Profits*. State College, PA: Wharton School Publishing.

Rankin, K. N. (2013) A Critical Geography of Poverty Finance. *Third World Quarterly* 34(4), 547–568.

Rittich, K. (2006) The Future of Law and Development: Second-Generation Reforms and the Incorporation of the Social, in D. M. Trubek and A. Santos (eds) *The New Law and Economic Development: A Critical Appraisal*. Cambridge: Cambridge University Press.

Roberts, A. (2012) Financial Social Reproduction: The Gendered Relations of Debt and Mortgage Finance in Twenty-first-century America. *New Political Economy* 18(1), 21–42.

Robertson, R. E. (1994) Measuring State Compliance with the Obligation to Devote the 'Maximum Available Resources' to Realising Economic, Social and Cultural Rights. *Human Rights Quarterly* 16, 693–714.

Roy, A. (2010) *Poverty Capital: Microfinance and the Making of Development*. New York: Routledge.

Schwittay, A. (2014) Designing Development: Humanitarian Design in the Financial Inclusion Assemblage. *Political and Legal Anthropology Review* 37(1), 29–47.

Shaw, E. (1973) *Financial Deepening in Economic Development*. Oxford: Oxford University Press.

Suri, T. and Jack, W. (2016) The Long-run Poverty and Gender Impacts of Mobile Money. *Science* 354(6317), 1288–1292.

Tamanaha, B. Z. (2011) The Rule of Law and Legal Pluralism in Development. *Hague Journal of the Rule of Law* 3(1), 1–17.

UN (2014) *A New Global Partnership: Eradicate Poverty and Transform Economies through Sustainable Development*. New York, www.post2015hlp.org/wp-content/uploads/2013/05/UN-Report.pdf

UNCDF (United Nations Capital Development Fund) (2018) *UNCDF and the SDGs: Financial Inclusion and the SDGs*, www.uncdf.org/financial-inclusion-and-the-sdgs

World Bank (2006) *Gender Equality as Smart Economics: A World Bank Group Gender Action Plan*. Washington, DC: World Bank Group.

World Bank (2008) *Finance for All? Policies and Pitfalls in Expanding Access*, World Bank Policy Research Report. Washington, DC: World Bank.

World Bank (2012a) *Information and Communications for Development: Maximising Mobile*. Washington, DC: World Bank.

World Bank (2012b) *World Development Report 2012: Gender Equality and Development*. Washington, DC: World Bank.

World Bank (2015) *Women, Business and the Law 2016: Getting to Equal*. Washington, DC: World Bank.

Young, B., Bakker, I. and Elson, D. (eds) (2011) *Questioning Financial Governance from a Feminist Perspective*. London, New York: Routledge.

LEGISLATION

Laws of Kenya, The National Payment System Regulations 2014, *Kenya Gazette* Supplement no. 119, Legislative Supplement no. 43.

Laws of Kenya, The Banking Act, Chapter 488, 1995 (as amended to 15 September 2015), Nairobi: Central Bank of Kenya.

Laws of Kenya, National Payment System Act, N. 39 of 2011.

Government of Kenya, *Kenya Vision 2030*, Nairobi: National Economic and Social Council of Kenya, 2007.

Government of Kenya, *The Constitution of Kenya*, Laws of Kenya, Revised Edition, Nairobi: National Council for Law Reporting, 2010.

United Nations, *International Covenant on Economic, Social and Cultural Rights, UNGA Res 2200 (XXI)*, 19 December 1966.

Conclusion

The exclusionary politics of digital financial inclusion

Digital financial inclusion has increasingly become a key feature of the global development project, promoted as an instrument for economic growth and the attainment of the Sustainable Development Goals (SDGs). Financial inclusion policies are premised on the assumption that people, particularly those living on low and irregular incomes, who do not have access to formal financial products and services such as credit, savings, insurance and money transfers, need such services to improve their livelihoods. While access to finance is not considered more important than access to basic resources such as food, clean water, healthcare or education, it is seen as useful or even necessary for achieving these goals. This idea is supported by international organisations, governments, donors, financial institutions and corporations, which have coined the term 'unbanked poor', suggesting a nexus between financial exclusion and the perpetuation of poverty. Digital technology has furthered the relationship between financial inclusion and development by providing new platforms for access to financial services, which are acclaimed as more secure and transparent than informal finance and more convenient and available than mainstream banking.

For various historical, socio-economic, political and regulatory reasons analysed throughout this book, the financially excluded population is seen as consisting predominantly of women and are therefore particularly targeted by financial inclusion projects and policies. While they are also portrayed as disproportionately excluded from digital technology, devices such as mobile phones have been shown to have low barriers to their access and use, and mobile phone-enabled money transfer systems have been acclaimed for facilitating financial inclusion and extending the purview of financial markets. The development project presents financial inclusion to women as a precondition of their own, their families and their communities' autonomy and future wellbeing. Financial exclusion, according to the international development agenda, undermines women's ability to manage money autonomously and efficiently; cope with uneven flows of income, lack of resources and unexpected events; engage in productive activities, and support their social reproduction work. By this logic, financial inclusion not only mitigates the precarity and vulnerability of poor women and households but also places them in a better position to secure access to basic resources and services and provides them with a variety of entrepreneurial opportunities. These ideas are in line with the 'gender equality as smart economics' framework (World Bank 2006, 2012), the governing narrative embraced by all of the institutions supporting digital financial inclusion.

This book has investigated digital financial inclusion as a development strategy for gender equality, looking at the institutions, narratives and regulations that frame mobile money, in particular M-Pesa in Kenya, as an archetype of digital financial inclusion in the Global South. The rapid growth of M-Pesa in a developing country of the Global South has been used to promote the idea that 'successful' financial inclusion initiatives such as M-Pesa are possible even in places with a dominant informal sector and limited infrastructure and resources. The book has explored and unravelled this notion of 'success' using gender as a relevant and revealing aspect of the relationship between digital financial inclusion and development. This analysis necessarily implies the examination of multiple interlocking layers of inequality and requires that elements such as Kenya's colonial and postcolonial history, gender, race, socio-economic status and poverty are taken into account.

To define the global context of this exploration, Chapter 1 provided an overview of financial inclusion and gender equality as two interrelated aspects of the international development project. First it examined the economic, social and legal norms introduced since colonialism that have excluded women from financial services, and then it analysed the progressive adoption of development measures aiming to include women in the formal financial sphere. It discussed the shift from microcredit to microfinance to universal financial inclusion and the recent turn to digital financial inclusion, arguing that the rhetoric of inclusion has been used to reframe rather than challenge the gendered socio-economic disadvantages that cause financial exclusion.

Drawing on these insights, Chapter 2 set out the conceptual framework of the analysis, engaging with feminist debates on development, unpaid work, empowerment and socio-economic rights. It examined financial inclusion across the nexus of finance, production and social reproduction, as shaped by the legacy of colonialism and development interventions. The analysis uses the interrelated concepts of autonomy and solidarity and of opportunity and redistribution to show how digital financial inclusion is based on a logic of opportunity that encourages women's autonomy, relying on and even profiting from their solidarity and survival practices. These practices are often promoted as resilience and even empowerment, instead of prompting the adoption of measures to ensure decent standards of living that consider and support women's disproportionate responsibility for social reproduction work. Such logic risks exacerbating gender inequality by imposing the further burden of transforming opportunity into success on women. The chapter argued that rethinking digital financial inclusion according to a politics of redistribution would contribute to a more equal distribution of power, resources and responsibilities, and thus more equal gender relations.

Chapter 3 focused on the case study of M-Pesa in Kenya, starting with the Kenyan context, mirroring the analysis of the international context in Chapter 1. The chapter showed how M-Pesa is the result of the interaction of global and local dynamics and examined the institutional arrangements and regulatory framework that have contributed to defining it as an archetype of digital financial inclusion. Unlike microcredit projects, M-Pesa does not specifically target women but its development is embedded in gendered political, economic and social relations and institutions. The chapter argued that the rapid expansion of the M-Pesa service has relied on gender and socio-economic inequalities and created new gendered responsibilities by promoting the idea that poor people can live well on a small and irregular income if they have access to a financial instrument such as M-Pesa to help them manage their small amount of money efficiently.

Chapters 4 and 5 illustrated the interaction between global and local dynamics in greater detail by looking at the narratives and governance of M-Pesa and how these have shaped the role of mobile money in the global financial inclusion agenda and in M-Pesa's further development in Kenya. Chapter 4 argued that M-Pesa is premised on a narrative of social entrepreneurship, promoting the idea that digital financial inclusion can both address social problems and produce profit. It analysed the articulations of this narrative in relation to digital financial inclusion, and traced the shift from social entrepreneurship to philanthrocapitalism, a type of philanthropy that emulates for-profit business in the capitalist world. It illustrated the gender implications of these narratives within the M-Pesa system by looking at the mobile money-enabled products and services and mobile money agents that constitute the M-Pesa ecosystem, and showed how M-Pesa has contributed to conceptualising access to basic needs as entrepreneurial opportunity, increasing gendered responsibilities for social reproduction work. The revenue produced by the expansion of the M-Pesa ecosystem is not redistributed to provide more vulnerable and marginalised people with the resources and social infrastructure that they need to be able to take advantage of financial inclusion.

Chapter 5 highlighted the gender aspects of the regulation and governance of mobile money, showing how Kenya's main legal and policy frameworks for financial inclusion and gender equality, Kenya Vision 2030 and the 2010 Kenyan Constitution, are the results of interaction between global influences and local norms. Kenya Vision emphasises the importance of economic growth and financial development, while the Constitution is seen as deriving from long-term grassroots struggle for national recognition of gender justice and socio-economic rights, among other principles. The chapter showed how the regulatory framework of M-Pesa focuses on creating an enabling environment for financial inclusion and expansion of the mobile money market according to the Kenya Vision, in preference to the more redistributive measures necessary for the realisation of the rights and purposes enshrined in the Constitution. This regulatory approach is endorsed by the various institutions involved in the global financial inclusion governance, which promote gender equality as a measurable and profitable goal to ensure their own social legitimacy rather than as a necessary aspect of social justice.

This book has argued that while the various institutional, commercial and regulatory arrangements that favoured the rapid development of M-Pesa have contributed to increasing the number of women with access to financial services and created opportunities within the mobile money market, they have not contributed to challenging unequal gender relations, particularly at the lower end of the income distribution. This is mainly due to the lack of corresponding redistributive measures addressing the gendered socio-economic inequalities that cause and reproduce financial exclusion. M-Pesa has brought its users various benefits including facilitating the movement of money across the country, overcoming infrastructural barriers; allowing greater autonomy and efficiency in money management; facilitating access to financial services, and creating new entrepreneurial opportunities. It has also revealed the richness of local ideas and initiatives, potentially giving to more marginalised groups the opportunity to make their voices heard via the new digital platforms that have proliferated since its launch. These dynamics have created grounds for the potential restructuring of socio-economic and political relations, possibly inspiring new forms of cooperation, engagement and distribution. However, this potential has not been used for the fairer redistribution of power, resources and gendered responsibilities that is necessary if social justice is to be achieved.

A main issue identified in this book is the role of colonialism and development institutions in shaping both the gender dynamics of financial exclusion and the rationales and conditions for inclusion. This argument may be familiar to postcolonial, decolonial and critical development scholars but it has rarely been considered in studies of M-Pesa or in the literature on mobile money. While a recent and growing body of critical literature questions digital finance's contribution to poverty reduction and local development (e.g. Gabor and Brooks 2016; Bateman, Duvendack and Loubere 2019), the responsibilities of colonialism and development interventions have been ignored in most of the widely cited studies on mobile money (see for example Mas and Morawczynski 2009; Mas and Radcliffe 2010; Jack and Suri 2011, 2014; Suri and Jack 2016). As discussed, most of these studies have been funded and coordinated by institutions, such as the Bill and Melinda Gates Foundation, which promote an inclusive capitalism approach to development and influence global dynamics and agendas through funding.

The mainstream development project has reinvented itself over the years, adopting a more social face but failing to challenge its own core assumptions. For instance, the development agenda that promotes financial inclusion does not see poverty or gender inequality as shaped by the colonial and development interventions that imposed discriminatory and limiting conditions on countries of the Global South, mitigated by ambiguous forms of aid and philanthropy. It does not consider people from former colonial countries the rightful owners of the vast amount of wealth of which they have been unjustly deprived through exploitation, extraction and unfair economic rules, or the debt that the Global North owes to the Global South for these reasons. One of the main problems with this is that development institutions, like the institutions now leading the financial inclusion agenda, present themselves as external to the situation rather than implicated in the production of the inequalities that cause financial exclusion. The responsibility for exclusion has increasingly been shifted from the countries and institutions that caused it to those on whom it has been structurally imposed. This research has used gender relations to illustrate this point, showing how approaches that seek to include and empower women through financial inclusion projects without adequate infrastructure, public services and legal measures aimed at realising socio-economic rights are highly unlikely to change gender relations, and that adding their further burden to the 'feminisation of responsibility' (Chant 2008) can even exacerbate the current gender inequality.

A central problem with the logic of financial inclusion for gender equality resides in the same idea of inclusion. Inclusive initiatives are built on existing inequalities: the structures of exclusion that have shaped socio-economic disadvantage according to gender, race, ethnicity, class and other power relation since colonialism are not addressed, but reshaped by a logic of inclusion that risks reproducing them. Inclusion can be simultaneously both transformative and the framework that allows the perpetuation of inequality. As Spivak (1993: 46) puts it, 'one cannot not want' strategies that secure greater independence, autonomy, safety and security for women and marginalised groups. What is ambivalent, however, is their inclusion in a social, political and economic order originally founded on their exclusion. The rhetoric of inclusion has often been used to reframe rather than challenge problematic development discourses and measures. The development project has renewed itself over the years, adapting to changes, criticism and the growing set of interests involved. The process of the convergence of economic growth, social goals and, increasingly, financial inclusion started with the adoption of the Millennium Development Goals (MDGs) framework and was institutionalised in the SDGs, which also encouraged new partnerships and forms of funding for development. The progressive expansion of the development framework to include social goals such as gender equality has resulted in the legitimisation of the provision of 'socially relevant' financial products and services by a variety of development agents who are not held accountable for the realisation of social objectives, deliberately framed as objectives rather than rights. The development agenda's expansion, aims and actions are supported by the narratives of social entrepreneurship, inclusive capitalism, shared values and the influential logic of philanthrocapitalism, all based on the overoptimistic claim that markets and social goals are commensurate goods. Inclusion of the 'social' in the development agenda has led to the privatisation, marketisation and financialisation of social needs and social provisioning, with the discussed negative consequences for gender equality. These are consequences of the increasing shift in the responsibility for social provisioning from government to civil society, and particularly women, and of the interest of some development institutions, corporations and philanthropic foundations in promoting gender equality mainly through market and financial inclusion measures.

Development measures tackling exclusion tend to focus on products and services that can economically include poorer people rather than on 'the inequalities in power and voice that keep poor populations systematically, socially and politically excluded' (Banks and Hulme 2014: 192). This understanding of exclusion simplifies policy and the calculation of development outcomes without the need to engage in more complex discussions about global and local structural inequalities, all people's entitlement to a decent livelihood and the public obligation to realise this purpose. Financial inclusion can easily be quantified as the number of people able to access formal financial services, and gender equality in relation to financial inclusion can be reduced to a simple, measurable and even profitable goal that can be achieved without challenging power structures and relations. More complex is the fact that there are differences and disadvantages among the financially included which are not addressed, but used as the criteria by which a person or group (as in the case of group lending in microcredit) is placed on a particular grid of risk and their access priced accordingly (Allon 2014: 23).

M-Pesa has also demonstrated that unlike its users, its providers have a secure source of revenue in the fees charged for each transaction, and very limited restrictions on creating and marketing new mobile money products and services. This has favoured the proliferation of mobile money opportunities for poor consumers, but such growth has not been matched by the adoption of parallel measures to ensure that people have sufficient resources to take advantage of these opportunities. Women living in poverty or on a low income with disproportionate responsibility for providing for their households bear the greatest insecurity and uncertainty in the system. Legal measures adopted in relation to M-Pesa have facilitated the growth of the mobile money market and philanthrocapitalist practices, but no relevant redistributive measures have been adopted to use the increased revenue, funding and investments that mobile money has secured to improve poor people's livelihoods and realise socio-economic rights through public services, social infrastructure, welfare assistance and other measures that can challenge gendered disadvantages and contribute to substantive equality. For example, while the interest on M-Pesa customers' funds, generated by the trust accounts that hold them, is used for charitable purposes, it is distributed according to a logic of entrepreneurial opportunity rather than a politics of redistribution.

The M-Pesa system has the potential to increase the resources available to the country to guarantee access to basic goods and services, ensure social support and facilitate the redistribution of resources and responsibilities. However, as this book has argued, M-Pesa is guided by a logic of opportunity rather than a politics of redistribution. This logic of opportunity tends to ignore past and present political, economic and legal dynamics that have impoverished people and reproduce inequality, favouring its providers and financial institutions over the target beneficiaries, the unbanked poor. The people who are marginalised and financially excluded because they live in poverty and on a low income are also those who have contributed to making M-Pesa a successful digital financial inclusion project, and could be considered the rightful owners of this growth. The centrality of opportunity, for instance the opportunity to access basic goods and services or start a micro-business, has been powered by narratives such as philanthrocapitalism and can reproduce or even increase gendered inequality and responsibilities. Its logic requires women to take advantage of opportunities not only to benefit themselves but also to improve the livelihoods of their family, community and country in line with the framework of 'gender equality as smart economics' supported by the institutions involved in mobile money governance. The focus on opportunity allows the instrumental use of gender equality to achieve other goals such as market and financial integration, often reproducing rather than challenging gender inequality.

The rapid growth of M-Pesa has been favoured by the integration of the service into existing everyday social and economic practices. More than simply facilitating support and solidarity among the population, M-Pesa has brought efficiency to people's everyday survival practices, encouraging them to take responsibility for their own improvement while integrating them with financial circuits, often serving other interests in addition or contradiction to their basic needs. In this process M-Pesa has even reinforced some existing gender inequalities without contributing to evident structural and relational changes. Autonomy, considered one of the most important gains for women that M-Pesa offers, in reality is the very entrepreneurial capacity that women are called upon to employ in order to negotiate their livelihoods by taking advantage of the numerous opportunities that mobile money offers. These opportunities can increase rather than reduce women's socio-economic insecurity. The livelihood strategies facilitated by M-Pesa have been instrumentally linked to the need for more mobile money products and services but are not seen as the expression of the substantive needs of people who should be supported per se rather than via financial services. The various forms of reward deriving from M-Pesa have not been redistributed to challenge unequal relations, including gender relations, but are awarded or invested according to entrepreneurial logic. What has been redistributed, however, is the hope and optimism attached to the opportunities created by M-Pesa and financial inclusion, which frame the idea of 'Africa rising' and ensure the functioning, sustainability and profitability of the mobile money (eco)system.

This analysis of M-Pesa has demonstrated how people in Kenya have developed highly imaginative modes of survival and exchange, although these 'innovations' are often institutionalised according to the values and interests of corporations and financial institutions that fund them. The view of the South as a place where new ideas take shape, often prefiguring the future of the Global North, has long been discussed by scholars working on epistemologies of the South (e.g. de Sousa Santos 2007; Comaroff and Comaroff 2012). For instance, Facebook has a project to create a digital currency, Libra, and a payment method integrated into everyday socio-economic relations that is similar to the M-Pesa system, but with global effect.

M-Pesa has also shed light on changes to global governance in favour of the multi-polar management of financial relations beyond the North/South divide. More investigation is needed to understand whether and how these patterns could contribute to a redistribution of power in global financial governance, or would increase the power of elites, but not of the people at the lower end of the income distribution in Southern countries, reinforcing the idea of a new global order divided not geographically but according to intersections of gender, race, socio-economic status and poverty across the South and the North. These factors are very important in thinking about redistribution and the need to target extreme wealth as much as extreme poverty for global justice. Extreme wealth and extreme poverty are increasingly emerging as interconnected global issues beyond the geopolitical divide. Digital platforms play a relevant role in this, as they have created new forms of governance, such as Blockchain, and because of their ability to control and produce a great amount of value that can potentially be redistributed.

This book has considered gender inequality as deriving more from a lack of redistributive approaches and measures than from a lack of financial services, and argues for a politics of redistribution to guide financial inclusion projects, policies and regulation. Digital finance is an instrument that can be organised and regulated according to different interests, and expanding access to financial services is one way of furthering those interests. It can be used to foster the interests of some, reproducing and increasing inequalities, or to contribute to a fundamental transformation oriented towards universal provisioning and social justice through the redistribution of power, resources and responsibilities.

References

Allon, F. (2014) The Feminisation of Finance. *Australian Feminist Studies* 29, 12–30.

Banks, N. and Hulme, D. (2014) New Development Alternatives or Business as Usual with a New Face? The Transformative Potential of New Actors and Alliances in Development. *Third World Quarterly* 35(1), 181–195.

Bateman, M., Duvendack, M. and Loubere, N. (2019) Is Fin-tech the New Panacea for Poverty Alleviation and Local Development? Contesting Suri and Jack's M-Pesa Findings Published in *Science*. *Review of African Political Economy*. DOI: 10.1080/03056244.2019.1614552

Chant, S. (2008) The 'Feminisation of Poverty' and the 'Feminisation' of Anti-Poverty Programmes: Room for Revision? *Journal of Development Studies* 44(2), 165–197.

Comaroff, J. and Comaroff, J. (2012) *Theory from the South: Or, How Euro-America is Evolving Toward Africa*. Boulder, CO: Paradigm Publishers.

De Sousa, Santos B. (2007) Beyond Abyssal Thinking: From Global Lines to Ecologies of Knowledges. *Review* 30(1), 45–89.

Gabor, D. and Brooks, S. (2016) The Digital Revolution in Financial Inclusion: International Development in the Fintech Era. *New Political Economy* 22(4), 423–436, DOI: 10.1080/13563467.2017.1259298

Jack, W. and Suri, T. (2011) *Mobile Money: The Economics of M-Pesa*, Cambridge, MA: MIT Sloan.

Jack, W. and Suri, T. (2014) Risk Sharing and Transactions Costs: Evidence from Kenya's Mobile Money Revolution. *American Economic Review* 104(1): 183–223.

Mas, I. and Radcliffe, D. (2010) *Mobile Payments go Viral: M-Pesa in Kenya*, Seattle, WA: Bill and Melinda Gates Foundation.

Mas, I. and Morawczynski, O. (2009) Designing Mobile Money Services: Lessons From M-Pesa. *Innovations* 4(2).

Spivak, G. C. (1993) *Outside in the Teaching Machine*. New York: Routledge.

Suri, T. and Jack, W. (2016) The Long-run Poverty and Gender Impacts of Mobile Money. *Science* 354(6317): 1288–1292.

World Bank (2006) *Gender Equality as Smart Economics: A World Bank Group Gender Action Plan*, Washington, DC: World Bank.

World Bank (2012) *World Development Report 2012: Gender Equality and Development*, Washington, DC: World Bank.

Index

For Product Safety Concerns and Information please contact our EU representative GPSR@taylorandfrancis.com
Taylor & Francis Verlag GmbH, Kaufingerstraße 24, 80331 München, Germany

www.ingramcontent.com/pod-product-compliance
Lightning Source LLC
LaVergne TN
LVHW021107300926
849160LV00009B/645
9781032175355